Praise for
Great Expectations
by Antonia van der Meer

"Incredibly informative, superbly supportive, this beautiful book will greatly enhance any pregnancy. I love it." —Louise Bates Ames, Associate Director, Gesell Institute of Human Development

"*Great Expectations* is a welcome addition to the crowded field of parenting books. It is complete, easy to read, and up-to-date, and should be of great help in raising the healthiest possible baby." —Alvin Eden, M.D.

"*Great Expectations* is a very pleasing and quite informative book for mothers or expectant ones. A wonderful, sensible and soothing approach to this phase of any woman's existence if it concerns pregnancy or motherhood. Wonderfully illustrated and instructive for expectant mothers, the book easily and quite completely covers the diagnosis, your anatomy, your prenatal visits, your chosen birthplace, your growing baby, your lifestyle, the birth itself, your delivery, your diet and any problems that may arrive." —"The Book World," *Neshoba Democrat* (Miss.)

Also by Antonia van der Meer

GREAT EXPECTATIONS
An Illustrated Guide to Your Pregnancy,
Your Birth, Your Baby

Great Beginnings

An Illustrated Guide to
You and Your Baby's First Year

ANTONIA VAN DER MEER

Foreword by
IAN R. HOLZMAN, M.D.

A Dell Trade Paperback

A DELL TRADE PAPERBACK
Published by
Dell Publishing
a division of
Bantam Doubleday Dell Publishing Group, Inc.
1540 Broadway
New York, New York 10036

Cartoon credits:

Pages 59, 104, 178 and 278. Copyright © 1977, 1992 by Lynn Johnston Productions, Inc. Reprinted from *Hi Mom! Hi Dad!* with permission of its publisher, Meadowbrook Press.

Page 211. Copyright © 1977, 1992 by Lynn Johnston Productions, Inc. reprinted from *David, We're Pregnant!* with permission of its publisher, Meadowbrook Press.

Pages 73, 84, 207, 234, and 262. Copyright © 1988 by David Sipress. Reprinted from *It's a Mom's Life* with permission of Sutton Signet, a division of Penguin Books USA, Inc.

Photo credits:

Pages 1, 16, 25, 72, 73, 85, 89, 98, 116, 122, 132, 135, 149, 163, 174, 180, 182, 197, 253, 272, and 279 by Superstock.

Pages 8, 9, and 12 by Gerry Baby Products.

Page 189 by R. Ming.

Illustration credits:

Pages 13, 29, 108, 134, 139, 164, 165, from *Caring for Your Baby and Young Child* by Dr. Art Ulene and The American Academy of Pediatrics. Copyright © 1991 by Feeling Fine Programs, Inc. Used by permission of Bantam Books, a division of Bantam Doubleday Dell Publishing Group, Inc.

Library of Congress Cataloging in Publication Data

Van der Meer, Antonia.
Great beginnings : an illustrated guide to you and your baby's first year / by Antonia van der Meer.
p.   cm.
Includes index.
ISBN 0-440-50634-4
1. Infants (Newborn)—Care.   2. Infants—Care.   3. Infants—Development.
4. Postnatal care—Popular works.   5. Puerperium—Popular works.   I. Title.
RJ253.V27   1994
649'.122—dc20   93-5608
                                                    CIP

Illustrations by Wendy Wray and Jackie Aher

Printed in the United States of America
Published simultaneously in Canada

May 1994

10   9   8   7   6   5   4   3   2
RRH

DEDICATION

To my mother, Billie Cretella, for filling my first year (and every year) of life with promise and love, and for helping me to see that every year can be a great beginning.

ACKNOWLEDGMENTS

Thanks to my editor, Emily Reichert, for helping to "parent" another book. I also wish to thank the following specialists for their time, expertise, and interest in healthy mothers/healthy babies:

Deborah L. Albert
Director of Public Relations
Juvenile Products Manufacturers Association, Inc.
Marlton, New Jersey

Louise Bates Ames
Associate Director
Gesell Institute of Human Development
New Haven, Connecticut

Thomas F. Anders, M.D.
Professor of Psychiatry
University of California, Davis Medical Center
Sacramento, California

Susanne L. Bathgate, M.D.
Assistant Professor of Obstetrics and Gynecology
Division of Maternal-Fetal Medicine
The George Washington University
Washington, D.C.

Dana A. Brown
Director
Women's Exercise Research Center
The George Washington University
Washington, D.C.

W. Keith Bryant, Ph.D.
Professor and Chair Consumer Economics and Housing
Cornell University
Ithaca, New York

Nancy F. Butte, Ph.D.
Associate Professor
Department of Pediatrics, Children's Nutrition Research Center
Baylor College of Medicine
Houston, Texas

Frank J. Courts, D.D.S., Ph.D.
Chairman
Department of Pediatric Dentistry
University of Florida
Gainesville, Florida

Keith Crnic, Ph.D.
Professor of Psychology
Pennsylvania State University
University Park, Pennsylvania

Alvin N. Eden, M.D.
Chairman, Department of Pediatrics
Wyckoff Heights Medical Center
Brooklyn, New York
    and
Associate Clinical Professor of Pediatrics
The New York Hospital—Cornell Medical Center
New York, New York

Hakim Elahi, M.D.
Medical Director,
Margaret Sanger Center
Planned Parenthood
New York, New York
    and
Director of Obstetrics and Gynecology
Laguardia Hospital
Forest Hills, New York

Tiffany Field, Ph.D.
Professor of Pediatrics, Psychology and Psychiatry
University of Miami School of Medicine
Miami, Florida

Barbara Frankowski, M.D.
Assistant Professor of Pediatrics
College of Medicine
University of Vermont
Burlington, Vermont

Gary L. Freed, M.D., M.P.H.
Assistant Professor of Pediatrics and Health Policy
    Administration
The Sheps Center for Health Services Research
The University of North Carolina at Chapel Hill
Chapel Hill, North Carolina

Ian R. Holzman, M.D.
Chief of Newborn Medicine
Mt. Sinai Hospital
New York, New York

Mary Howell, M.D.
Assistant Clinical Professor of Pediatrics
Harvard Medical School
Boston, Massachusetts

Max Kahn, M.D.
Clinical Associate Professor of Pediatrics
New York University School of Medicine
New York, New York

Ronald E. Kleinman, M.D.
Associate Chief of Children's Services
Chief, Division of Pediatric Gastroenterology and
    Nutrition
Massachusetts General Hospital
    and
Associate Professor of Pediatrics
Harvard Medical School
Boston, Massachusetts

Linda J. Kobokovich, R.N.C., M.Sc.N.
Clinical Nurse Specialist
The Birthing Pavilion
Dartmouth Hitchcock Medical Center
Lebanon, New Hampshire

Michael Lewis, Ph.D.
Professor, Pediatrics, Psychiatry and Psychology
Robert Wood Johnson Medical School
New Brunswick, New Jersey

Diane Lye, Ph.D.
Assistant Professor of Sociology
University of Washington
Seattle, Washington

Denise Nelson
Community Coordinator
Childcare Aware Project
National Association of Childcare Resource and
    Referral Agencies

Barbara Watson, M.D.
Director of the Vaccine Evaluation Center
The Children's Hospital of Philadelphia
  and
Assistant Professor of Pediatrics and Infectious
  Diseases
University of Pennsylvania School of Medicine
Philadelphia, Pennsylvania

Modena Wilson, M.D., M.P.H.
Director, Division of General Pediatrics
Johns Hopkins Children's Center
Johns Hopkins University School of Medicine
Baltimore, Maryland

THANKS ALSO TO

The American Academy of Pediatrics, Elk Grove, Illinois
The American College of Obstetricians and Gynecologists, Washington, D.C.
Juvenile Products Manufacturers Association, Inc., Marlton, New Jersey
Toy Manufacturers of America, New York, New York
The Sudden Infant Death Syndrome Alliance, Columbia, Maryland
American Cleft Palate–Craniofacial Association, Pittsburgh, Pennsylvania
American Psychological Association, Washington, D.C.
The Independent Order of Foresters, Solana Beach, California
Cystic Fibrosis Foundation, Bethesda, Maryland
Spina Bifida Association of America, Washington, D.C.
National Down Syndrome Congress, Park Ridge, Illinois

AN IMPORTANT NOTE

The information given in this book is meant only to aid you in your discussions with your child's pediatrician and other doctors. It is not intended as a substitute for baby care by a qualified medical expert. The book should not be used for home diagnosis or home treatment. In reading about developmental stages, the reader should keep in mind that normal individual child development varies greatly and should not use this book to diagnose perceived developmental delays.

For *Great Beginnings,* I enlisted the help of some 25 experienced and knowledgeable specialists to compile a book which addresses your general concerns and needs. But your own postpartum health and your baby's growth and development are very individual things. Only your family's doctors know your unique health situation and therefore must be looked to as the final authority.

Medical science and child development research are constantly evolving and subject to reinterpretation. Although every effort has been made to include the most up-to-date and accurate information, there can be no guarantee that future research won't change some of the material presented here.

✢ Contents ✢

Foreword   xvii

PART I: YOUR BABY   1

Introduction   3

1. Baby Gear   5
  Layette   5
  Bassinet   6
  Crib   6
  Portable Crib   7
  Infant Seat   8
  Infant Carrier   9
  Stroller   10
  Stroller Accessories   10
  Changing Table   10
  Baby Bath   11
  Rocking Chair   11
  Car Seat   11
  Baby Intercom   12
  Night-light   12
  Mobiles and Early Toys   13
  Baby Swing   13

2. Your Caregiver Connection   15
  Pediatricians   15
  Family Practice Physicians   17
  Obstetricians/Gynecologists   17
  Certified Nurse-Midwives   17
  Baby Nurses   18
  Doulas   18

3. To Have and to Hold: The First
    Twenty-four Hours   21

Cutting the Cord   22
Suctioning the Baby   22
The First Breath   23
Apgar Score   24
Brazelton Neonatal Behavior Assessment
    Scale   24
Birth Weight   25
Birth Length   26
Head Circumference   26
Chest Circumference   26
Bonding   26
Feeding on the Delivery Table   27
Footprinting the Baby   28
Hospital ID Bracelet   28
Temperature Control   28
Reflexes   29
Eyedrops   30
Vitamin K Injection   30
Hepatitis B Vaccine   31
PKU and CH Test   31
Vision   31
Meconium Passage   32
Diapering Duties   32

4. Early Choices   35
  Rooming In   35
  Visitors   36
  Circumcision   36

Human Milk vs. Formula   37
Naming the Baby   39
Disposable vs. Cloth Diapers   40

5. Oh, You Beautiful Baby!   41
Facial Appearance   41
Head Shape   41
Soft Spot (Fontanel)   42
Hair   42
Eyes   43
Eye Discharge   43
Ears   43
Nails   43
Skin Color   44
Vernix   44
Milia   44
Erythema Toxicum
    (Red Blotches)   44
Birthmarks   45
Male Genitalia   46
Female Genitalia   46
Bowlegs   47
Cradle Cap   47
Prickly Heat   47

6. Your Baby's First Month   49
The First Checkup   49
Personality   50
Newborn Behavior   51
Playtime   52
Crying   52
Baby Noises   54
Daytime Sleeping   55
Nighttime Sleeping   56
Swaddling   57
Pacifiers   57
Infant Massage   58

Spoiling   58
Routines   59
Umbilical Cord Care   60
Bowel Movements   60
Thrush   60
Sponge Baths   61
Immersion Baths   61
Toiletries   63
Dressing   63
Outings   64
Carrying Baby   64
Time Alone for Parents   65
Toys for the First Month   66
Happy Baby's Hit Parade   66

7. Your Baby's Second Month   67
The Second-Month Checkup   67
DTP Immunization   68
Oral Polio Vaccine   69
HIB Vaccine   69
Your Personal Immunization
    Chart   70
Weight Gain   70
Muscle Control   71
Learning   72
Vision   72
Routines   72
Sleeping in the Second Month   73
Sudden Infant Death Syndrome   74
Cooing   75
Smiling   75
Sucking   76
Colic   76
Diaper Rash   78
Baby Carrier or Stroller?   79
Playtime   79
Toys for the Second Month   80
Happy Baby's Hit Parade   81

8. Your Baby's Third Month   83
   When to Call the Pediatrician   83
   Muscle Control   85
   Vision   85
   Gurgling and Chuckling   85
   Learning   85
   Sleeping   86
   The Family Bed   87
   Safety Tips for the Third Month   88
   Playtime   88
   Toys for the Third Month   88
   Happy Baby's Hit Parade   89

9. Your Baby's Fourth Month   91
   The Fourth-Month Checkup   91
   Muscle Control   92
   Vision   93
   Laughing and Babbling   93
   Learning   93
   Thumb Sucking and Pacifier Use   94
   Interrupted Feedings   94
   Safety Tips for the Fourth Month   95
   Playtime   95
   Toys for the Fourth Month   96
   Happy Baby's Hit Parade   96

10. Your Baby's Fifth Month   97
    Pediatric Care by Phone   97
    Muscle Control   98
    Rolling Over   98
    Weight Gain   99
    Language   99
    Learning   100
    Sleeping   100
    Teething   101
    Starting Solid Foods   102
    Safety Tips for the Fifth Month   103
    Playtime   103

    Toys for the Fifth Month   104
    Happy Baby's Hit Parade   104

11. Your Baby's Sixth Month   105
    The Sixth-Month Checkup   105
    Language Development   106
    Creeping   107
    Sitting Up   107
    The First Tooth   108
    Drooling   109
    Cleaning Teeth   109
    Fluoride   110
    Early Waking   110
    Night Waking   111
    Safety Tips for the Sixth Month   112
    Playtime   112
    Toys for the Sixth Month   113
    Happy Baby's Hit Parade   114

12. Your Baby's Seventh Month   115
    Books   115
    Music   116
    Left-handed or Right-handed   117
    Security Blankets   117
    Taking a Trip with Baby   118
    Likes and Dislikes   119
    Toys for the Seventh Month   119
    Happy Baby's Hit Parade   119

13. Your Baby's Eighth Month   121
    Creeping, Scooting, or
        Crawling   121
    Standing with Support   123
    Walkers   123
    Clinging   123
    Stranger Anxiety   124
    Separation Anxiety   125
    Napping   126

Bottle Mouth (Nursing Caries)   126
Finger Foods   127
Dirt and Germs   127
Interest in Genitalia   128
Safety Tips for the Eighth Month   128
Toys for the Eighth Month   129
Happy Baby's Hit Parade   129

14. Your Baby's Ninth Month   131
The Ninth-Month Checkup   131
Pulling to a Stand   132
First Words?   132
Freewheelin' Fun   133
Pincer Grasp   134
Self-feeding   134
Sugary Foods   135
Hair Care   135
Bedtime   136
Playtime   136
Safety Tips for the Ninth Month   137
Toys for the Ninth Month   137
Happy Baby's Hit Parade   138

15. Your Baby's Tenth Month   139
Cruising   139
Feet   140
Messy Babies   140
Baby's Body Language   141
Head Banging   141
Hair Pulling/Teeth Grinding/
    Ear Tugging   142
Newfound Fears   143
Toys for the Tenth Month   143
Happy Baby's Hit Parade   144

16. Your Baby's Eleventh Month   145
Standing Alone   145
More First Words   146

Understanding Language   146
Mental Skills   147
Fussy Eaters   147
Accidents   148
Safety Tips for the End of the
    First Year   148
Toys for the Eleventh Month   149
Happy Baby's Hit Parade   149

17. Your Baby's Twelfth Month   151
The Twelfth-Month Checkup   151
Walking/Not Walking   152
Shoes   152
The First Visit to the Dentist   153
Sharing   153
Biting   154
Your Girl: Sugar and Spice?   155
Your Boy: Puppy Dog Tails?   156
TV Shows and Videos   156
Crib or Bed?   157
"No!" Baby's New Word   157
The First Birthday Party   158
Safety Tips for the Twelfth
    Month   158
Toys for the Twelfth Month   159
Happy Baby's Hit Parade   160

18. Feeding in the First Year   161
Breastfeeding Made Simple   161
Breastfeeding Positions   164
Constant Nursing   166
Enough Milk   166
Demand Feeding vs. Scheduled
    Feeding   167
Vitamin Supplements   167
Breastfeeding Problems   168
Expressing Breast Milk   170
Drying Up Your Breast Milk   172

Formula Feeding   172
Warming Bottles   173
Bottle-feeding Equipment   174
Keeping Bottles Clean   175
Preparing Bottles   176
Offering the Bottle   176
Burping   176
Spitting Up   177
When to Wean   177
Introducing Solid Foods   179
Changes in Bowel Movements   179
Homemade Foods   180
Commercially Prepared
    Baby Foods   180
Additives   181
Allergies   181
Cholesterol   182
Water   182
Cups   182
Plates   183
Spoons   183
Bibs   183

19. Medical Problems You and Your
       Baby May Be Facing   185
Newborn Intensive and Intermediate
    Care Units   185
The Low-Birth-Weight Baby   186
The Premature Baby   187
Meconium Aspiration   188
Jaundice   188
Cerebral Palsy   189
Cleft Lip/Cleft Palate   190
Clubfoot   191
Down Syndrome   191
Spina Bifida Manifesta   191
Heart Defect   192
Celiac Disease   192
Cystic Fibrosis   192
Sickle Cell Anemia   193
Tay-Sachs Disease   193
Thalassemia   193
Pyloric Stenosis   194
Inguinal Hernia   194
Undescended Testicles   194
Hydrocele   194
Emergency Rooms   195

PART II: YOUR BODY   197

Introduction   199

20. You: The First Twenty-four Hours   201
Delivery Repair   201
Cesarean Section Repair   202
Urinary Catheter Use
    and Removal   203
Postpartum Painkillers   204
Intravenous Oxytocin   204

Hunger   205
Eating After a Cesarean   205
Afterpains   206
The Delivery in Retrospect   206
Hospital Necessities   207
Lochia (Bleeding After Birth)   208
Perineal Swelling   208
Getting Out of Bed   209
Urinating   209
The First Bowel Movement   210

21. Continued Postpartum Recovery: The First Six Weeks 213
  Uterine Involution 213
  Healing of Episiotomy or Tear 213
  Sitz Baths 214
  Pelvic Floor Exercises 214
  Recovery from Cesarean 215
  Bathing 215
  Postpartum Checkup 215
  Menstruation 216

22. Your Most Common Postpartum Concerns 217
  Backache 217
  Hair Loss 218
  Urinary Incontinence 218
  Frequent Urination 219
  Fatigue 219
  Common Cold 219
  Pigmentation 220
  Skin Breakouts 220
  Hemorrhoids 220
  Leaky Breasts 221
  Engorged Breasts 221
  Bigger Bust 222
  Nursing Bras 222
  Stretch Marks 223
  Hot Flashes 223
  Sweating 223
  Flabby Belly 223
  Postpartum Fashions 224

23. Healthful Food for New Mothers 225
  Weight Loss 225
  Nursing Mom's Diet 226
  Dietary Restrictions for the Nursing Mother 227
  Needed Nutrients 227
  Vitamins 228
  Best Bites 228
  Water 229
  Caffeine 229
  No Smoking 230
  Alcohol 230

24. Exercises for the New Mother 231
  First Exercises 231
  Exercises in the First Six Weeks 232
  Exercise During the First Year 233
  How to Choose an Exercise Class 234
  Body Image 235

25. Postpartum Sex and Contraception 237
  Feeling Sexy Again 237
  Postpartum Sex 238
  Sex and the Single Episiotomy 238
  Contraceptive Needs 238
  Diaphragm 239
  The Pill 240
  IUDs 242
  Contraceptive Sponge 243
  Cervical Cap 243
  Condom and Foam 244
  Contraceptive Implants 244
  Injectable Depo-Provera 245
  Withdrawal 245
  Rhythm 245
  LAM (Lactation Amenorrhea Method) 246
  Morning-after Pills 246
  RU 486 247
  Sterilization 247

26. Your Feelings 249
  Baby Blues 249
  Postpartum Depression 250
  Worrying 250
  Your Energy Level 251

PART III: YOUR NEW FAMILY   253

Introduction   255

27. Your Partner Is Now a Dad   257
Paternity Leave   257
Father-Time   258
Still a Mate   259
Jealousy   260
Support of Breastfeeding   261
A Father's Financial Worries   261
Fair Shares   262
When Dad Is Not Around:
    Single Mothers   264

28. Full House   265
Siblings at the Birth   265
Homecoming of Mother and
    Newborn   266
Sibling Interaction   267
Regressive Behavior in Older
    Sibling   267
Sibling Rivalry   268
Birth Order   269
The Only Child   271
Twins   271
The Family Pet and Your
    New Baby   271

29. Grandparents Are Grand   273
Grandparents as Parents   273
Long-distance Grandparents   273
Next-door Grandparents   274
Divorced Grandparents   274
Interfering   275
Special Names   275
New Roles   276

30. Child-care Arrangements   277
Relatives Who Babysit   277
In-Your-Home Babysitters   277
Day-care Centers   278
Family Child Care   280
Mom-and-Tot Groups   280

31. Returning to Work   283
Maternity Leave   283
The Transition from Home
    to Work   284
Working Moms and
    Breastfeeding   285
Working Mother Guilt Busters   286

Conclusion   287

Index   289

✦ Foreword ✦

Ian R. Holzman, M.D.

No single act is more profound or meaningful than bringing a child into the world. As a pediatrician, neonatologist, teacher of child care, and parent of three, I know firsthand that every journey of parenthood is a unique and memorable experience. It has been almost twenty years since I completed my residency in pediatrics, during which time I have cared for thousands of children from Colorado to Pennsylvania and New York. Yet even if you have been a parent for only a day, you already have something perhaps as important as all my years of medical expertise: parental instincts. I always advise parents to trust these, and to go with what they know. When good parental instincts are combined with timely pediatric consultations and care, and rounded out by the parenting knowledge that can be obtained from a book like this one, your new family has all the seeds for success.

In this informative and lively book, Antonia van der Meer deftly fills the special needs that all new parents have: the need for reassurance that their instincts are correct, the need for accurate, up-to-date information, the need to understand the medical and parenting choices and decisions that lie ahead. *Great Beginnings* is a practical guide that allows easy access to age-specific information about your baby and provides details on hundreds of topics of interest to new mothers and fathers. With this book in hand, you'll be able to gracefully cope with the myriad of worries, wonderings, and friendly (but often conflicting) advice from family and friends that can quickly overwhelm new parents. Antonia van der Meer is careful to present medically accurate information while still allowing parents to make their own decisions with the advice of their doctors, where controversies arise. As a doctor and a parent, I know there is often no one "right way" to parent all children or nurture all families. Once prepared and fortified with the information in this book, you'll be able to ask questions and discuss issues of concern with your baby's doctor and within your own family.

I recommend *Great Beginnings* to all new parents, whether this is your first baby or your fourth. Just don't leave it on your bookshelf—it should be kept out somewhere between the half-used box of Pampers and the baby rice cereal. You'll be using it often and with increasing confidence!

PART I
✤ Your Baby ✤

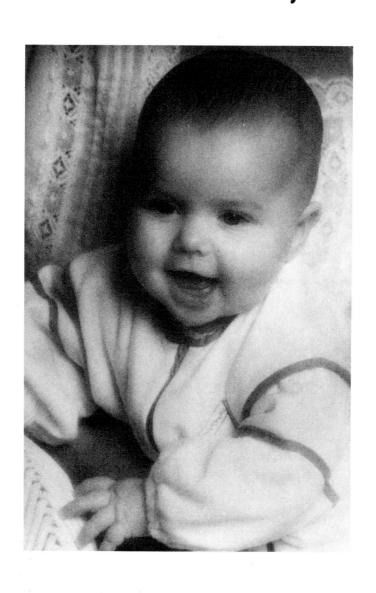

✤ Introduction ✤

The first year with your new baby is a challenging and exciting time. You are beginning a journey that will provide you with many new adventures and new feelings. Unlike pregnancy, which was a journey that had an end, parenting continues. The first year is only the beginning, but it is an important one. Both parent and child deserve a great start. This year builds the foundation of parent-child bonding and trust that will continue to grow and develop over a lifetime.

During the first year, you will see (and have to adapt to) an amazing number of changes. You begin the first year by caring for an essentially helpless and dependent newborn who can be carried like a package wherever you go. You end the first year with a mobile, determined, and curious little creature who is just beginning to express his independence from you. The first year can bring first teeth, first words, first smiles, and maybe even first steps. When you have a baby under one, the world is a new and exciting place. You will want to build on all these firsts and set the stage for your child's continued growth and development. Clearly, this is a remarkable and significant year—not just for your baby, but for you.

Once you become a parent, you have joined a very large club—with over 4 million babies born in the United States in 1991, that adds up to over 8 million moms and dads. Even so, you can sometimes feel alone with the day-to-day problems, the choices, and the challenges of bringing up baby. Most parents need a book to help them understand and cope with their new role and their new addition to the family. Having a place to turn to for information and comfort is important during the sometimes confusing first year.

This book is divided into three parts: "Your Baby," "Your Body," and "Your New Family." In order to make the first year as good as it can be, you'll need to concentrate on all three facets of your life—neglecting any one of them can make it hard to enjoy the other two. This first part, "Your Baby," is divided into nineteen chapters, beginning with a chapter on baby equipment and furniture you'll need to have on hand (after all, you won't want to take baby home to an empty nest), plus a chapter on how to choose a pediatrician and other support people, followed by a look at the first twenty-four hours with your newborn, and a month-by-month guide to your baby's first year. This part also includes a long chapter giving lots of advice on how to happily feed your baby throughout the first year—from breastfeeding and bottle feeding through solid foods.

CHAPTER 1

✦ Baby Gear ✦

You may have begun getting your home and life prepared for your baby before the birth, or you may have waited until after your baby was born. If you've waited until now, the planning and purchasing that was put off during pregnancy can be postponed no longer. One stroll through a juvenile furniture store or infant section of a major department store can make your head spin. The choices! The prices! What do you really need? Which brands are best? What will the baby outgrow all too soon? What will make life with a new baby easiest? Do you have to buy it all at once? These are just some of the questions you'll have as you go about assembling baby clothes and cribs. Taking along an experienced friend can be a great help. This chapter is the next-best thing. It includes everything you need to know about strollers, bassinets, baby clothes, bedding, car seats, changing tables, baby baths, and more.

✦   ✦   ✦

LAYETTE

"Layette" is a fancy word for the collection of baby clothes you'll need to get through the first couple of months. Newborns tend to drool, spit up, and have runny bowel movements, which all add up to frequent clothing changes. Some babies need their clothes changed two or three times a day! In the week or two preceding your due date, you'll want to go out and get a few essentials. If money is tight, remember that they need not be new. Newborn clothes can often be found at secondhand clothing stores, as well as church and school secondhand clothing events. Because newborn clothes are quickly outgrown, these secondhand items are often like new. You may also

For the layette, assemble an assortment of practical items.

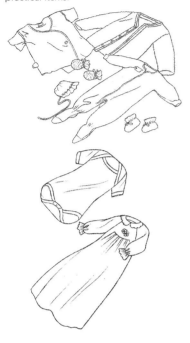

inherit some newborn clothes from other moms and can expect to receive some baby gifts after the baby is born, so don't overbuy items in the newborn to 3-month sizes. This list should give you some basic guidelines to follow:

- Three snap front or envelope collar T-shirts
- Three onesies (T-shirts with snap crotch)
- Two to three drawstring sleep sacks (nightgowns)
- Three to six stretchies (pajamas with snaps and feet)
- Two to three dressier outfits (soft overalls or romper)
- One to two bibs (optional)
- One cardigan sweater
- One hat (seasonal)
- Six receiving blankets
- Diapers (cloth or disposables)
- Three pairs booties or infant socks
- Snowsuit or lighter bunting (depending on season)

BASSINET

Bassinets or cradles are essentially small baskets. Some sit up on a stand. Some have wheels. Some rock. In the first few weeks, a bassinet may be the ideal spot for your baby to sleep. It's a smaller and cozier space than a crib, helping many babies to feel more secure. They are also easier to place in a corner of your bedroom or to move and bring downstairs to the living room for the day. On the other hand, many babies happily begin sleeping in cribs the first day home from the hospital. If you are trying to press an antique back into service, check it carefully to make sure it is sturdy, stable, and in good condition.

CRIB

Most parents, even those who start out with bassinets or with baby sleeping in the parents' bed, eventually put their babies to sleep in cribs. When purchasing a new crib, make sure it conforms to all Juvenile Products Manufacturers Association safety regulations.

Laundry Duty
Once you have a baby in the house, get ready for laundry duty! According to *The Harper's Index Book*, the average American family of four washes one ton of laundry per year!

- Avoid decorative cutouts.
- Slats should be no less than 2⅜ inches apart and the mattress should fit snugly.
- Releases and latches on the dropside must be safe and secure from accidental release by the baby.
- Avoid cribs with high corner posts, as children's clothing may catch on them.
- If you place a crib near a window, keep drapery cords out of reach by tying them to a cleat on the wall.
- Keep the mattress at its highest setting for an infant, lowering it as the baby grows and learns to sit up or stand.

Although used cribs are not recommended by safety experts, if you must use one, be sure to look it over carefully. Measure an older crib to make sure side slats are no more than 2⅜ inches apart. The paint on the crib must be lead free and nontoxic. The mattress should fit snugly into the crib frame. Decorative cutout areas on crib end panels are dangerous.

Cribs call for some special bedding accessories. You'll need:

- A waterproof mattress pad.
- Several fitted crib sheets for covering the mattress. (No top sheet is needed.)
- A crib-size quilt or baby blanket to cover your child.
- Cloth bumper pads running completely around the inside of the crib. (These will keep the baby from bumping his head against the hard slats.)

PORTABLE CRIB

There is an assortment of portable cribs today which make visiting Grandma or going on an overnight trip with baby so much easier. Most fold into their own bags for carrying and assemble quickly. They have thin mattresses for baby's comfort and netted sides for safety. They can be used throughout the first year. Even smaller and easier to tote than a portable crib are portable bassinets. Some unfold from a diaper bag, with stiff, vinyl-covered cardboard sides

A Father's Reflections
"When I was born, my parents didn't have enough money to buy a fancy cradle or crib, so during the first month, I slept in a dresser drawer. I imagine it was quite cozy. All the same, I bought a crib for my baby."

An Expert's Opinion
Although you may want to use an antique crib or bassinet, this may not be a practical or safe idea.

"Stay away from secondhand products for the baby. Crib safety standards have changed so much in past years. An old crib may have loose or missing screws, chipped paint, or other problems. Used cribs are not recommended by the Juvenile Products Manufacturers Association [JPMA]."
—Deborah Albert, Director of Public Relations, JPMA

Safety Tip
Do not use any pillows in a crib. Because a newborn is unable to raise his head up or roll over, a pillow could smother him.

✦

Visual Interest
A mobile hanging from the ceiling above the crib, or attached to the side of the crib, is a perfect first visual toy for newborns. Once your child is able to sit up or stand, the mobile should be removed.

✦

Warning
Never leave an infant unattended in a seat. Be sure straps are well below the baby's neck. And remember, these seats are not acceptable substitutes for car seats.

that can be secured with Velcro to form a box. With a receiving blanket thrown down as a sheet, a newborn (up until about 3 months of age) can sleep quite nicely in here. (The setup is similar to the sky cradles airlines sometimes offer on long flights.)

INFANT SEAT

When your baby isn't asleep in his crib, dozing in his bassinet, or being held securely in your arms, where can you put him down? Infant seats offer a change of scenery for baby and a rest for your arms when baby is quietly alert. Some have a convenient carrying handle that can be flipped back to secure the base when you put it down. They can be adjusted for sitting up or placed at a slight recline. They come with seat belts for securing the infant. Use care in where you place the baby and never leave him unattended. Beware of placing an infant seat on top of an island counter or table where the seat could be bumped, causing it to fall. Likewise, don't put the

infant seat on top of a bed, because this is not a stable surface for the seat. During the early weeks, a rolled-up receiving blanket works well to keep baby's head from rolling unsupported from side to side. An added bonus: This can be a great position for your baby to be in when you want to snap a few photos!

INFANT CARRIER

There are many soft front carriers available today which enable mothers and fathers to carry babies while leaving their hands free for other tasks. Some take a little practice to use, but once you get the hang of putting it on and getting baby in, it's all worth it. Your baby may fuss a little while he's being maneuvered into this contraption, but once in, most babies love the snug feeling of being carried strapped to your chest and often fall asleep in there on walks. Parents of colicky babies sometimes swear by this method as the only thing that relieves the crying.

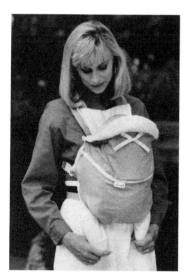

Beanbag Pillow Recall
Beanbag pillows have been shown to be dangerous to sleeping infants. Never put a baby to sleep facedown on a pillow or infant beanbag cushion. Infant beanbags filled with plastic foam beads or pellets have been associated with infant deaths caused by suffocation. All beanbag pillows sold for infant use have been recalled.

✦

Free Safety Information
For your copy of "Safe and Sound for Baby," send a stamped, self-addressed business-size envelope to the Juvenile Products Manufacturers Association, Baby Safety Brochure, 2 Greentree Centre, Suite 225, P.O. Box 955, Marlton, NJ 08053.

A Look Ahead

The stroller you choose should last through the first year. Toward the toddler years when your child no longer needs the back support or the recline feature, you may opt for an umbrella-style stroller that's even more lightweight.

✦

Safety Tip

You can check on baby equipment recalls or make a complaint about a product by calling the U.S. Consumer Product Safety Commission Hotline at 1-800-638-2772.

STROLLER

If you are using a baby carrier, you may not need a baby carriage or stroller during the early weeks. You may want to wait and buy one later when you know firsthand the importance of ease, convenience, and lightweight maneuverability. The stroller should be safety certified by the Juvenile Products Manufacturers Association. The seat should recline for a newborn who can't yet sit up. (Make sure the stroller won't tip when in a reclining position.) Choose a stroller with a base wide enough to prevent tipping, even if an older baby leaned out over the side. Try folding and unfolding it in the store. If you live in a city and need to get on and off buses with a stroller, you'll want to make sure that the stroller is lightweight, folds small, and can be opened with one hand (because that's all you'll have if your baby is in your other arm). Follow the manufacturer's instructions and don't overload the stroller with packages or extra children. Make sure the child is strapped in properly. The stroller should have wheel locks, which you'll need to use whenever the stroller is stopped. You can get brand recommendations from friends and relatives but the only way to decide what's best for you is to try out a few models in the store. Strollers are quite expensive, often costing more than a hundred dollars, so you'll want to choose wisely.

STROLLER ACCESSORIES

If you live in a rainy area, you may want to get the rain hood that fits your model. Make sure it's easy to put on and take off, and that it stays in place when in use. For sunny climes, an umbrella or shade help shield baby from too much sun. You can also buy thick, decorative stroller seat covers for added cushioning. These are removable for washing. Matching stroller bags are sometimes also available and can be convenient, offering a place to put an extra diaper or stash your wallet.

CHANGING TABLE

Changing tables can be purchased at juvenile furniture stores. Usually, they have a top with a guard rail and thin mattress. Shelves underneath can hold diapers, clothes, and other changing supplies. A changing table is used only for the first two years of life, however, so you may want to choose one that will serve some other purpose later on. Some of them can be used later to hold toys or books. Some changing tables open out from the top of a baby dresser and hide away when not in use. If you don't have the money or room for an official "changing table," you can easily do without. The indented foam pads sold for baby bath time make an excellent nonslip changing surface for infant diaper changes. You can put it on top of your bathroom counter. Never turn your back on an infant you're changing. Always keep one hand on her for added security. You can also change your baby by leaning into her crib. Changes can also be accomplished on a bed, or on a receiving blanket spread out on the floor. One of the benefits of changing a baby on the floor: There's no way she can fall off!

BABY BATH

A small plastic tub can be purchased for baby's bath. You can place it in the bathtub or on a counter top. This is another piece of baby equipment that isn't entirely necessary. You can give a baby a bath in the kitchen sink, for example, without a baby tub. A large, indented sponge pad for bathing can be purchased in a children's store and used under baby to keep him from slipping. See page 61 for more on how to bathe baby.

ROCKING CHAIR

There is something very soothing about sitting with an infant in a rocking chair. If you don't have one, you might want to consider adding this piece of furniture to the nursery ensemble. The rocking can soothe both mother and baby and is a perfect place for breast-feeding or bottle feeding. Make sure that the arms of the rocking chair are at a comfortable height for you and that you will be able to rest against them if you have a baby in your arms.

CAR SEAT

New parents have to think ahead and buy a car seat before baby is born. That way, you'll have it on hand for the first car trip home from the hospital or birthing center. A baby in an approved and properly used car safety seat is much better protected than a baby in a parent's

Safety Tip
Changing tables should have straps to prevent falls. Make sure you'll be able to easily reach the place where you keep the diapers while attending the baby.

Who to Call
For consumer safety information on car seats or car seat recalls, call the National Highway Traffic Safety Administration 1-800-424-9393 [in Washington, D.C., the number is (202) 366-0123].

Increased Safety Belt Use
From 1980 to 1990, seat belt use rose from 11 to 49 percent. The National Highway Traffic Safety Administration hopes to continue to increase safety belt use. Do your part. Make sure you and your child are buckled up 100 percent of the time.

lap. A child is likely to fly out of his mother's arms during a crash and strike the interior of the car, dashboard, or windshield. Although holding your child may "feel safe," it is not. The use of child safety seats in cars has been the law in all fifty states since 1989.

Many brands, fabrics, sizes, and types of car seats exist, offering various conveniences and prices. There are small bucket-style infant seats, made especially for the very young baby, up to 20 pounds. These seem quite comfortable and appropriate for the newborn but, obviously, your baby will soon outgrow it, and you'll ultimately need to purchase another child safety seat. For this reason, some parents prefer to start out with a full-size car safety seat, used in the recommended rear-facing position for a newborn. This seat can be used until the baby weighs 40 pounds. A few rolled-up receiving blankets or cloth diapers can be used to help support your newborn's head in this seat. Your seat will come with instructions on installation and recommendations on when the seat can be used in the forward-facing position. Be sure to follow all instructions carefully. Leave your child in the seat as long as you are driving. Although it may be tempting, a passenger should not remove a fussy child from the seat while the driver continues to drive. Pull over and stop the car if you need to change, feed, or comfort the infant.

BABY INTERCOM

A helpful new addition to the baby care scene, nursery monitors are now in use throughout America. They often put parents' minds at ease and keep their bodies firmly planted in the living room instead of jumping up every five minutes to check on baby's breathing in the nursery. The intercom is placed next to baby's crib and plugged into the wall, where it picks up almost every little sound the baby makes. Meanwhile, you can place the receiver anywhere you are in the house. It can be plugged in or used with batteries. With an on-off switch and volume control, you can monitor the baby from another room. Some even light up when baby cries, to give a visual clue if you are vacuuming or listening to music.

NIGHT-LIGHT

During the early months, the night-light probably helps the parent more than the baby. Plug it into the wall and you can (hopefully) find your way to baby's crib for middle-of-the-night feedings!

MOBILES AND EARLY TOYS

Throughout the first year, your baby will want to play with toys. As a newborn, she is basically passive and enjoys toys that she can see or listen to. Later, as her skills and abilities change, she will prefer active, hands-on toys. During the early weeks, babies like to look at patterns and some enjoy listening to music. For this reason, you might consider getting a musical mobile and attaching it to the crib. There are a lot of black-and-white geometric toys and mobiles now available for infants. Better than any toy during the early weeks, of course, is the human face—of most interest to the baby (as she is to you!). For specific suggestions on appropriate toys throughout the first year, see the "Toys" section at the end of each monthly chapter.

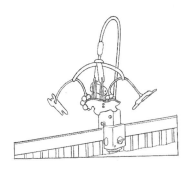

BABY SWING

Many parents swear by baby swings, which can help to lull little ones to sleep. Other parents never own (and never miss) them. When purchasing a new one, look for a sturdy, stable base and smooth, soft edges. They are not recommended for babies under six weeks.

CHAPTER 2

✤ Your Caregiver Connection ✤

You may be the only mother your baby will ever have, but you need not be alone in caring for her. There is support out there for you: in the form of doctors and nurses and other health care professionals. This chapter covers the basics of choosing the right pediatrician and other health care providers to help keep you and your baby healthy and happy throughout the first year. (For information on babysitters and other child-care arrangements, see Chapter 30.)

✤   ✤   ✤

PEDIATRICIANS

You've barely gotten used to your obstetrician and already you're worrying about a pediatrician. Finding the right pediatrician for your family is an important step. Even if you have a healthy baby with no problems, this is someone you'll see and talk to a great deal during this first year of your baby's life. Well-baby checkups are frequent during the first year, when developmental stages need to be marked and immunization schedules begin. This is also the person you will be turning to for advice on personal and sometimes subjective matters such as breastfeeding, returning to work, starting solid foods, dealing with sibling rivalry, and so on. For this reason, you'll want to find a pediatrician whose advice you can trust and whose beliefs are similar to your own.

To begin your search, get the names of pediatricians in your area from your obstetrician, from other moms, or from hospital referral services. Your state chapter of the American Academy of Pediatrics is also a good source. You'll probably find that you get your best

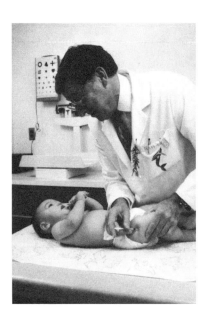

referral from someone who thinks most like you do. While you are still pregnant, call one or more of these names to arrange for a prenatal visit. There may be a fee for this initial consultation/interview. (If you have already had the baby, make a regular appointment for a well-baby checkup and use the appointment to decide how you feel about this doctor.)

When determining whether or not this pediatrician is right for you, ask yourself:

- Does he or she make me feel comfortable? Do I feel at ease asking this person questions?
- Are my questions answered fully and with patience?
- Do we seem to agree/disagree on various childrearing topics like breastfeeding, rooming in?
- Are the office hours and location convenient for me?
- When can I call with questions or concerns? Are there scheduled telephone hours?
- Does the doctor seem to schedule enough time for each patient?
- Are sick children seen separately from healthy children?
- Is the pediatrician affiliated with a hospital near me?
- What are the pediatrician's fees for regular checkups?

The first meeting is a time for gathering facts. Give your doctor background medical histories on both families. If this is a prenatal visit, bring up any special delivery concerns (twins, high-risk pregnancy) you may have and discuss your plans for delivery and the intended length of your hospital stay. If you have some early questions now about a newborn's needs, breastfeeding, or circumcision, ask.

If the pediatrician you choose has privileges in the same hospital in which you plan to deliver, he or she can be at the delivery if necessary (in the event of serious maternal disease, prematurity, or other medical problem). Following a normal birth, your pediatrician would be able to perform a checkup on your baby before discharge. All babies are routinely examined by a pediatrician within twenty-four hours of birth. If the pediatrician you choose does not have hospital privileges at this hospital, a staff pediatrician will check out your baby at birth and you may bring your newborn to see your regular pediatrician after discharge.

FAMILY PRACTICE PHYSICIANS

There are about 70,000 family and general practice physicians in the United States today. These are M.D.s with a specialty in family practice. One of them may be right for your baby and family. They provide an alternative to a pediatrician for primary care of children. Family practice physicians handle well-baby visits as well as common, acute, or even chronic illnesses. Like the pediatrician, there may be times when they need to refer you to specialists.

OBSTETRICIANS/GYNECOLOGISTS

If you were happy with the way your pregnancy and birth were handled, you will probably want to return to see the same doctor who delivered your baby. Although the pregnancy is over, the need for a gynecologist remains. You may have questions about your postpartum recovery in the early weeks. Your doctor is there to answer those questions. You also need to be seen six weeks after the birth for a complete checkup to make sure your body has fully recovered from the birth. Contraception methods will probably also be discussed and chosen at that time with the help of your doctor.

If you were, for some reason, extremely unhappy with the care you received at the birth of your baby, you may decide not to return to your doctor for follow-up visits during baby's first year. Do not neglect your health, however. You must see someone for a six-week checkup to make sure your body has healed. Choose a new doctor with the help of a hospital or university's referral service or get a name from a friend or relative whose opinion you value. When switching doctors, it's a good idea to call and leave a message for the old doctor, briefly advising him of the switch, and asking that the records from your pregnancy and birth be sent to the new doctor. All you need to say is that you have decided to continue your medical treatment elsewhere. If you want to give a reason, you may. If such a call seems like too much for you to handle in the early weeks, have your partner do it for you.

CERTIFIED NURSE-MIDWIVES

A CNM, or certified nurse-midwife, is a registered nurse who has undergone at least two years of extra schooling and training in pregnancy, birth, gynecology, and family planning. A CNM must

Woman to Woman
Looking for a female gynecologist? The hunt may soon get easier. Although in 1991 only 22 percent of the members of the American College of Obstetricians and Gynecologists were female, in 1992 more than half of all first-year residents were women. Once their training is complete, there should be a lot more women doctors for us to choose from. For now, you might also consider using a nurse-midwife. Nurse-midwives are almost always women and provide pregnancy, postpartum, and routine gynecological care.

Locating a Midwife
For the name of a midwife near you, call the American College of Nurse-Midwives at (202) 289-0171. In Canada, contact a regional midwifery association in your province.

Mothers' Reflections
"I loved having a baby nurse because it meant I could spend more time with my two-year-old. I think it helped to avoid any problems of sibling jealousy in her."

✦

"I felt like having a nurse in the house was an intrusion on my privacy. I wouldn't use one again."

complete an accredited program as well as pass rigorous national boards. State requirements must also be met. According to the American College of Nurse-Midwives, there are about 4,000 CNMs delivering babies in the United States today. You may have used a CNM for your pregnancy and birth or you may be interested in switching to a CNM now for postpartum care, contraceptive counseling, and well-woman gynecology.

BABY NURSES

A baby nurse is a person who is skilled at taking care of newborns. A baby nurse can be hired to care for the newborn and assist the new mother during the early weeks of baby's life. Nurses may be hired to work on a live-in, 24-hour-a-day basis. Or they may be hired strictly to help out at night. Some women feel they can use this extra help, especially if they are bottle feeding (not because bottle feeding is more difficult, but because the nurse can feed the baby). Others prefer to mother alone. If you decide to hire a nurse, contact a recommended agency and tell them your due date. Ask your pediatrician or obstetrician for a recommendation. You can also look in the yellow pages under nurses or sitters.

When you call, find out about fees and ask questions about their pool of nurses. What type of experience does this agency require them to have? In what ways would they be able to assist you? Because due dates are never exact, they usually can't guarantee you a particular nurse, who may be on another job when you deliver. Once you have a baby nurse in your home, explain your particular needs and expectations. Even though they have done this many times before, each household is different. This is the time to make guidelines clear. For example, if you are breastfeeding, you may want to make it clear that the nurse should not give the baby any bottles. Or you may want her to screen phone calls for you while you sleep or breastfeed.

For information on hiring a full-time babysitter or on finding a day-care center, see Chapter 30.

DOULAS

Doulas, from the Greek word meaning "servant," are usually experienced mothers who can assist you with baby care and your own postpartum recovery.

Doulas usually come four hours a day for about two weeks and their sole job is to "mother the mother." Doulas believe that moms are special people who deserve lots of extra attention and TLC. They will do your laundry, watch older children, make nutritious meals, go grocery shopping, even clean your bathroom: in short, whatever it takes to keep moms at peace, rested, and enjoying their newborn. A doula may make more sense than a baby nurse for breastfeeding mothers who want the lion's share of the baby care but have little time or energy left over for household chores.

If you would like to find a doula in your area, ask your hospital, obstetrician, or midwife for a suggestion. If they are unfamiliar with doulas, contact the National Association of Postpartum Care Services for a referral at P.O. Box 1012, Edmonds, Washington 98020 (include a self-addressed stamped envelope). Unfortunately, there are only about 400 doulas practicing right now (most of them in the coastal states or in large cities). There is not yet any standard certification or training procedures for doulas, although there may soon be.

On the Lighter Side
Here's a quick, humorous dictionary of the caregivers in your life: "Pediatrician: The doctor who treats Mom's anxiety attacks. Nurse: The only person who truly cares about a new mother's bowel movements. Baby-sitter: A teenager who will eat your food and watch your TV for money unless she gets a last-minute date. Wet Nurse: A nurse who changes a diaper too slowly."
—Copyright © 1989 by Joyce Armor, *The Dictionary According to Mommy* (Meadowbrook Press, Deephaven, MN)

Chapter 3

To Have and to Hold:
✤ The First Twenty-four Hours ✤

Almost more amazing than the birth itself is the fact that you are now the parent of a precious newborn baby. Although you spent nine months preparing for that role, nothing prepares you for the intensity of that first twenty-four hours with your new baby. This baby which, only a few minutes ago, was so much a part of you has suddenly emerged as his own separate little being—with distinct physical features and a distinct personality, able to see, taste, hear, smell. Your identity, too, has changed and you can now add "mother" to the list of words that best describe who you are.

During these early hours in your new roles, both you and your baby are guided more or less by instinct—your baby knowing how to breathe for air, turn his head in your direction, suck for food, swallow, get rid of wastes, cry for attention. You, too, will immediately find yourself performing many parental tasks instinctively—reaching for your baby when he cries, protecting him against unnecessary noise, patting his back, stroking, talking to your little one, wrapping the receiving blanket a little tighter against a draft. Parenting is foreign and yet natural, a little scary but exciting, tiring and yet invigorating all at the same time.

To help you relax and enjoy your new baby during the first twenty-four hours, read through the information presented in this chapter, including everything from Apgar scores and birth weight to bonding and newborn abilities. As each minute of this first day with your baby passes, you will become more and more amazed at all this tiny baby can do and at the same time, how much he needs you.

✤   ✤   ✤

In-y or Out-y?
The way the cord is cut, and the type of clamp or tie used to secure it, has no bearing on the type of belly button your child will grow up to have. So don't blame (or thank) Dad or your doctor for your child's in-y or out-y.

CUTTING THE CORD

The umbilical cord is a thick, whitish, glossy cord which connected your baby to the placenta during your pregnancy. Throughout your pregnancy, the cord served as your baby's connection for nutrition and oxygen. The cord can range from twelve to thirty-six inches in length! With so much cord and so little space, it is easy to imagine why the cord sometimes gets wrapped around the baby's neck. Usually, your doctor or midwife will be able to easily slip the cord over the baby's head and out of danger's way. This may have occurred at your delivery. In rare cases, however, the cord is wrapped too tightly and the baby must be born by cesarean.

Once the cord is cut, the baby is officially his own, separate entity, ready to take on the world in his own limited way. Many caregivers allow the father to cut the cord, a ceremonious way of including dad and ending the mother-fetus relationship. Your doctor or midwife will show your partner exactly where to cut. Surgical scissors are used, but cutting the cord does not hurt you or the baby.

Practitioners differ on when to cut the cord. One school of thought suggests that it is wise to wait until the blood in the cord has stopped pulsing. Others believe it should be cut right away. There is no real medical consensus on this point. Doctors seem to agree, however, that the cord should be clamped before the baby is raised above the level of the birth canal. Otherwise, some of the baby's blood may drain out of the baby and back into the placenta, possibly causing anemia.

After the cord is cut, you will see that a stump remains. The stump may have a clip or tie around it. For more information on the umbilical cord stump, see page 60.

Your Baby's Reaction to Aggressive Suctioning
If your baby needs aggressive suctioning, it can be a little unpleasant to watch. Your baby is going to let everyone in the room know what she thinks of the process as well! Your baby will quiet down (and breathe a lot easier) as soon as you get her back in your arms.

SUCTIONING THE BABY

Most babies are born with a certain amount of fluid in their nose and mouth. Lung secretions and swallowed amniotic fluid are squeezed out of the baby during a vaginal delivery and may end up in the nose and mouth. Liquids in the baby's nose and mouth can sometimes interfere with a baby's breathing, especially if any of the fluid contains meconium. Usually, your baby's airways will be cleared as soon as the head appears at the delivery. In a quick delivery, the baby may not be suctioned until after delivery. Suctioning involves the use of a bulb syringe to pull fluids from the baby's nose, enabling the newborn to breathe more easily. Not all newborns need to be suctioned. When more aggressive suctioning is needed, your doctor may turn to a suction machine mounted on the wall. A thin tube may be inserted into the baby's nasal passages or mouth while the machine works to pull out fluids.

THE FIRST BREATH

As soon as the baby is born, everyone in the room is waiting to hear the baby take the first breath or make his first cry. There are many new stimuli that cause a newborn to take those first breaths: light, the feeling of air on the skin, the sounds around him, the sudden coolness of a 72-degree room after the warmth of a 98-degree womb. Although doctors no longer hang babies upside down by their heels and slap them to elicit that first cry, they still need to pay close attention to early respiratory attempts. The first breath is taken in the first few seconds following birth and normal, effective respiration should be achieved within one minute after birth. In a normal vaginal birth, the baby's chest was squeezed by the pressure of the birth canal, helping to express a certain amount of fetal lung fluid. This helps the newborn to breathe immediately after birth. By crying, the newborn helps to fill the tiny collapsed airspaces in his lungs with air. This helps to get the airways open and working.

Occasionally, a baby will take gasping breaths before his head emerges from the vaginal canal. It is not known why some babies do this but some doctors believe it is a sign of distress. Unfortunately, the gasping breaths can cause baby to inhale amniotic fluid, which may get into his nose, mouth, or even his lungs. See the section on suctioning (page 22), which helps rid the baby of excess fluids in nose and mouth. Babies who have amniotic fluid in their lungs, especially if tainted with meconium, are transferred to intensive care for testing, oxygen, and observation, and are closely monitored for twenty-four to forty-eight hours. See page 188 for more on meconium aspiration.

A Doctor's Thoughts
"The most amazing thing about a newborn is the way he or she quiets down right after birth. At first the baby is crying and looks yucky, and the next thing you know the infant is wide-eyed and alert, quiet, ready to eat, and primed to receive human contact and be loved."—Dr. Ian Holzman, Chief of Newborn Medicine, Mt. Sinai Hospital, New York

✛

Rapid Breathing
It may seem to you that your baby is breathing too quickly. Rapid, irregular breaths are normal in the first few days of life. A newborn baby takes as many as sixty breaths a minute. An adult takes only about thirteen!

All Systems Go
Babies arrive surprisingly well equipped to handle the independence so recently thrust upon them. In the first twenty-four hours after birth, your baby's circulatory, respiratory, and hormonal systems will begin to function effectively.

APGAR SCORE

Your baby's general health is assessed at one minute and five minutes after birth. Usually, the rating is done by a doctor, midwife, or nurse in attendance at the birth. A score is given, ranging from 0 to 10, with 10 being the healthiest. The Apgar tests evaluate your newborn's color, heart rate, respiration, muscle tone, and reflex irritability. All these things give clues as to your newborn's well-being. A score of 0, 1, or 2 is given for each test. For example, a pinkish baby gets a 2 while a baby with tinges of blue rates a 1. The scores are then added and totaled. A score of 7–10 is considered normal. These babies usually require only routine care. Scores under 7 may indicate the need for resuscitative or other emergency measures. Happily, at least one study has shown that the Apgar score at birth has no bearing on intelligence in later life, so even babies who get off to a shaky start can end up doing just as well as those who start out life problem-free.

BRAZELTON NEONATAL BEHAVIOR ASSESSMENT SCALE

With so many more skills now expected of the newborn, the Brazelton behavior assessment scale can provide a more in-depth look at baby's abilities. The Brazelton behavior assessment is not routinely used for normal newborns, although it can be. Such surveillance would be more likely ordered in the case of a baby with a birth injury or other problem, or a newborn recovering from the effects of drugs taken by the mother during delivery. The assessment takes about thirty minutes. A baby might also be looked at over a period of a few days. It is often used to test an infant's motor, social, self-calming, and reflexive skills. Often, the test is performed in front of the mother and father, who can use this time to learn some interesting things about infant behavior. The nurse or doctor tests the way in which the baby responds to his environment. The test giver may, for example, shake a rattle to see if a baby will turn to look at it. He may note the newborn's response to the human face, voices, speech, and smells. The scale is based on environmental interactions such as alertness, consolability, and cuddliness. It also notes the newborn's response to stress, in terms of skin color, startling, and trembling. Motor skills are looked at as well—specifically hand-to-mouth movements, reflexes, muscle tone, and activity. Lastly the baby's physiological state is observed, as the clinician notes the baby's ability to calm himself when upset and the ability to get used to certain stimuli (for example, a newborn may react to a loud noise the first time he hears it but then shut it out as the noise is repeated a second or third time).

BIRTH WEIGHT

Soon after the birth, your baby will be weighed. The average birth weight is 7½ pounds. In the first few days, babies may lose some of that weight. This is normal. Babies arrive ready for action, full of fluids and fat meant to sustain them through the birth and during the first day or two of life. Don't worry if your baby weighs less when you check out of the hospital than he did when he was born. Your baby's weight will begin to increase again over the next couple of weeks.

If your baby is well below the average birth weight or well above it, and is considered to be low birth weight or high birth weight, he may need some extra attention. A full-term baby who weighs less than 2,500 grams is considered to be a low-birth-weight baby. Some babies are not only low birth weight but also premature. The two groups face some of the same problems but they are, at the same time, quite different.

Large babies (once safely out!) usually pose a danger only if their size is due to maternal diabetes. This condition, known as macrosomia, may warrant some time in the nursery where doctors and nurses can monitor the newborn, and keep an eye on the baby's blood sugar levels.

Losing Weight
Babies can lose as much as 10 percent of their body weight in their first few days of life, but this will be regained shortly thereafter.

Gaining Weight
Assuming your baby weighs in somewhere around the average of 7½ pounds, you can probably count on him doubling his birth weight in the first five months and tripling it by year end.

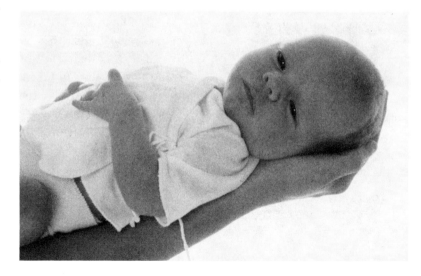

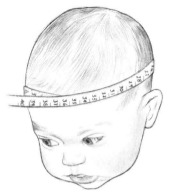

The baby's head circumference is taken and recorded.

BIRTH LENGTH

A nurse will measure the length of your baby soon after birth and this figure, along with the weight, will be recorded. The average length at birth is 20 inches. Your baby will likely measure anywhere from 18 to 22 inches. Although interesting to know, it cannot predict the future. A long baby does not necessarily mean a tall adult!

HEAD CIRCUMFERENCE

The head circumference is measured at birth, using a disposable paper tape measure. The head circumference will continue to be measured and recorded over the first two years, the period of most active brain growth. The average newborn head circumference is 13.8 inches. If the head is unusually large, extremely small, or if changes in size over the coming months do not take place as expected, your doctor will want to speak with you about possible medical concerns.

CHEST CIRCUMFERENCE

Right now, your baby has a narrow little chest, compared with his oversized head and protruding abdomen. The chest circumference will be measured with a tape measure. The chest circumference should be less than the head circumference in a newborn. By age one, the chest circumference will be larger than the head circumference. You may notice that your baby seems to have little breasts. This is normal swelling due to the amount of the mother's hormone still in the newborn's system. It will decrease and disappear in both boys and girls.

BONDING

Bonding is that special process of becoming close to your child. It is wonderful if you can spend the first twenty-four hours with your new baby, getting to know one another. If you can't, do not despair. Bonding will occur even if, for medical reasons, you are unable to be with your child for the first twenty-four hours. It does not need to occur on schedule or on cue. Parents of newborns in the intensive care unit know what all parents know—that the ties that bind parent and child continue to grow, develop, and change over the first few weeks and, in fact, throughout all the years of childhood.

Assuming your baby is healthy, however, you will likely want to keep that baby with you, not because you read some academic study on bonding but because emotion and instinct tell you to. You have just spent hours working harder physically and emotionally than you ever have in your life, all for the opportunity to see and hold and kiss this newborn in your arms. Now that she is here, you may not want to let her go. Most hospitals now provide well-baby checkups and monitoring right at your bedside out of respect for your desire to stay in close contact with this brand-new baby. If all goes well, this means you have been the primary caretaker of your baby from minute one. While this is undeniably a major responsibility, it also brings major good feelings as you begin to see yourself in the role of capable provider. The magic cement that holds parent and baby together should begin to set.

It stands to reason that the more time you spend with your newborn and the more responsibility you take for his care, the sooner the two of you will get to know one another. This is the case even if you are the parent of a baby in intensive care. Simply sitting next to and watching your baby through the Isolette brings the two of you closer. Bonding occurs every time you pick up a newborn who is crying and find that the crying stops when you hold her, every time you watch your child fall into a satisfied sleep at your breast following a feeding, every time you dress her and see how perfect she is, every time she looks at you with those expectant eyes, every time you stroke her skin and feel its soft smoothness.

FEEDING ON THE DELIVERY TABLE

As soon as the baby is delivered, he will probably be offered to you for nursing, unless you have specifically requested otherwise. Your obstetrician or delivery nurse will usually help you to get started. Your newborn will enjoy the comfort that sucking naturally brings and you will enjoy the automatic physical benefits. The act of breastfeeding helps your uterus to contract and stop the flow of blood. During the first twenty-four hours, you may put your baby to your breast many times. Feed your baby whenever you think he wants to suck. Switch sides uniformly during the feedings, so the baby doesn't drink only from one breast. Drink plenty of extra fluids yourself.

A Proverb
There is an African proverb which says, "Children are the reward of life."

✤

A Mother's Reflections
"As soon as my daughter was born, the nurse helped me hold her and feed her. She had to be suctioned a few times but the nurse did it right next to the delivery bed, so the baby never had to leave my side. When I held her, she seemed to look right at me, not crying, just staring in wonder. Even though she obviously couldn't understand what I was saying, I couldn't help talking to her."

✤

Your One and Only
The footprint and hospital ID bracelet give black and white proof of a fact all parents realize right away: that this baby is unique. Every newborn looks, feels, moves, reacts, and affects his parents differently. Your baby is one of a kind and, already, you know him best.

Letting Off Steam
One third of body heat loss is through the head. This is why a cap can help keep baby warm.

✦

Is Baby Cold?
New parents may make the mistake of keeping baby warmer than necessary. A newborn's hands and feet may feel cold while the rest of him is quite warm. Check the back of his neck for a more accurate idea of his body temperature and then remove or add a blanket as necessary.

During the first twenty-four hours, your baby will be drinking a premilk substance known as colostrum. Don't let anyone tell you this is inferior to milk or worthless. Colostrum is the perfect drink for your baby right now and contains all that he needs, including antibodies that will protect him from the germs and illnesses lurking in his new environment.

If you are not breastfeeding, and have chosen to begin bottle feeding right away, make sure the staff at the hospital knows of your decision, so they can provide you with bottles of water and formula for feeding. For more on breastfeeding and bottle feeding, please see Chapter 18, "Feeding in the First Year." To help you decide whether to choose breastfeeding or bottle feeding, see page 37.

FOOTPRINTING THE BABY

Hospitals take a footprint of your baby for positive identification purposes. These are kept with the record of height, weight, name, time of birth, and so on. After the birth, there's a lot of paperwork like this to be filled out by your attendants but you're usually blissfully unaware of the work going on around you, so entranced are you by that new little face in your arms.

HOSPITAL ID BRACELET

Hospitals will place a plastic bracelet on your newborn's wrist to match your own. The bracelet identifies your newborn by sex and last name as well as date and time of birth. It is checked against your own each time baby is brought to you. At the end of your stay at the hospital, the bracelet will be removed. Most hospitals will give it to you if you want to keep it as a memento.

TEMPERATURE CONTROL

Immediately after delivery, your newborn will be wrapped in prewarmed receiving blankets and placed on your chest. Your own body heat should help to keep your baby warm. Remember, the outside air temperature is almost 20 degrees lower than the warm, snug environment your baby just came from. Furthermore, since infants are born wet, they cool off very quickly in the outside air. Some infants need a little extra warming in the early hours after birth and may be given a stocking cap to wear on their heads or placed under a radiant warmer in the nursery.

REFLEXES

Newborns exhibit a range of reflexes in response to certain stimuli. For example, a loud noise or loss of balance may cause an infant to stiffen and thrust her arms outward in the *Moro reflex*. The Moro reflex is also referred to as the startle reflex because the baby is tensing and arching her little body, as though she is trying to grab on to something. You can calm her just by putting your hand firmly and gently on her arm or shoulder. A full-term baby will have a healthy *hand grip* to go along with this and can squeeze your finger. Newborns usually also exhibit the *righting reflex*. If you put a healthy term baby on her back and then pull her up to a sitting position, she will try to hold her head forward in an attempt to right herself. Without the righting reflex, the head would lag behind with no support or control. The *rooting reflex* is a strong instinctual reflex designed to ensure baby's survival in the outside world. Almost as soon as your baby is born, she will begin to hunt for a nipple. No one can explain how a baby, thrust into a completely foreign environment, has any knowledge of a way to get food or comfort, but they seem to come prepared for just that. Called *rooting*, it is this reflex that allows your baby to find her new food supply. If you put your baby to your breast, she will instinctively turn her head toward the nipple and try to latch on and suck. If you even stroke a newborn's cheek with your finger, she will again instinctively turn in the direction of your finger, thinking it might be a food source. As more evidence of the marvelous perfection of nature, newborns have a *gag reflex* which protects them against choking. Newborns are designed only for liquid diets. If they get something besides liquid in their mouths, they will not swallow it, but instead, automatically gag. Likewise, if they get too much milk in their mouths at once (this might be the case in a bottle-fed baby with a free-flowing nipple), the gag reflex will kick in. The gag reflex also helps them to spit up some of the mucus they may have swallowed during the birth. Your pediatrician may test this reflex with a tongue depressor. Much to the delight of many new parents, your newborn also has a *stepping reflex*. If you hold her in a

The Moro (startle) reflex

The grasp reflex

The stepping reflex

The tonic neck (fencer's) reflex

standing position on the bed, and allow a little weight to fall on one foot and then the other, she will begin to instinctively draw up and put down each leg, as though walking. This reflex vanishes fairly quickly. The *tonic neck reflex* can be seen if you put your infant down on her stomach. She will turn her head to one side and bring her arm up so that her hand is in her line of sight. One leg will bend and the opposite arm will bend down like a fencer.

EYEDROPS

In the first hour after birth, your baby's eyes will be treated with silver nitrate drops or antibiotic ointment. This is routine although parents who are opposed may refuse the treatment. You would probably be asked to sign something, since this decision would be against medical advice. The eye treatment prevents blindness that can occur in a baby born to a woman with gonorrhea. Even though you may be confident that you do not have gonorrhea or chlamydia, the American medical community has instituted this routine for all newborns because tests to detect gonorrhea are not always accurate. Rather than run the risk of even one unnecessarily blind baby, the United States prefers to treat all newborns with this preventative measure. Some practitioners like to wait a few minutes before administering the drops or ointment, allowing the infant to see his parents and his new world with clear eyes. Use of the eyedrops or ointment tends to blur baby's vision temporarily.

VITAMIN K INJECTION

Here is this perfect little creature you adore and are aching to protect . . . and already he needs his first shot! The old adage is probably true here. It'll hurt you more than it'll hurt your baby. Try to keep in mind that the vitamin K shot is a protective measure. It helps newborn blood to clot. Babies do not begin to make their own vitamin K until five to eight days after birth. To help fill in the blank space here, babies are routinely injected with vitamin K. Although it is unlikely that your baby will get a cut during those early days (unless you are planning a circumcision), the thinking is that it is better to be safe than sorry.

A Note
Although it can be fun to see all the "tricks" your baby can do, don't make yourself overanxious by trying to "test" all your baby's reflexes. He may not do what you want him to. For example, a perfectly normal baby may not exhibit a Moro reflex because he's just not interested right then. If, however, as you continue to observe your newborn, you feel your baby responds inappropriately to certain stimuli, it wouldn't hurt to mention this to your pediatrician.

HEPATITIS B VACCINE

A relatively new vaccine, HepB protects your child against hepatitis B, which causes liver infection and can even lead to liver cancer and a shortened life expectancy. The vaccine was made mandatory for children when the medical community began to see a rise in hepatitis B among people with no risk factors for the illness. Since its introduction, the incidence of the disease has, as expected, been going down. Unlike other immunizations, this one is recommended to be given at birth. This early inoculation helps to safeguard against infected mothers who may unknowingly pass the disease to their infants in the first months of life. You will typically be asked by the hospital to sign a consent form and then the shot will be given to your child. The hepatitis B vaccine is repeated one month later and again between six and eighteen months, depending on the schedule your pediatrician has worked out. For information on other immunizations, see pages 68–70.

PKU AND CH TEST

Around day two or three, your baby will be given a blood test to detect PKU. (This would not be done in the first twenty-four hours after birth.) PKU stands for phenylketonuria and the test screens for a congenital condition in which a protein-metabolizing enzyme is missing from the infant's makeup. Untreated, PKU can lead to seizures and mental retardation. If PKU is discovered, a special diet is necessary which can circumvent the problem and prevent the condition. The blood which is drawn from the heel can also be used to screen your child for other conditions, including thyroid malfunction (congenital hypothyroidism, or CH) and bilirubin levels.

VISION

No matter what you may have heard, newborns *can* see immediately after birth. As you hold them in your arms, you will notice how they concentrate on your face. Research has shown that babies will respond to a sketch of eyes, nose, and mouth over more random drawings. They are drawn to the human face and see it best when

---

A Doctor's Thoughts
Many people worry about the additional costs of yet another vaccine. But look at it this way: "The cost of giving a hepatitis B shot to a newborn and preventing the disease is about $10. We spend $350 million a year on the disease itself."—Dr. Barbara Watson, Director of the Vaccine Evaluation Center, The Children's Hospital of Philadelphia

Pretty as a Picture
Babies seem to prefer looking at patterns with stripes and angles as opposed to solid color patterns or even circular patterns.

Smile Power
Do babies actually smile in the first few days following birth? Although it may not be considered a voluntary response, babies do smile in response to your gentle touch and crooning. They also smile to themselves in their sleep. Later their smiles will become more meaningful.

Over and Over Again
You and your baby will go through about 5,000 diaper changes before he is toilet-trained!

Cloth Diapering

Fold cotton diaper in thirds and place it on opened diaper cover.

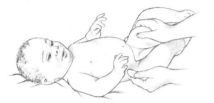

Place baby's bottom on the diaper, fold the diaper between baby's legs and adjust Velcro tabs at sides for a good fit.

held at a distance of about 12 inches, roughly the length from their face to yours when held in your arms. Objects farther than a foot away may appear hazy. They can follow an object of interest with their eyes and even turn their head to continue tracking it. They will close their eyes to bright lights and squint if the lighting in the room changes.

MECONIUM PASSAGE

The very first "dirty diaper" you change may come as a shock. How did this black goo come out of your perfect little baby when next to nothing has gone in? Newborns pass meconium during the first twelve to twenty-four hours. Meconium represents the waste from products they received from you while still in utero, combined with any fluids and mucus they swallowed during the birth. Meconium is very black and sticky, almost like tar, but has no smell. Sometimes, babies pass meconium during the birth. This is considered by some to be a sign of fetal distress but can apparently also occur in the absence of fetal distress. In fact, breech babies often pass meconium even though they're perfectly fine. After birth, meconium passage is normal and expected, and not a sign of any problems. Once you have changed a couple of meconium-filled diapers, bowel movements change to a loose, watery consistency with a yellowish color. Bottle-fed babies will have a browner, more solid stool.

DIAPERING DUTIES

You're not likely to get through the first twenty-four hours without having to change a diaper! In fact, a newborn may urinate as many as twenty times in one day. Don't worry. You needn't change baby every single time. Change her every two to three hours, and as soon as possible after every bowel movement. Feces are much more irritating to the skin than urine.

For some women who babysat as teens, diapering may be old hat. For others, remember: Simply having female genes does not mean you're an automatic expert at baby care basics like diapering. To change a disposable diaper:

1. Place the baby on your hospital bed or lean over her bassinet. Never let go of a baby who's lying on a bed.
2. Undo the tapes on the old diaper, and lifting the baby with

one of your hands around both ankles, slide the old diaper out from underneath the baby.

3. Before you put her bottom back down, quickly wipe it clean with a wet cotton pad or a commercially prepared wipe.
4. Slide a clean, open diaper underneath baby, with tapes at the back, and lower baby's bottom down onto it.
5. Center the baby on the diaper.
6. Pull the front of the diaper up between baby's legs.
7. If necessary, fold the diaper down slightly so it doesn't rub on the umbilical cord stump.
8. Secure sides with sticky tapes.

There is no need to use any powder or lotions. Baby's skin needs no more than simple water to get clean. If you do opt for powder, however, cornstarch is recommended, as talc can be breathed into the lungs. Lotions and creams may come in handy in later weeks and months, in the event of a diaper rash, but there is no need to use them before this.

Don't be alarmed if your baby fusses at diaper changes. You are not doing anything wrong. The simple act of unwrapping a securely bundled little newborn and exposing his skin to air and a cool wipe can be unsettling and annoying to this little newcomer. Try to keep everything on hand, to make diaper changes as smooth and speedy as possible.

For information on cloth vs. disposable diapers, see page 40.

Sticky Problem
If the tab on a disposable won't stick, you can always use a little masking tape or even a Band-Aid!

✛

A Mother's Reflections
"The first day or two in the hospital, my husband roomed in and changed every single diaper. I was breastfeeding so I guess he wanted to be doing everything else. When he left to go back to work, I panicked . . . my baby was three days old and I didn't even know how to change a diaper! In a real reversal of stereotypical roles, Peter had to quickly show me how to do it before heading out to the office."

CHAPTER 4

✦ Early Choices ✦

Within hours of your baby's birth, you are making decisions regarding your baby's care. Advice and opinions are to be had everywhere, but your child's upbringing is ultimately up to you. This chapter helps you to tackle some of the earliest decisions you will be making regarding your child: whether to take advantage of rooming in or the hospital nursery, how and whether to limit visitors, whether or not to circumcise your baby boy, whether to breastfeed or bottle feed, whether to use cloth or disposable diapers, and even what to name your baby!

✦   ✦   ✦

ROOMING IN

After you and your baby have been monitored closely for a few hours, the two of you will be shown to your hospital room. At some hospitals, you will be able to stay in the same room you delivered in. At other hospitals you will be moved to a new room. Depending on your hospital's policies, you may be able to keep your baby with you throughout your stay. This is known as rooming in. Other hospitals have only partial rooming in allowed. This means that the baby is occasionally taken to the nursery along with other babies. This may be at visiting hours or between midnight and 6 A.M. If the hospital is flexible about its rules, make sure you let your wishes be known. You may be able to keep your baby with you when most are being taken away.

This is a wonderful time to get to know your new baby. Meals are being served to you, your sheets are being changed by someone else, and help is only a holler away. You can really concentrate on the baby. Even though you may be tired from the delivery, you're probably also

A Doctor's Thoughts
"I am very pro–rooming in. I think babies and mothers ought to be together. I trust mothers' observations of their babies during this period."—Dr. Ian Holzman, Chief of Newborn Services, Mt. Sinai Hospital, New York

on a high, with a sudden feeling of energy and a strong desire to see the product of your labor lying right next to you. If, however, you really feel like you need a little time to yourself, take advantage of the nursing staff's offer to care for the baby in the nursery.

VISITORS

Your partner, your parents, and your older children will all want to be at the hospital, spending time with you and your baby. Friends and neighbors will be calling too, wondering when they can come and visit. The hospital you are in may have specific rules about who can visit and when. Check on these before you invite people over, so that there are no surprises. Some hospitals allow immediate family to visit at any time. Others impose strict regulations on anyone other than the father. Some hospitals remove the baby from your room and place the baby in the nursery during visiting hours. Others leave it up to you.

To the extent that you have a choice, you may enjoy having visitors or not. Some women feel uncomfortable in a hospital setting and would rather wait until they're home (and in street clothes) to receive friends. Others are feeling energetic and lively and can't wait to show off the new baby and talk to close friends and relatives about the birth. You may even feel one way one day and another way the next. Abide by your own feelings (not other people's wishes) and tell your friends what to do. If you feel uncomfortable doing so, ask your partner to handle calls and schedule visits, politely reminding people to stay only a half hour, if that's all you think you can handle.

Remember—you're a mom now and you have a right to control who you and your baby see and when.

CIRCUMCISION

You may still be wondering whether or not to circumcise your baby boy. This is a decision a lot of parents try to make before the birth but some do not make until after they have their baby. Circumcision should not be performed in the first twenty-four hours. You need to wait until the baby's condition has been stable for at least that long. Discuss the issue with your pediatrician and family if you have questions or concerns. Not everyone will reach the same conclusions. For some, circumcision is an important part of their religious faith. For others, circumcision is no longer a routine procedure. Parents are arriving at their own, very personal decisions regarding this matter. Circumcision involves the surgical removal of foreskin from a baby boy's penis. Studies are ongoing to determine whether there are any benefits to this procedure, with at least one study pointing to a possible connection between the uncircumcised penis and an increase in urinary tract infections among boys. Dangers and side effects of circumcision are also being explored, including the always-present dangers of infection which are a possibility in any surgery. Some tout the benefits of an intact foreskin, which they surmise is there to protect the delicate and very sensitive end, or glans, of the penis. The American Academy of Pediatrics sits on the fence, able only to list the current pros and cons. Opponents of circumcision, meanwhile, have pointed out that we do not routinely cut off any other part of our bodies for preventative (or possibly preventative) reasons.

Outside the medical community, parents may be weighing other, more social or psychological, factors. Some parents have expressed a concern that the child should look like the father. There is no evidence that a maturing boy would be psychologically hurt by the thought that his penis looks different from his father's. A straightforward explanation regarding beliefs about circumcision when Dad was a boy compared with the change in beliefs by the time Junior was born is all that would be needed to answer any question that may come up. Similarly, imagined locker room scenes should not present a worry to parents, who can at the very least rest assured that there will be a mixture of circumcised and uncircumcised penises in locker rooms across the country.

Recent attention has been paid to the pain of circumcision, which is often performed without any anesthesia. Parents who choose to circumcise may want to discuss pain relief with their doctors before the operation. Find out what, if any, painkiller is offered and discuss the benefits, as well as possible side effects of its use.

HUMAN MILK VS. FORMULA

For a long time now, the medical community has been in agreement over one thing: breast milk is the best milk for normal, full-term babies. Many mothers, therefore, choose to provide nothing but breast milk for their infants for the first year. The American

Circumcision Rates
Although circumcision is still popular in the United States, 85 percent of the world's male population is not circumcised. Circumcision rates within the United States have been declining since the 1960s. Within the United States now, about 40 percent of newborn boys are *not* circumcised (according to a November 1992 issue of *American Baby*).

Academy of Pediatrics specifically recommends that babies be given breast milk for the first six to twelve months of life. With the possible exceptions of vitamin D and iron, breast milk from a healthy mother contains everything a baby needs to grow and thrive. Breast milk contains every nutrient, in the proper balance, at the proper temperature and in the proper amounts for your newborn. You never hear of a baby "allergic" to breast milk, a universally well-tolerated substance. Breast milk also hides another gem: the ability to protect newborns, with their still immature immune systems, from germs and illnesses that lurk in the outside world. The mechanisms of this protection are not fully understood and cannot be duplicated by formula. The health benefits can continue throughout early childhood, long after breastfeeding has stopped. For the mother, there are other benefits: from the undocumented belief that breastfeeding can help you to lose weight to the possible link between breastfeeding and lower rates of breast cancer among premenopausal women and lowered risk of osteoporosis. Lastly, breastfeeding is convenient, always available, always sterile, and costs nothing. Furthermore, if you choose to breastfeed, you can know that you alone are providing your baby with the excellent nutrition he needs to accomplish amazing feats of growth during the first year. You are also helping to fuel his emotional growth just by responding to his needs, and holding the infant close to feed him. It's a wonderful feeling to know that not only did you give birth (and life) to this baby, you have the power to sustain that life throughout the first six months with no outside help at all and throughout the rest of the first year with the addition of some solid foods.

The American Academy of Pediatrics, while advising breast milk, adds that the only acceptable substitute during the first year is iron-fortified infant formula. Formulas have been expertly created to mimic the qualities and properties of breast milk and remain as a suitable alternative to breastfeeding for many families. Although no formula has been able to equal breast milk, babies can be bottle-fed with safety and love. Bottle feeding has presented a danger only to babies in undeveloped areas of the world with impure running water and poor hygienic conditions. If you choose to bottle-feed, you and your baby can enjoy some of the same closeness at feeding times that nursing moms and babies do. Holding your baby in your arms and watching her drain her bottle is satisfying for both of you. Bottle feeding allows you greater freedom to leave your baby and spend time apart because someone else can always offer the baby a bottle in your absence.

The Academy advises against whole cow's milk and low-iron formula during the first year of life.

NAMING THE BABY

Be it Dean or Derek, Karen or Kristen, the name you give your baby will last for a lifetime! It may seem like it's taking you a lifetime to decide on it, too! Sometimes, of course, parents have a name all picked out and ready to go, but you needn't count it as your first parental failure if your newborn is still unnamed on day two. The awesome responsibility, power, and sheer fun of naming your baby can cause the process to drag on. Customs of naming differ in different cultures and religions. It helps to get suggestions from books of baby names. These books often tell you the meaning of the name as well as the origin and the nicknames commonly associated with it. You may decide for or against a name based on names already held by family members, meanings, popularity or originality, the nickname, or the memory of someone you knew in grade school with the same name. Remember: No matter how hard you try to avoid it, the name you choose will inevitably end up being twisted into a nasty rhyme by some grade school tyrant somewhere, so it's almost useless to worry about it! It's also useless to worry about pleasing everyone in the family. One grandparent may love the sound of the name "Larissa," while the other one may complain he can't even spell it! Speaking of spelling, unusual spellings may mean a lifetime of corrections for your child but need not be avoided. It's not terrible for a child to learn early on that being a little different can add beautiful and interesting dimensions to the ordinary.

Once you're close to deciding on a name, write down the initials. Do they form a word or stand for anything? If so, is that word likely to be a positive or negative addition to your child's self-esteem?

For those of you with serious protocol questions, a son may ... named after his father, as in John Ray Smith, Jr. He would ... called John Ray Smith II. If there is also a grandfather by ... name, however, the father is John Ray Smith, Jr., and ... becomes John Ray Smith III. If the baby is not named aft... but is named after his grandfather, uncle, or cousin, ... called John Ray Smith II.

A Mother's Reflections

"My firstborn was a boy, named Austin. Out of curiosity, my mother asked me what I would have named him if he had been a girl. I answered, 'Vanessa,' to which my mother breathed a huge sigh of relief and added, 'Thank God it wasn't a girl!' Naturally, I told her, 'Don't count your blessings yet!' Two years later I had a girl, and in spite of my mother's opinion, I went ahead and named her Vanessa."

Tradition, Tradition!

Your family may have a tradition you want to uphold. If you come from an Irish f... ily, for example, you m... wish to consider na... as Conor, Bridge... Maeve. Of cour... your family ... land, yo... differe... Acc... c...

Fill 'Er Up
Environmentalists point to the fact that 2 percent of our landfills are already made up of disposable diapers. And disposable diapers have been in use for only about thirty years!

✛

By Popular Demand
According to a recent article in *Working Mother* magazine, 90 percent of American mothers use disposables!

✛

ost Comparison
'll spend about $50 to
onth buying dispos-
aper service is
nonth also. If
s yourself,
d energy
ou to

DISPOSABLE VS. CLOTH DIAPERS

During the first twenty-four hours, your choice of diaper will be largely decided by the hospital where you had your baby. A number of hospitals have switched to the more ecologically sound cloth diaper. Others continue to offer newborn-size disposables. Both are easy to use. These days, it is more a matter of preference than convenience. Cloth diapers are now used in combination with Velcro enclosures, making changes not only simple but also adorable (the outer "pants" can be purchased in a variety of colors and prints). There are no pins or tapes. The folded cloth diaper is placed inside the outer cotton diaper, put on just like a disposable, then adhered by Velcro. Some cloth diapers come already in one piece—a cloth diaper with attached nylon outer shell. Instead of throwing the cloth diaper into the garbage, you throw it into a pail of sudsy water, to await its turn in the washer-dryer. At the hospital, of course, the care and cleaning of these cloth diapers is the hospital's responsibility and they will instruct you as to proper placement for pickup. Disposables have the benefit of being, of course, disposable. No washing, drying, or folding is involved. Both choices seem equally amenable to baby's skin, although in your own personal use, you may discover that one or the other leads to fewer rashes for your baby. (Some people argue that cloth diapers breathe and cause fewer rashes; opponents say they tend to hold the wet, irritating urine against baby's skin rather than drawing it away like the disposables can. As with many other aspects of parenthood, testing out the claims for yourself and choosing the method that best suits your lifestyle is the only right answer.)

For information on how to use the diaper of your choice, see "Diapering Duties," page 32.

CHAPTER 5

✤ Oh, You Beautiful Baby! ✤

Just one look and most parents are convinced that theirs is the most beautiful baby of all—and rightly so. There are some unusual things about a newborn's appearance, however, and parents may have some questions about what will change and what will remain the same. There's nothing quite so wonderful as sitting back and admiring your baby's unique looks. This chapter includes everything from head shape to eye color and birthmarks.

✤   ✤   ✤

FACIAL APPEARANCE

Who does this baby look like? It may be hard to tell during those first twenty-four hours when your baby's face is still a little flattened by birth. Your baby will look a whole lot more like her true self in a week or so. Even so, you may already see a few telltale features from your family or your partner's. More likely, however, your baby will simply look like herself. There are a few things about your newborn's face that may look odd to you and that will change within the next few days. For example, the nose may look a little squashed or your newborn's chin may be pushed in. Ears may be folded over, eyelids may be puffy. The act of birth can be hard on a baby's soft little features. Don't worry. Everything returns to the shape and size it was meant to be within a week or two.

HEAD SHAPE

First of all, the head looks quite large compared with the rest of the baby's tiny body. The head is, in fact, about one quarter of the length of the whole body! This is normal. Second, the tight squeeze through the birth canal can mold a newborn's head, sometimes noticeably, other times not. Even if it looks a little out of shape to you at first, this

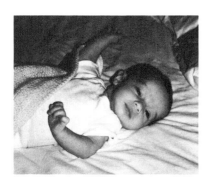

is really Mother Nature at its cleverest. The bones of the head are malleable and not firmly joined together, enabling them to adapt to the pressures of the birth canal, and allowing the head to fit through the mother's pelvis. If you think birth was a tough process, imagine what it would have been like if nature didn't have this trick up its sleeve! The end result after birth, of course, is a temporarily elongated head which, to some, looks pointed. A posterior birth, in which the baby was born with his back against his mother's back, may cause more molding than the more common anterior birth in which the front of the baby's body faces the mother's back. The natural head shape should reappear soon.

Occasionally, the head is even bruised or swollen. This is called *caput succadaneum* and is a raised bump caused as the baby's head pushed against the dilating cervix during labor. It will disappear in about a week and does not signify any health problem for the baby. If forceps were used, you may also notice slight indentations in the sides of the head. These, too, will disappear in a matter of weeks, if not in a few days.

Babies' heads are quite large and yet the muscle strength in the neck is still quite weak. Your baby will need your help supporting her head for a while.

SOFT SPOT (FONTANEL)

The top of your baby's head will have a "soft spot," or fontanel. The "soft spot" is the point where the bones of the head don't quite join. There isn't really anything "soft" about the soft spot. The area is covered with a tough membrane which protects the brain until the bones join together and fully close over the spot by eighteen months of age. To you, the area will simply feel slightly indented. You don't really need to worry about the fontanel or live in fear of your own baby as too fragile to handle. Your doctor will check the fontanel at well-baby visits.

HAIR

Some babies have a full head of hair, others a few wisps, while still others are born bald or with no more than a downy fuzz. Hair color can range from blond to black but is not necessarily the color that your child will have throughout life. Often, the newborn hair will fall out over the coming weeks, only to be replaced by a different-color

A Mother's Reflections
"Natalie was a very rosy-skinned baby with lots of jet black hair. Within a couple of weeks of her birth, however, she had blond hair and much fairer skin! We joked that every time we bathed her, we washed some of her coloring away! Pretty soon, all her black newborn hair had fallen out and she stayed blond until she was three. Now it's getting a little darker again!"

hair. Your baby may also have body hair, which will fall out. The body hair is known as *lanugo*. Lanugo, which appears on babies while still in the womb, disappears with maturity. Many term babies are born without it.

EYES

A newborn's eyes may seem small or swollen. Again, owing to the tight passage through the birth canal, some swelling is normal. This will decrease over the next few days and your baby's inherited eye shape should come more clearly into focus. Eyes can also be blood-shot from the pressure of delivery. Hemorrhages in the whites of the eyes are normal and will resolve themselves. It is not easily determined what color your baby's eyes will be. Right now, they may appear blue, only to end up being brown. Eye color often changes up until six months, or beyond.

EYE DISCHARGE

You may notice some sticky white gunk in the corners of your baby's eyes. Newborn tear ducts clog easily. Your baby will soon grow out of this stage. In the meantime, you can clean the eye by using sterile water on a sterile cotton ball. Use a fresh cotton ball on the other eye. Wipe from the inside of the eye, at the bridge of the nose, to the outside. If the discharge becomes yellowish, advise your pediatrician as this may be a sign of an infection.

A Convenient Option
Freshly expressed breast milk (assuming it hasn't touched anything else) is sterile. To clean the eye, you can express a little milk straight onto a sterile cotton ball and wipe from the inside of the eye toward the outside. Use a new cotton ball for each eye.

EARS

The ears are very soft and may have been squashed or even bent a little during the delivery. They will return to their normal shape very soon. Even as you hold your baby, you may notice that an ear can get folded over by accident. This is nothing to worry about. It will pop back up in a few seconds.

NAILS

Some babies are born with long nails. Others will quickly catch up and you will soon note the need for clipping. Long nails can be a problem because a baby can inadvertently scratch himself as he

Fashion with a Purpose
In between nail trims, you might want to use the baby "mittens" that are often found at the end of the sleeves on newborn nighties. These cover the hands and reduce the likelihood of baby cutting himself with his own nails.

waves his arms around. Use special baby clippers or scissors. Make sure you have only the nail in its grasp and then snip. You won't need to use much pressure, as baby's nails are very thin and easily cut. Try cutting the nails during a quiet moment, such as when the baby is asleep. Better yet, make nail clipping a two-person job. Perhaps your partner can do it while you're feeding or holding the baby. (Although some parents find it easy simply to bite the nails off, this has been known to cause skin infections in young babies and should be avoided.)

SKIN COLOR

Newborns often have a ruddy-colored complexion at birth, sometimes with bluish hands and feet during the first twenty-four hours. Skin color may continue to change over the first few days. Black babies may appear light-colored at birth. The pigment will continue to deepen over the coming weeks and months.

VERNIX

Babies will have creamy paste on them when they are born, known as vernix, although it may or may not be a noticeable amount. The vernix helped to protect their skin during the last nine months as they floated in the liquid of the amniotic sac. It also has the added benefit of greasing their exit through the birth canal. (Every little bit helps!) The vernix can be wiped off right after birth, although it is not necessary to do so.

MILIA

Some babies get what look like tiny white pimples on their faces, usually concentrated on the nose, cheeks, and forehead. This is known as milia and is caused by the working of the sebaceous glands. No treatment is necessary and the milia will simply disappear over the next few weeks.

ERYTHEMA TOXICUM (RED BLOTCHES)

Some newborns may get erythema toxicum, which look like red blotches and, again, are no cause for concern. On closer inspection, you can see yellowish-white pimples at the center, surrounded by a reddened area. They most commonly appear by the second day of life and disappear again by day five.

BIRTHMARKS

Birthmarks are not uncommon during the newborn period. They are rarely anything to be concerned about. Some babies are born with red birthmarks. You may wonder what causes them and whether they will grow, shrink, or remain. The various types of birthmarks are as follows:

Strawberry Hemangioma: This birthmark is, true to its name, red and slightly raised. It is quite common in newborns and likely occurred during fetal development. Most often, these strawberry hemangiomas are not apparent until the infant is a few weeks old. An infant may have only one mark or more than one. They can occur on any part of the body. Although the hemangioma may grow during the first six months, it will eventually begin to fade and disappear. Treatment is rarely if ever necessary. Eventually, the birthmark will be visible only in old photos.

Don't be concerned if a hemangioma bleeds slightly when bumped. This birthmark is made up of vascular materials that broke away from the circulatory system during development, and contains some blood.

Cavernous Hemangioma: Although not nearly so common as the strawberry hemangioma, the cavernous hemangioma also disappears with age. It is larger and more bluish than the strawberry hemangioma, with indistinct borders.

Stork Bites (Nevus Simplex): Stork bites is the fond nickname given to these salmon-colored patches which appear on baby's neck and face. Known medically as nevus simplex, these salmon patches will disappear as baby grows. No treatment is necessary.

Port Wine Stain (Nevus Flammeus): The port wine stain is a flat deep red or purplish red hemangioma. This mark may be present at birth and will continue to grow along with the child. Flat hemangiomas usually do not fade. Depending on the location, your doctor may discuss the medical significance and implications of these birth-

Quotable Quote
"Love is a great beautifier."
—Louisa May Alcott

marks with you. Rarely, the port wine stain is associated with some health problems.

Cafe-au-Lait Spots: Present at birth or soon after, these light brown spots are flat and sharply bordered. An infant may have one or several spots. While a single spot is not indicative of any underlying problem, the presence of multiple cafe-au-lait spots may suggest a health problem and should be mentioned to your doctor.

Mongolian Spots: Mongolian spots are large, flat, bluish-black areas, usually covering the buttocks and lower back, and resembling bruises. They are caused by pigment-producing cells. They cause no problems and disappear by late childhood. Mongolian spots are more common in Native American, Asian, and black newborns than in white newborns.

MALE GENITALIA

Genitalia can be a little swollen at birth, making them appear larger than normal.

In a full-term boy, the testes should have descended into the scrotum (they move from the fetal abdomen down the inguinal canal and into the scrotum around the eighth month of pregnancy). About 3 to 4 percent of the time, the testes do not descend. For more on this, see page 194 in Chapter 19, which discusses medical problems.

The testicles hang down from the baby when they are warm and retreat back up into the body when they are cold. You may notice such a shift during diapering. One testicle commonly hangs a little lower than the other, but that does not mean that one is undescended.

The foreskin of the uncircumcised penis is not yet retractable and should not be forcibly pulled back.

FEMALE GENITALIA

The genitalia may be a bit swollen at birth and therefore may appear larger than normal. In a full-term girl, the labia majora completely cover the labia minora and clitoris. In girls, there may be a white vaginal discharge or even a slight bloody discharge from the vagina, a result of the mother's hormones still circulating in the baby's body. This needs no treatment and will soon cease on its own.

When changing your daughter's diaper, be sure to wipe from the front to the back. The female anatomy being what it is, it is easy to get infection-causing fecal matter into the urinary tract if you wipe the wrong way.

BOWLEGS

After nine months tucked in a fetal position within your womb, newborns' legs are bowed. Newborns usually keep their legs in this tucked, or frog, position throughout the early weeks of life. Feet sometimes also seem bent in strange directions, depending on baby's position in the uterus. Legs and feet will straighten out on their own within a week or so. Your pediatrician will continue to check legs, hips, and feet for any problems which may need an expert's attention. For information on clubfeet, see page 191.

CRADLE CAP

If you notice small crusty patches on your baby's scalp, you are facing cradle cap, a common seborrheic dermatitis. Brushing the hair daily with a soft baby brush can help keep it under control. For more stubborn patches, try rubbing a little baby oil into the scalp. Leave it on until bath time when a thorough shampooing should be able to wash away the grease and the patches. If flaking is heavy or patches are resistant to this treatment, you might want to speak with your pediatrician about a topical ointment or other type of shampoo.

A Cosmetic Problem
Cradle cap has no side effects and doesn't bother your baby, so there is no real reason to treat it aggressively. The "problem" is purely cosmetic.

PRICKLY HEAT

A baby who gets overheated or sweaty may break out in little pink pimples. Normally found around the neck, they are not bothersome to the baby. Just use a little cornstarch to help dry up the area, and be sure you are not overdressing your baby.

CHAPTER 6

✤ Your Baby's First Month ✤

After the first twenty-four hours with your baby, the reality of a baby in your life is starting to sink in. Your joy and excitement may be mixed with apprehension and anxiety. You may wonder how you'll manage to do everything right and worry about mistakes you may make. Look back and see just how much you've already accomplished in twenty-four short hours as a parent. You have already held him, comforted him, fed him, made him feel secure and happy and full. You have changed him, talked to him, watched him respond to your face and your touch. You may already have dressed him, swaddled him, offered him a pacifier, or sponge bathed him. Not bad for a beginner! If you could handle all that in a day, just imagine how much you'll know about your baby in a month.

This chapter includes information about what your baby will be doing: how he sleeps, eats, plays, reacts.

✤   ✤   ✤

THE FIRST CHECKUP

Your baby was seen by a pediatrician during your hospital stay. It may have been a staff pediatrician or your own doctor who did the exam. Now that you are at home, your pediatrician will want to schedule a visit with you and your baby at some point during the first month. If you left the hospital shortly after delivery, you may be asked to make a visit within the next few days. Your doctor will check to make sure your baby is thriving and that feeding is going well. Your

Your Views Are Important
You may have been a mother for only a very short time, but do not underestimate the importance of your role.

"Although we examine the babies, the most important part of the visit is talking to the parents and counseling them. Most problems announce themselves by the way the child is behaving at home with the parents. Doctors can often find out more from this than from a routine physical exam. The physical exam can then be targeted to particular problems or symptoms."—Dr. Modena Wilson, Director, Division of General Pediatrics, Johns Hopkins Children's Center

✦

Type A Babies?
According to a March 1992 article in *Pediatrics*, competitive, hardworking, impatient (type A) mothers are more likely to have type A babies (babies who cry more and are harder to soothe). Authors Parker and Barrett caution, however, that "As the first study of type A behaviors during pregnancy, its conclusions should be considered tentative."

baby will be weighed and measured and given a thorough physical exam. Your baby will also be given his second hepatitis B vaccine at one month assuming he received the first dose at birth (see page 31 for more information on the HepB vaccine). If you visit your pediatrician for a checkup at two weeks, as many parents do, it is too early for the second HepB and you will have to return at one month from delivery for the shot. (You won't need another exam at this time. Just arrange with your pediatrician's office for a quick stop-in for the vaccine.)

Don't be surprised at checkups by your pediatrician's interest in your health and well-being, as well as your baby's. A good pediatrician knows that baby's health depends on your health right now. Your pediatrician will be interested to know how you are handling motherhood, whether or not you're getting any rest or are overtired, and how you are managing your health.

This is your turn to ask questions too. Pediatricians are used to parents who ask a lot of questions; they know that parents worry and wonder and worry some more. So, feel free to use the office time to express any fears or concerns and get questions answered. Unlike other doctors who may be interested only in your specific medical problem, the pediatrician wants to hear about baby's personality, ways of playing, interest in sounds, love of the bath, and so on. All these things are related to your baby's health and give the pediatrician a good idea of how you and the baby are coping. Good communication helps your doctor to help you.

PERSONALITY

You don't need a book to tell you that your newborn has a personality. You've known it since he was first born. If this is your second or third child, you probably saw personality differences between your children right away, even at the delivery itself. Undeniably, babies are individuals. This means that another experienced mother or even a book on early child care cannot tell you everything about your baby. There's so much you'll have to learn straight from the baby himself. You need to settle into your own parenting style and find the best ways to relate to your baby. For example, while rocking and dancing may calm other babies, maybe your baby doesn't like so much stimulation. There are active babies and quiet babies, sleepy babies and wakeful babies, babies who love to look at things and babies who love to listen. There are babies who like slow movement and babies who appreciate a little gentle bouncing.

There are babies who are extroverts and babies who are introverts. Your baby may have come into this world wearing his heart on his sleeve, exhibiting very active physical reactions to the world around him. Or he may react on the inside but show a poker face to those around him. The extrovert baby approaches sounds and sights happily, and can be easily distracted and amused by them. A more introverted baby will be more likely to withdraw from these same stimuli because they're a little too much to handle. As a parent, part of your job will be to determine how much stimulation (playing, talking, handling, noise) your baby enjoys and where he draws the line. You'll soon learn to provide the right amount for your baby. As your new family spends more time together, you'll discover the little things your baby likes, the little personality quirks that make your baby who he is.

NEWBORN BEHAVIOR

Much of your baby's behavior may seem random and even purposeless to you during the first month. He may wave his arm through the air, clench his fist, then open it, kick out, move his lips, jerk his body. What does it all mean? Your baby's behavior is not so simplistic as it may at first seem. Many of the skills your baby will eventually master have their root in this early behavior.

The newborn is actually quite a complex and interesting little fellow. He can see, play, hear, and respond to the world around him in much more sophisticated ways than we ever believed possible. From the beginning, he craves comfort and good feelings, avoids pain and unpleasant sensations. He shows some early social skills as well: staring into your eyes, quieting down in response to your voice or touch, perhaps even pausing in the middle of a feed to listen to an interesting sound nearby. Even in the first twenty-four hours of life, babies have been observed doing many very sophisticated things: discriminating between smells, recognizing the mother's voice, understanding basic facial expressions, imitating facial expressions, recognizing the mother's face, understanding the basics of math,

Now and Later

The little personality you view now in the cradle may have real staying power. You will probably note that, even as the child grows, much of his basic temperament remains the same. In one study of 136 children from birth through age twelve, the researchers discovered an amazing consistency in the child's responsiveness, irritability, and adaptability—especially during the first two years of life. For example, irregularities in sleep, slow adaptability to new situations, or a tendency for bad moods—noted in some newborns—persisted throughout childhood, leading researchers to conclude that personality may have a hereditary base, although the specific behaviors can be shaped by social interaction, particularly early interaction with the family (Thomas, Chess et al., *Behavioral Individuality in Early Childhood,* New York: New York University Press, 1963).

Baby Preferences
Your baby has a strong sense of taste and smell and prefers sweetness to bitter tastes, good smells to bad. Newborns are especially attuned to the smell of their own mother's breast milk. Studies have shown that babies are able to make the sensitive distinction between the smell of their own mother's breast milk and someone else's milk.

recognizing musical scale notes and more. By the end of the first four weeks, the newborn can appear excited by a certain toy, may kick or stick his tongue out just for the fun of it, may visibly cheer up in response to the mother's voice, may suck on his own fist to soothe himself, and may even smile to himself.

Crying, feeding, and sleeping times remain disorganized but seem to require less energy and effort on his part as the first month draws to a close. Physical immaturities do fill up most of the infant's time in the early weeks, as he tries to regulate the rhythms of sleeping, waking, and eating.

PLAYTIME

One of the best times to get to know your new little baby is during those alert moments, when he's neither asleep nor drowsy, nor hungry, wet or crying. This is your baby's playtime, and the play that interests him most is simply looking at your face and hearing you talk to him. During the first month, babies will also delight in a small toy that you dangle in front of their eyes or the sound of a tinkling bell or rattle. It may last only for a few minutes or the two of you may amuse one another quietly for a whole half hour. These short unscheduled play periods will become longer and more interesting as your baby grows. Play as long as your baby seems to enjoy it. If the baby becomes quiet and looks away, you'll know that it's time to stop the game.

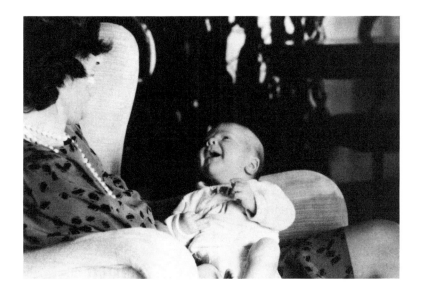

CRYING

All newborns cry, some for longer periods than others. This is normal. A baby can't be kept in a constant state of quiet contentment. In spite of their tiny size and helpless appearance, babies are capable of the most irritating and demanding cries in the world. This grating cry may be a part of their wonderful package of survival skills: certainly, a newborn's cries are hard to ignore. A baby's cry will bring Mom or Dad on the run, proving that baby's rudimentary communication skills are successful.

You probably already know that babies cry when they are hungry. Hunger is a new and very unpleasant sensation for a baby. He can't be sure just yet that anyone will come to relieve that hunger, so he cries out angrily until his need is taken care of. Some babies continue to scream even after they have been picked up and put to the breast or bottle. Until the first drops of milk find their way into their mouths, all they can think about is the hunger that drives them. Take heart: Toward the end of the first few months, you may start to notice a miraculous change in your baby's crying behavior. Fussy periods may become shorter. Cries that signify urgent needs (like hunger) may become shorter as well. He may cry out lustily, then stop, waiting for you to come. The consistent attention you give now will pay off later, as your baby comes to understand that his cries will be answered and that you are on your way. When your baby cries for you, call to him. This can sometimes stem the tide of wails. When he hears your voice, he is already somewhat comforted, and seems to understand that you are nearby. He will hold his cries for a second in anticipation of your arrival. Of course, if you take too long, you'll hear about it!

During the first month, you will also discover that babies cry for many other reasons besides hunger. Unfortunately, it is sometimes hard, if not impossible, to find the hidden reason behind the unhappiness. Here are some clues that may help:

- Is the diaper wet or dirty? Some babies get very uncomfortable when left in a dirty diaper. Check it and see if changing the nappie changes baby's disposition.
- Is the stomach distended? Is the baby pulling up his knees to his chest? This, coupled with crying, may be a sign of gas pain. Try burping the baby. This may relieve some gas. You can also try putting a little pressure on baby's tummy by sitting down and placing the baby, stomach down, across your knees and gently rubbing the back.
- Is the cry piercing? Something may be hurting her. Check to make sure clothes aren't too tight, diaper pins are not jabbing, sticky tape is not stuck to skin and so on. You may have to

An Expert's Thoughts
"Once parent and baby are comfortable with the first important interaction—breast or bottle feeding, they can begin to spend a lot of time in face-to-face interactions. This is something parents tend to do spontaneously. It is impressive how important (even critical) this is. The infant learns to read your vocal cues, how not to talk when someone else is talking, how to respond. Some easy things for a parent to keep in mind during playtime: When in doubt, imitate the baby's behavior. When the baby goes silent and looks away, this is a signal that the baby needs a break. You can describe what the baby is doing as he does it, like a sports announcer. Or talk for yourself and the baby. Babies enjoy a lot more stimulation than what was originally thought. At the same time, the primary role of the parent is to serve as a barrier to too much stimulation."—Dr. Tiffany Field, Professor of Pediatrics, Psychology and Psychiatry, University of Miami Medical School

Attuned to Mom's Voice
Research has shown that babies are more likely to quiet down and become alert when they hear higher-pitched voices than lower-pitched ones. It is believed that even at this early age, babies can differentiate between their mother's voice (which usually signals food and care) and their father's. In studies, they also show a preference for Mother's face over a stranger's.

undress the baby completely to get to the root of the problem.

- Is the baby screaming and becoming red in the face? If this occurs around the same time every day, it may be colic. Knowing the name of the problem isn't much help. No one really knows the reason (or the cure) for this periodic crying, but there are some comforting solutions you can try. See the sidebar on page 55 or turn to "Colic," page 76.

- Does she seem to visibly startle and then start crying? Her cries may be connected to loud noises such as a doorbell, phone, or tea kettle. Some babies are very sensitive to outside stimuli, even smells. You may want to respond by toning down the environment—turning down lights, reducing noise, speaking softly, moving more slowly.

- Is your baby crying during early-evening hours? This fussy period unfortunately often coincides with the hardest part of your day. You are tired by now, other children need to be fed, your partner may be coming home from work, the TV may be on, the phone may be ringing with end-of-the-day calls from relatives or close friends. Babies, too, experience a buildup of tension during the day and may simply have to let off some steam before they can bed down for the night. Regular evening cries may or may not be considered colic. Of course, it really doesn't matter what you call it: the cries are just as insistent and demanding and very hard for parents to listen to. Picking the child up, rocking him, and lavishing attention on him works sometimes but not always. If you have already determined that the cries are not being caused by hunger or a wet diaper or any physical pain, there may not be much more you can do. You may have to put him down and allow him to cry by himself a bit, then return to the bassinet and pick him up calmly. Sitting in a rocking chair with him and letting him cry on your shoulder is another alternative, but doesn't allow you to do anything else except hold the baby.

BABY NOISES

Baby's breathing often sounds somewhat irregular. Newborns sneeze, gasp, grunt, wheeze, hiccup, and take occasional rapid breaths. Although these variations can frighten a new mother, they are normal for newborns. The respiratory system is still immature and a newborn may forget to take a breath, then make up for it with some quick breathing. Dust irritates his nose and he sneezes, even though he doesn't have a cold. The little gasps and chokes are his way of adapting to the new work at hand: breathing for himself. They may also still be the result of swallowed liquids from the birth itself. Your baby may cough up a little mucousy liquid over the first few days. For information on spitting up, see Chapter 18, page 177.

DAYTIME SLEEPING

During the first month, babies seem to sleep everywhere and anywhere: in cribs, in bassinets, in your arms, in their infant seats, in their car seats. Unfortunately, you can never be quite sure when your baby will be asleep and when he might suddenly wake up for a look around. Newborns take frequent naps, some as long as three to four hours, but sleep time is often interrupted by crying and fussing. They do not always sleep peacefully through from feeding to feeding.

There may not be a lot of rhyme and reason to your baby's sleeping patterns yet, so the best thing to do is to go with the flow. Have patience. Your baby needs some adjustment time. Everything is brand new for him and this still foreign environment demands a lot of his energy.

Babies are individuals, and they need varying amounts of sleep. Some parents get very sleepy babies. Other parents say it seems like the baby is always awake. There can be tremendous differences between how long your newborn sleeps and how long your sister's same-age baby sleeps. Most babies sleep sixteen to eighteen hours out of every twenty-four. By the third month, however, some babies will be sleeping as little as ten hours a day, while others continue to sleep sixteen. Both babies are normal. One baby might nap four or five times a day, while another might nap seven or eight times a day. Unfortunately, some babies may nap for only twenty minutes at a time, leaving you feeling as if you never have any time off.

Newborns are fairly light and restless sleepers and may be easily roused by noise or commotion around them. Some babies, on the other hand, appear to always be asleep the first month and parents may be left either wondering about their good luck or worrying

An End to Crying
These soothers might help:
- Swaddle the baby (see page 57).
- Wheel the baby around the house in her stroller.
- Take the baby outside (the change of temperature, breeze in her hair, new smells and sights may stop the crying.
- Put the baby in a front carrier and walk around.
- Offer a pacifier (assuming it's sucking time and not real food she needs).
- Play some music—spin the dial until you determine whether your baby likes rock, country, or classical.
- Dance with the baby in your arms. Many babies love the movement and you get exercise too.
- Cry back at her. Hearing you mimic her sounds can silence a baby for a few minutes—maybe long enough to get her interested in something else.
- ———(fill in the blank with your own ideas). Remember, as this baby's mother, you will soon know the best ways to soothe your own infant.

Safe Sleep
The American Academy of
Pediatrics now recommends
that babies be put to sleep
on their sides or their backs.
The stomach-down position,
long favored by the medical
community in the United
States, has recently been
called into question, be-
cause of its possible link to
sudden infant death syn-
drome (SIDS), a little
understood tragedy in which
babies simply stop breathing. If you wish to put your
baby to sleep on his side,
use a rolled-up receiving
blanket tucked behind his
back to keep him from rolling onto his stomach or
back. SIDS is rare after five
months of age, so you could
presumably allow your baby
to sleep stomach down once
she is older than five
months. For more on SIDS
see page 74.

✦

Fairy Kisses?
According to Welsh folklore,
when babies smile or frown
in their sleep, it is a sign that
fairies are kissing them.

about whether their baby is all right. It is perfectly normal for new babies to have long sleeps, and then wake only to doze off again. The problem is that some babies in the early weeks sleep right through mealtime! You may have to wake the baby up for feedings. This is important, because otherwise your breasts may get engorged during the long naps.

As your baby sleeps, you may notice him smiling, frowning, grunting, wheezing, whimpering, or even sucking. You may also see his eyes darting back and forth behind his closed lids. Babies also may move their mouths while sleeping or breathe irregularly. This is all normal during your newborn's light catnaps.

NIGHTTIME SLEEPING

Don't expect your newborn baby to fall into a pattern or to sleep through the night yet—no matter what a neighbor says *her* baby does! Few babies sleep through the night during the first month. (In the early months, sleeping through the night would be considered a straight-through sleep from midnight to 5 or 6 A.M.) Many babies continue to wake up at night throughout the first year.

It may take a couple of weeks or more for babies to differentiate between night and day. Until that time, you may feel that you have been placed on duty for him twenty-four hours a day. You can begin to impose a day-night order on your baby by following certain daily rituals. For example, change the baby into pajamas, turn down lights, turn off TVs and radio. Use only the night-light when you get up to answer the baby's cries in the middle of the night. Use hushed tones when you talk to him at night. Let him feel the quiet and begin to associate it with nighttime.

Some babies cry a little when they are first put down. This fussy few seconds of crying can be baby's way of settling down into sleep. You will soon learn to recognize this as a tired cry that doesn't demand immediate action on your part but is better left alone. Likewise, if your baby is asleep and begins to whimper a bit, don't rush in and swoop her up. She may still be happily asleep, but making normal newborn noises. Of course, babies one month of age should not be left to cry themselves to sleep. If the few seconds of fussing or grumbling turns into full-scale or persistent crying, you'll want to respond rather than ignore it. At this time in their lives, their cries usually mean they need something. They may be hungry or wet or lonely. Their cries are a signal to you that they need attention. Instead of spoiling your baby, you will be teaching him that the world is a safe place, where needs are met and cries are answered. Answering the cries makes him a more relaxed, confident baby.

SWADDLING

Learning how to swaddle a baby is an important soothing technique that may earn you many precious minutes of blissful quiet. Wrapping your baby snugly into a receiving blanket can give him a sense of warmth and comfort. The wrapping also prevents him from being disturbed by his own sudden movements. Your baby will feel secure in his little package and will often drift off to sleep when swaddled. You needn't be too concerned about the wrap being too tight, since the blanket is held in place only by the baby's own weight. See the illustrations in the sidebar on the right for instructions on how to swaddle a baby.

PACIFIERS

While some babies immediately gravitate to a thumb or fist when they need something to suck on, other babies prefer a pacifier. Over the years, the pacifier has fallen in and out of favor. As long as it doesn't become a substitute for your attention, a pacifier is today considered to be a perfectly acceptable method of soothing a fussy baby during the early months. Used in the first year, pacifiers will not damage a child's dental bite.

Some parents, however, prefer not to use the pacifier because they just don't like the way it looks. If you feel this way and your baby is happy without the pacifier, then you have no problems. If you have an unusually fussy or colicky baby, however, you may need to give in and see if a pacifier can help. Some babies take to them right away; others want no part of them. You'll have to leave it up to your baby to decide.

In the early weeks, pacifiers should be kept clean and sterilized between uses. If you have questions or concerns, you might want to ask your pediatrician about pacifier use and for a brand recommendation.

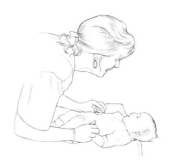

Place baby on his back on receiving blanket.

Pull one side up and bring it down diagonally across baby's shoulder and tuck it under baby's knees.

Tautly pull up the other side and fold straight down over baby.

Tuck the end securely under baby's body to create a snug little newborn bundle.

INFANT MASSAGE

Infant massage can soothe and calm your baby, and make him feel good about touch. It can work to soothe a colicky baby, help an irritable baby get to sleep, and if done before bed, may even keep him asleep longer at night. All pleasant touch is important. It doesn't have to be an all-out massage. You can stroke your baby's leg or arm as you nurse her or change a diaper. After the bath, when baby's dry and lying on the floor on an open towel, you can apply a little baby oil or vitamin E oil to your hands and give a more complete massage. Take your time with your baby. (If your infant has sensitive skin, ask your pediatrician which type of body oil is best.) If your infant is in a particularly fussy mood or doesn't seem to want to be massaged right now, don't do it. Always respect her cues and find other ways to comfort her. The massage should be something the baby enjoys. With your baby on her back, stroke the legs, from ankle to thigh. Then gently massage the abdomen and chest, using the palm of your hand. Massage the arms and hands, working from the wrists toward the armpits. You can even lightly stroke your baby's face, using your thumb to make smooth circles over the forehead and cheeks. Babies also like a back massage. Your loving touch, done at your baby's own tempo and when she is in the mood, can be a relaxing and enjoyable experience for your baby.

SPOILING

It is not possible to spoil a baby in the early months. Holding him in your arms, going to him whenever he cries, feeding him on demand will not turn him into a little tyrant. At this age he has no other way to tell you he needs you than a full-volume, demanding cry. The best response to a newborn's demands is reaction on your part, and an attempt to calm him. This is not spoiling; it is loving attention. When you lavish attention and affection on a baby, you are doing as much for his spirit and mind as food does for his body. In institutional settings where babies had proper nutrition but no one to hold and cuddle them in response to their cries, their development was significantly delayed. Rather than teaching your baby that he can have whatever he cries for, you are teaching him that he is a worthwhile and important person who is loved and deserves to be happy. He knows that he is able to communicate with his parents, get his message across, and is responded to accordingly. The lessons he learns from your attention are much more likely to make him a pleasant little person to live with than to turn him into the mythical spoiled baby who doesn't know who's boss.

ROUTINES

A newborn's basic pattern of activity is circular: he sleeps until hunger wakes him, cries, eats, feels better, looks alert, gets drowsy, falls asleep again. This pattern may repeat itself seven or more times a day. Even though there is a primitive pattern to his day, there isn't really a routine in the first four weeks. Babies are not always predictable in the first month of life, when immature digestive, neurological, and respiratory systems make the simplest things in life (getting rid of waste, falling asleep, etc.) momentous chores for baby. Your baby is very busy adapting to life outside the womb. Some days your newborn may be active; other days he may be quiet. Eating and sleeping times can be erratic.

You can, however, begin to impose some order on your baby in gentle ways. If you are breastfeeding on demand and notice that he is eating every couple of hours, for example, you may want to make the environment conducive to sleeping in between. Even though you may be feeding on demand, it will begin to approximate a schedule. Your job then is to reinforce that schedule, assuming having a routine is important to you. Most parents' lifestyles are eventually reflected in a baby's routine, anyway. Some parents are determined to get the baby to sleep all night. Others want to keep baby up late at night because of work schedules. Over time, the baby's behavior and routine usually adapt to these constraints, as they do if a baby is placed in day care early where all babies may be put down to nap or fed at the same time.

No Pillows
Never use a pillow under the baby's head. Pillows can interfere with a baby's ability to breathe. On a firm, flat mattress, the baby is able to turn his head and find a clear space for breathing.

No Honey
Never dip a pacifier in honey to encourage its use. Honey is very dangerous for children under one because it has been associated with infant botulism, a type of poisoning.

UMBILICAL CORD CARE

The stump from the umbilical cord will remain for about a week to ten days. Then it simply falls off on its own. The stump may look blackened, unattractive, and uncomfortable, but does not appear to bother the baby. Your only job is to keep the area around the stump clean and dry. You can wipe the stump with a little alcohol on a sterile gauze or a commercially prepared alcohol wipe. Turn the diaper back at the waist so that it doesn't rub against the stump, or use a newborn diaper with a notched waistline. You may see a little bleeding now and again at the base as the stump is falling off. This is normal, but redness, bleeding that continues, or a foul smell should be reported to your pediatrician, as these may be signs of infection.

BOWEL MOVEMENTS

Before you had a baby, you would never have believed how much interest you would take in what appears in baby's diaper. Now you actually spend time worrying about the timing, color, consistency, and frequency of dirty diapers. Some breastfed babies have a movement after every feeding. Others have only one bowel movement a day. It is usually a pasty consistency and a light yellow color. The number of bowel movements may change or become less frequent as the baby gets older. Your baby may even go two to three days without a movement. This is fine, as long as the bowel movement your baby does have is soft. If you are feeding your baby formula, you can expect between one and four movements a day, although your baby might have more. As your baby grows, the frequency of movements may decline. The movements may be pasty or curdlike and usually are light yellow or tan in color.

Some babies (more likely bottle-fed) can become constipated. Once they have a movement, you may notice a trace of blood in the stool if there are anal fissures. Anal fissures are tiny tears in the anus caused by the passage of very hard stools. Report this to your pediatrician.

THRUSH

Thrush is a fungus which generally appears in the baby's mouth. You may notice white patches on the tongue, cheeks, and roof of the

To Each His Own

As long as your baby is thriving and movements are not too hard or too loose, there is probably no need to worry about bowel movements. There is a great deal of variation in normal movements from baby to baby. If you notice a major change in your baby's bowel movements, especially their consistency or smell, call your pediatrician to find out about it.

mouth. Do not confuse this with the milky tongue that all newborns have right after feeding. Milk on a tongue can easily be wiped off. Although thrush is not serious, it does make the baby uncomfortable and can interfere with nursing or bottle feeding. Thrush should be treated with an antifungal medication, so call your doctor if you see signs of this fungus.

SPONGE BATHS

Until the umbilical cord stump falls off, babies should be given sponge baths. Full-immersion baths are avoided because of the slight chance of infection. Even after you are giving baby real baths, the sponge bath still has its place. A newborn won't necessarily need a full bath every day. In the early days, wiping his bottom with clean water and under his chin with a clean, wet washcloth may be more than enough. Newborn skin is delicate and keeping it clean helps to prevent rashes. Milk dribbles can hide in the folds of the skin; feces can hide in the folds of the genitalia.

Sponge baths can be given on a changing table, on the counter next to the sink, or even in the baby's bassinet. Sometimes referred to as "topping and tailing," a sponge bath lets you concentrate on the only parts of baby's body that really get dirty: the top and the bottom. Keep the baby in a T-shirt and diaper. Fill a bowl with warm water and get some sterile cotton pads or cotton wipes. Using warm water on a cotton wipe, gently clean the folds of her neck and outer ears. Wash eyes with a fresh piece of cotton for each eye. Be gentle. Never poke or push. With a fresh piece of cotton, you may want to unfold her little hands and give them a wipe too. Next, remove the diaper and clean her bottom. Be sure you get into all the folds and crevices. Clean gently around the umbilical cord stump. For more on umbilical stump care, see page 60. When you have finished, dry her bottom, put on a fresh diaper, and dress her. Put on a dry T-shirt if any of the water dripped onto her shirt.

IMMERSION BATHS

Immersion baths can be given in the bathtub, in the sink, or in one of the many, commercially available smaller baby baths. The first time you bathe your baby, you may be a little nervous. Your baby may

Bath Time Anytime
You can bathe your baby at any time of the day and you do not need to bathe at the same time every day.

Wipe eyes with a sterile wet cotton ball. With another, wipe around ears and neck. Use a third to clean mouth and chin.

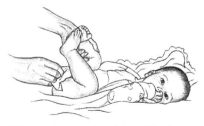

Remove diaper and wash baby's bottom with a wet washcloth. Be sure to get into all the skin folds. Dry well.

Sweet-Smelling Babies
During the Middle Ages, newborn babies were anointed with oil of myrtle and roses after their baths.—According to *Mamatoto,* by Carroll Dunham and The Body Shop Team

Safety Tip
Never bathe a baby in the kitchen sink while the dishwasher is running. Apparently, in some homes the plumbing is connected and steaming hot water from the dishwasher may back up into the kitchen sink. Some babies have been burned by this.

Using both hands, gently lower baby into the bathwater, allowing him to adjust to the new experience.

Support baby's head with one arm securely under and around baby, leaving your other hand free for washing.

Lift baby out with one hand around his shoulders and the other under his bottom. Baby can be slippery, so take care.

Wrap baby in a towel. Be sure to dry in all the creases.

sense this and tense up too. Some babies love the experience but others tend to fuss throughout. This is more likely due to an innate dislike of being undressed than to any improper handling on your part.

To make the first baths easier, choose a warm room and keep soap, a washcloth, a towel, and a change of clothes close at hand. Fill the bath with warm water. Test the temperature with your wrist or elbow. Don't overfill the sink or tub. The water only needs to be deep enough to keep some of your baby's body immersed. To make the bath less slippery, line the sink with a towel or use a rubber mat. You'll want to be able to maintain a good hold on her with her shoulders and head out of the water. Place one hand under baby's bottom and the other under the head and shoulders. If you are bathing your baby in a tub or large sink, an oversize sponge mat indented for baby's body makes a good secure place to rest baby as you wash. If you are using a small plastic baby bath, lower the baby into the bath slowly, then remove the hand that was under her bottom, and while continuing to support your baby around the neck and head, use your free hand to wash her gently with the water. Use mild baby soap and, if desired, a little baby shampoo for the hair. Remember, soap can make your baby slippery, so use very little. If you prefer, water alone will get your baby nicely clean.

If you decide to bathe your baby in the family tub, it's easiest if you or your partner gets into the bath first; then one of you can simply pass the baby to the person in the tub and take the baby back when bath time is over. As you sit in the bath, cradle your baby in your arms and allow the water to clean him.

As soon as you lift your baby from the bath, you'll want to wrap her in a warm dry towel. Use a regular towel or a baby towel. Baby towels have a triangle of material at one corner for the head. If getting a hold of the towel presents logistical difficulties for you, you can lay the towel out on the floor or on the changing table if it's nearby and lay the infant down on the towel as soon as you lift her out of the bath. Then wrap her up. Or find your own tricks—holding the towel under your chin, for example, as you lift her out onto your chest and wrap. Just be sure that you keep a firm hold on your baby and feel comfortable with the setup. The first few times you bathe your baby, it helps to have an extra pair of hands at the ready—your partner or mother, for example.

TOILETRIES

Newborn needs are few. They smell absolutely perfect without any cosmetic or commercial additions. For the most part, bathing can consist of warm-water washes and diaper changes can be accomplished with warm water on a cotton wipe. There are dozens of baby toiletry products on the market, however, from baby shampoo and conditioner to soaps, lotions, and powders. You can use these in moderation if you like, as long as your baby's skin shows no sign of irritation. If you want to use a powder, plain cornstarch is recommended over other powders. Although newborn hair can be washed with water alone, a baby shampoo may be a good idea if your baby happens to have a lot of hair. Baby shampoos are made to be gentle to baby's skin and eyes, but some brands may be better at living up to this promise than others.

DRESSING

Babies don't lie immobile like little dolls, so dressing can sometimes present a problem. At this age, however, they are pretty docile, which is a good thing considering you're new to this job and may make plenty of goofs. Some babies dislike having their clothes taken on and off. Others seem more resigned to their fate. Clothing that gets pulled over the head can be especially difficult for you and trying for the baby. Opt for jacketlike or envelope-neck T's during the early weeks. Undershirts that tie or snap at the sides may be easiest for you. Clothing should be comfortable and roomy. Nightgowns, rompers, and snap coveralls work well and are easy to get on and off. Clothing with snap crotches and legs allow you to change diapers without taking off all their clothes. Don't overdress your baby. If you feel hot, she probably does too. Use your own good sense to determine whether or not she needs a sweater or hat. Little socks or booties are a good idea indoors. Some clothing comes with feet or has a drawstring bottom to keep baby warm. See the section on layettes (page 5) to determine what you'll need the first month.

Babies grow out of clothes quickly, so stay a step ahead with something on hand in the next size up. Clothing sizes can be deceptive. A

Bath Resistance
If your baby hates the bath, don't insist on it. You can always keep her clean with sponge bath techniques for a few days and try a real bath again later.

✢

Safety Tip
When running the bath, turn the hot water off first and the cold water off last. That way, if the faucet is still dripping a little when you put your baby into the sink or bath, the water won't burn her.

month-old baby might fit into some 6-month-size clothes. Hold them up or try them on occasionally or you may end up with clothes she outgrows before she ever wears them.

Stretch the neck of the garment open wide.

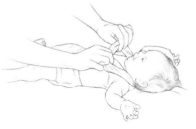

Quickly pull it over baby's head and face, keeping the garment stretched so that it doesn't get caught on nose or ears.

Put your hand inside the sleeve to grasp baby's hand and gently pull it through.

Pull shirt down over arm and chest. Repeat on other side.

OUTINGS

No matter what month your baby is born in, you can take her outside. As long as she is dressed appropriately for the weather, an outing is healthful for her and for you. Both of you will enjoy the fresh air and sunshine.

CARRYING BABY

Cradle your baby in your arms, with her head resting in the crook of one arm and her bottom supported by your other hand. You can also hold your baby over your shoulder with two hands, one to support the back and neck and the other to support the bottom. You will soon settle in to a comfortable way to carry her, and you will feel more secure with it each day. Be careful going down steps. Try to carry your baby in such a way that you can still see the steps and your feet in front of you. See the illustrations at right for more ideas on how to carry baby comfortably.

A soft, front carrier (such as a Snugli) can be an ideal way to carry your baby during the early weeks. Like swaddling, a front carrier gives a newborn a feeling of warmth and security. The close contact with your body combined with the gentle motion as you walk and move usually lulls your baby into a peaceful state, if not to sleep. Front carriers come in a variety of styles and offer varying support and comfort. See the section on front carriers on page 9. Don't overdress a baby who will be in a front carrier and periodically check your baby to make sure she's not sweating. Do not go for a run with a baby in a front carrier (that's too much bouncing for baby) and never use a front carrier in a car in place of a car seat.

The stroller or carriage is another way to take baby out. You don't have an extra load to carry and your baby gets a view of the world. To make your baby feel secure in the seat of his carriage, you can try swaddling him before laying him down in it. Make sure not to hang too many bags off the stroller or it will tip. Your baby's weight and the stroller's construction are not conducive to a lot of counterweights. See the section on choosing a stroller on page 10.

In the car, of course, a child's auto restraint is a necessity. Used correctly, the car seat will provide your baby with the safe ride he deserves. See page 11 for more on how to choose a car safety seat.

If you are going out for a short walk, it's best to travel unencumbered. You will be returning home before needing any bottles, clothes, or diapers. If you are planning to be out with your baby for a few hours, however, you will want to pack your baby bag with some essentials. Bring diapers and wipes, a change of clothes, a receiving blanket or cloth diaper for spitups, a soft rattle, and a pacifier (if your baby uses one). If you bottle-feed rather than breastfeed, you'll need to have along your formula, water in a thermos, bottle, and knife and scoop for measuring and stirring. The first few times you and your baby go out, you may feel you've taken the entire house with you! Over the next few months, you'll relax a little and get to know your baby's needs better and you will probably be able to travel a lot lighter.

TIME ALONE FOR PARENTS

Even during the first month, you may need to squeeze in a little time to yourself. You might find this time with the help of a willing spouse who can take over while you go out to get some fresh air

The sit carry allows a slightly older baby to look around while comfortably nestled back against your body.

The neck nestle is a cozy way to carry and comfort a newborn.

alone. Or you may need to hire a sitter so you can have some time with your spouse. See page 277 for information on how to choose a babysitter. The need for time alone is nothing to apologize for. Parenting is a demanding job, and as with all jobs, time off helps us to return to our duties with a fresh mind and new insights. It may not be easy to take that first step away from baby's side, but sometimes it's just what the doctor ordered.

TOYS FOR THE FIRST MONTH

Mobile
Soft toy
Soft rattle

HAPPY BABY'S HIT PARADE

High on this month's list of the top happiness inducers for baby include:

- Being swaddled (see page 57)
- Being carried in a front carrier
- Eye contact
- Looking at your face
- Listening to your voice
- Feeding times
- Being massaged (see page 58)
- Being rhythmically patted and rocked

CHAPTER 7

✛ Your Baby's Second Month ✛

As you head into the second month, a number of happy surprises await you, including big, wonderful smiles and happy, cooing noises. With better muscle control, perhaps some longer periods of nighttime sleeping, and a little more patience when she's hungry, your baby is becoming a more sociable child. In such an amazingly short period of time on this earth, she is already beginning to come to terms with the world around her. Your baby is daily more eager to explore and more responsive to the sights and sounds around her. Unfortunately, the second month can also bring with it bouts of unexplained crying or colic that can last through the third month. This chapter covers everything from daily routines and playtime activities to early language skills and ways to cope with colic.

✛   ✛   ✛

THE SECOND-MONTH CHECKUP

Schedule an appointment with the pediatrician for the end of baby's second month. For a new mother and her baby, visits to the pediatrician can be pleasant outings. The two of you have a real purpose for getting up and getting dressed on the day of the visit. It's fun to find out how much baby has grown and reassuring to know that your baby's progress is being followed so carefully. Many mothers look forward to these visits because it gives them the chance to talk with a truly interested party about their babies. Any questions or concerns you have been harboring since the last visit can be brought up now. It helps if you can make a list of these so you don't forget anything. If possible, the baby's father should try to join you on some of these first visits to the pediatrician. It's helpful for him to get to know the doctor as well as you do, in case he needs to call

A Look to the Future
A new, milder version of the DTP shot is already in use for the fourth and fifth injections (at eighteen months and four to six years). Recently approved by the Food and Drug Administration, the new vaccine does not include the whole cell of the pertussis bacterium and is deemed less likely to cause intense side effects than the current vaccine. In the future, this safer acellular pertussis vaccine may also be available to younger children.

An Expert's Thoughts
"There is a difference between controlling a disease and wiping it out. With hepatitis B we have a chance of wiping it out because it is found only in humans. With diphtheria and tetanus, which is in the soil, you can only control it."
—*Dr. Barbara Watson, Director of the Vaccine Evaluation Center at The Children's Hospital of Philadelphia*

when you're not around. Also, he will be able to pick up some valuable tips on parenting while he's there or he may be moved to ask some of his own questions (ones you didn't even know were on his mind). The pediatrician will also appreciate the chance to see and understand the dynamics of the whole family. At later visits, your doctor may also suggest that you bring an older sibling along as well. If you have a babysitter working for you by now, bring her with you as well. She will feel more comfortable calling the doctor with a question while you're out if she has already met the doctor and feels she is known to her.

At this month's checkup, your doctor will weigh, measure, take head circumference, and check reflexes and development. This is also the time for the first round of immunizations: usually the DTP, oral polio, and HIB vaccines.

DTP IMMUNIZATION

The American Academy of Pediatrics recommends that the first DTP (diphtheria, tetanus, pertussis) immunization be given at two months of age. The DTP shot is given again at four months, six months, fifteen or eighteen months, and four to six years, for a total of five injections. The vaccine is very effective against these dangerous childhood diseases, but it does have possible side effects. Your child may experience local reactions, such as redness and tenderness at the site of the shot. There may also be mild fever or irritability. It is recommended that you give your child Tylenol at the time of the injection and again four hours later. This should help keep the mild side effects from making your baby uncomfortable. Rarer but more serious side effects that necessitate a call to your doctor include:

- High fever
- Inconsolable crying
- Collapse or a limp, shocklike state

However remote and unlikely, these are, without a doubt, frightening possibilities for a new parent to face. Unfortunately, the alternative of not giving the shots isn't a pretty one either. According to the medical community, the dangers of acquiring a disease like pertussis can outweigh the dangers of the immunization. If your baby experiences any side effects from the first vaccine, let your doctor know.

Some doctors will opt not to repeat the shots; others may leave the pertussis part out next time. New wisdom, however, suggests that such symptoms do not represent an absolute reason to discontinue the shots. However, if your baby has a past history of convulsions or seizures, is taking drugs for a health condition or has a neurological disease such as epilepsy, the pertussis vaccine may not be given.

In general, if your baby should ever miss a vaccine, don't worry. You do not have to begin the immunization schedule all over again but you should go in for the shot as soon as you remember. Your doctor can simply pick up where you left off and give the next recommended shot.

ORAL POLIO VACCINE

The widespread use of a polio vaccine has just about eradicated a disease that was once a killer. Oral polio vaccine is given at two months, four months, fifteen to eighteen months, and between four and six years. The vaccine is considered relatively safe and has no reactions. The vaccine is given orally. It comes in individual tubes and is squirted into the child's mouth. Children with compromised immune systems or those who live with an adult with an immune system problem would not be given the live, oral vaccine. They might instead be given an injectable, inactivated vaccine (IPV). (It is not possible to get polio from the inactivated IPV vaccine.) In fact, all children may eventually receive the IPV as opposed to the oral polio vaccine. The oral polio currently given is a live vaccine whose strength may no longer be necessary in light of the fact that the disease is now so rare.

HIB VACCINE

The relatively new HIB vaccine protects children against a potentially deadly bacterium known as haemophilus influenzae B. This is the bacterium that is at the root of meningitis, epiglottitis, and septicemia—all potentially fatal infections. The vaccine was introduced in 1990 and appears to be safe and effective. Because the deadly bacterium it fights is more likely to strike children under age two, the AAP recommends that the first HIB vaccine be given at two months of age. The vaccine is given again at four months, possibly again at six months, and fifteen months. (Note: There are two

The Computer Generation
Can't remember which twin had the tetanus? Eventually, all immunizations may be computerized, helping parents and pediatricians to know who was immunized and when. Parents could be sent computerized notices reminding them of the next round of shots.

✛

Chicken Pox Vaccine
The long-awaited varicella vaccine may at last be ready for use in the near future. It would be given at the same time as the MMR vaccine in a combined MMRV shot at the age of 12–15 months. Although chicken pox may not sound dangerous, there are about 100 deaths from chicken pox each year.

✛

Fewer Shots
In two to five years' time, your child may only receive one shot at each scheduled immunization. Researchers are working to combine DTP, IPV, HIB and the upcoming pneumococcal vaccine into one syringe.

Vaccine Shorthand
DTP: diphtheria, tetanus, pertussis

APDT: acellular pertussis, diphtheria, tetanus

OPV: oral polio vaccine

IPV: inactivated polio vaccine

HIB: haemophilus influenzae B

HepB: hepatitis B

MMR: measles, mumps, rubella

✦

A Mother's Reflections
"I was really impressed with the weight gain during those first few months. I was breastfeeding and it made me feel wonderful (even proud!) to see my baby thriving and growing fat all because of me. It made me feel more secure in my new role as provider."

brands of HIB vaccine on the market, one requiring shots at two and four months, the other at two, four, and six months. There is no difference in their effectiveness.) This vaccine has already helped to virtually wipe out meningitis. There are other types of meningitis that must be guarded against, now, however—meningacoccal and pneumococcal. A vaccine against these is in the works and could hopefully be combined into one HIB shot.

YOUR PERSONAL IMMUNIZATION CHART

To help you keep track of when your child was vaccinated, you might want to use this chart. Your pediatrician will also keep records of these shots at her office. For the latest immunization recommendations, send a self-addressed stamped envelope to the American Academy of Pediatrics, Dept. C—Immunization Materials, 141 Northwest Point Boulevard, Box 927, Elk Grove Village, IL 60009-0927.

	DTP	Polio	MMR	Hepatitis B	HIB	Other
DATE						
DATE						
DATE						
DATE						
DATE						
DATE						
DATE						
DATE						
DATE						
DATE						
DATE						
DATE						

WEIGHT GAIN

Your baby will be weighed at every pediatric visit so that your doctor can monitor his progress. Your baby may gain as much as two pounds this month. Mothers often find themselves comparing weight gain with other mothers or even against charts. As long as your baby is gaining appropriately, according to your pediatrician, there is no reason to feel your baby is "too thin" or "too fat." Remember, too, that if you are breastfeeding, your baby may not weigh as much as a bottle-fed baby. (According to a study published in the June 1992 issue of *Pediatrics,* the weight difference between bottle-fed and breastfed babies is more evident in the last six months of the first year.) The slower weight gain is not a sign that the breastfed baby isn't getting enough nourishment, nor is it a sign that formula-fed babies are better nourished. The authors of the study believe that if parents and their doctors are aware of the slight differences in the growth patterns between these two groups, mothers and doctors may be less likely to conclude that a healthy, thriving breastfed newborn needs formula supplementation.

MUSCLE CONTROL

Heading into the second month, your baby has more control over his head and neck. His control is steadier now and he can hold his head up at a 45-degree angle for a brief look around. A two-month-old, when rolled onto his tummy, will try to pick his head up to look around. Neck and back muscles still do need support, however, so guard these areas with your hands when you lift and hold your newborn. When you place your infant over your shoulder, you'll begin to notice that he can hold his head to look around at things of interest.

Movements, in general, become smoother and less jerky during this month. If upset, hungry or crying, however, your baby's old jerky movements may return. The Moro reflex (page 29) is still in evidence when the baby is startled.

Your baby may even surprise you with some early crawling movements. If you put him on his tummy and then press against his feet, he will push back against your hands and try to scoot forward. This is probably just a reflex and not a real willful decision on the baby's part to go anywhere. On his back, he may bicycle his legs and wave his arms. Your baby can also twist, arch, and flex, making it possible (although not too likely) for him to suddenly flip himself over or propel himself off a bed or other flat surface. If you have an active baby, be cautious.

Most babies at this age keep their fists closed. If you press a toy into the palm of their hands, they can usually hold on to the object for a

Pain Thresholds
Did your newborn have a strong negative response to the heel stick done in the hospital at two or three days? If so, you might expect an equally distressed response to the first inoculation. Observations of infants (reported on by Dr. Michael Lewis in Part II of *Pediatrics,* September 1992) have shown that the infant with a low threshold for pain typically remains sensitive to uncomfortable stimuli. A 1990 study, also by Dr. Lewis, indicates that infants who react strongly to painful events like an inoculation have a higher incidence of illness. Those who are blasé about their shots may be more likely to stay healthy.

few seconds. This is a grasping reflex and will disappear by next month, when it is replaced by open hands and more voluntary reaching and grasping. At two months, he may enjoy swiping at dangling toys of interest. Batting at colorful toys that make a sound when hit are fun for baby and give him good practice for the reaching and grasping skill he will begin to demonstrate in coming months.

LEARNING

Even at this very young age, learning is already in progress. There is evidence that babies can remember certain toys, recognize familiar items, and enjoy and will repeat certain successful actions. In one experiment, babies as young as two months were able to learn how to control a mobile by turning their heads. They remembered this "trick" when presented with the same mobile two weeks later. They cooed and smiled more at this mobile simply because they enjoyed the feeling of control over something. Although memory is definitely in place, and babies will try to cause things to happen, it is unclear whether babies really understand cause and effect. He may not realize he is controlling the event until about four or five months of age.

VISION

Babies stare so earnestly and seriously that it cannot help making you smile. Given the newness of their surroundings, their stares should be expected but are often a surprise to parents. Just what can the baby see at two months? He still needs to be close to objects to see them well—about ten to twelve inches away. He can focus on these objects and track them with his eyes. Your baby still prefers the human face to other objects. Just as you love gazing into his tiny face, he gets a lot of pleasure gazing back at yours.

ROUTINES

There is now hope on the horizon for what last month seemed like an impossibility: some rhyme or reason to your days and nights! Your baby is not so new; she is becoming a full-fledged member of the house and family. There is some feeling that things are getting back to "normal." Although she's still a frequent eater, you may find more three-hour stretches between feedings. Some babies will even sleep six- or seven-hour stretches at night, although most continue to wake from sleep a number of times. She may begin to eat and sleep a little more regularly. Nighttime crying spells may still be fairly regular too, but will hopefully taper off by the end of the second month. By the end of the second month, awake periods are longer—she may be awake for as many as ten out of twenty-four hours by then (though not, of course, in a solid block).

SLEEPING IN THE SECOND MONTH

Although some infants will sleep as long as six or seven hours during the night by now, others continue to wake during the night. Actually, all infants wake briefly during the night—the difference is that some wake you up too. No one knows quite how some babies manage to calm themselves and put themselves back to sleep or why others tend to call for assistance with a cry. It may be that those who wake and need help falling back asleep associate sleep with your presence. Usually these are babies who fall asleep in your arms or at the breast and are then placed in the crib asleep. For more on this theory, see page 100.

There has also been some indication that breastfed babies wake up more often than bottle-fed babies at night. According to at least one study, however, breastfed infants can be taught to sleep through the night. In a method described in the February 1993 *Pediatrics,* parents were instructed to feed the baby between 10 P.M. and 12 A.M. and then to swaddle, diaper, and/or carry baby during a middle-of-the-night awakening rather than breastfeed baby. By the end of the first eight weeks, all the infants in this group were sleeping through the night (defined as sleeping from 12 to 5 A.M.). Of those in the control group, only 23 percent were sleeping through the night.

Of course, when your baby wakes up, you often are woken too. Some parents take turns going to the baby, especially if the baby takes a bottle. If you are breastfeeding, you may be the only one on night duty. Even though you are the only one who can feed the baby, you might want to ask your partner to go as a "front runner." He may

Well, if it's not your turn, and it's not my turn, then whose turn is it??!!

be able to coax the baby back to sleep so that a feeding is not necessary. It can also be worth waiting a few seconds before you rush cribside. Some babies will make noise, then find a finger or fist, and settle back to sleep without your help.

With interrupted sleep during the night, it is a good idea to nap during the day. Try to catch a few winks when your baby does.

SUDDEN INFANT DEATH SYNDROME

All parents who have heard of SIDS tend to regard their baby's peaceful sleep with suspicion. With so little known about how and why SIDS strikes, it's easy to understand why the syndrome evokes so much fear. Sudden infant death syndrome is the name given to infant death that occurs during sleep for no apparent medical reason. Happily, the threat of SIDS passes after the first year. Still, it takes the lives of 7,000 American babies each year. It is most likely to strike infants between the ages of two and six months. According to a recent study in *Pediatrics* (May 1992), it is most likely to occur during the early-morning hours, between 3 A.M. and 7 A.M. Apparently, some SIDS victims show altered patterns of sleep, and in this way, they are different from other infants. They also tend to have higher heart rates and an increased incidence of tachycardic episodes (moments of very rapid heartbeat). There is a higher incidence of SIDS among premature and low-birthweight babies. Statistically, they are more likely to be born to women who had no prenatal care during pregnancy, or who smoked or took drugs during pregnancy. Many, if not most, SIDS victims had few or none of these risk factors, however. Although nothing you can do as a parent can guarantee that your baby won't be a victim of SIDS, the medical community is beginning to compile a few possibly preventative measures. It is now believed that putting your baby to sleep on his back or side is preferable to a tummy-down position. (Check with your doctor first, however, as there are some children who for other medical reasons may benefit from a tummy-down position.) Some experts also believe that breast-feeding, being sure not to overheat the baby, and not smoking around the baby can all be preventative measures as well. Much more research is needed before any real conclusions can be drawn. For now, there are no adequate medical explanations for this bewil-

SIDS Resource

For more information, contact the SIDS Alliance, 10500 Little Patuxent Parkway, Suite 420, Columbia, MD 21044 or call 1-800-221-SIDS. They have general information brochures, including information on high risk factors and literature for grieving family members of SIDS victims.

dering syndrome, and there is no accurate way to predict or prevent SIDS. We do know, however, that SIDS is *not* caused by suffocation, child abuse, or immunizations. It is not contagious or hereditary.

COOING

As any new parent can tell you, communication still consists mainly of crying. But usually by two months of age, a baby also makes some small throaty noises, which may be called cooing. Sometimes, it sounds like a vowel sound: a, e, o, or u. Babies seem to actively enjoy making these sounds and listening to their own voices. It's not all an ego trip, however. Many of their vocal sounds are made for your benefit: you're likely to notice more cooing when you're facing your baby and talking to him. Your baby at this age is also more attentive to sounds around him: a tinkling bell or even the wind rustling the leaves of a tree. Musical sounds may be a favorite with your baby. Loud or high-pitched sounds (sirens, door buzzers, a slamming door) may cause a baby to stop whatever he or she was doing for the moment (these noises usually have the same effect on us). Body language and facial expression round out the picture and help your baby to get "messages" across to you or to siblings.

SMILING

This is one of the most important developmental milestones—from a parent's perspective. The feeling of having your little baby smile back at you is unbeatable! Sometime during the second month, the fleeting smiles you have noticed since birth will become more social and purposeful. Once, parents were told that these very early smiles were just "gas." We now know that it is not true. But fleeting smiles passing over the lips during a nap cannot be called social smiles either. They are thought to be reactions of the nervous system. By eight weeks, however, the social smile begins to blossom. Your baby will give you a big toothless grin as you stare into her eyes, talking and playing with her. There is no mistaking this smile which is plainly meant for you. Social smiles come when the baby is awake and alert and engaged in face-to-face "communication" with a sibling, parent, or other caregiver.

Developmental Milestones
Babies develop at many different speeds. They may be "early" at one thing, "late" at another. Developmental milestones are only loose guideposts that help caregivers spot possible health problems along the way. There can be many differences among perfectly normal babies, however, so don't spend too much time worrying and comparing notes with other moms. Your doctor can always reassure you if you think a milestone is being missed.

One of the nicest things about a baby's smile is, of course, the feeling it gives to new parents. After the work of birth and the sleepless nights of the first month and the colicky crying, isn't it nice to be rewarded with a simple but ever-so-engaging smile? The smiles help to cement the growing bond between parent and child and cause you to fall deeper in love with your baby. For some parents who might have felt intimidated by their demanding newborn during the early weeks, this smile helps them to realize that they are in a two-way relationship and that, yes, they are appreciated and loved. Some babies are more smiley than others, however, so don't worry if yours doesn't seem to smile too often. This is not a reflection of her feelings toward you—just her age, temperament, and personality.

SUCKING

Your baby is born knowing how to suck, an important survival reflex. By two months, your baby has made sucking an art. Sucking has never been for food alone. Your baby may suck his fingers or pacifier to reduce tension, stave off hunger, and replay the happy feelings associated with feedings. Sucking is for pleasure. (For more on pacifiers, see page 57.)

The mouth is central to the baby's feelings of well-being and baby uses it to learn about his environment. Eventually, most toys will end up in his mouth. Your baby can look at something and suck at the same time. If something startles or interests him, the sucking may stop momentarily while he focuses on that.

Many mothers find the finger sucking behavior a plus. Infants can often quiet themselves by turning to their own fingers for satisfaction. This ability to calm themselves can be a real help in the middle of the night when a little sucking can mean the difference between a baby who calls for you and a baby who puts himself back to sleep.

COLIC

Colic is usually described as regular periods of unexplained crying. The infant usually screams, is difficult to comfort, and draws his knees up to his chest. No one knows what really causes colic or why it mysteriously starts a few weeks after birth or magically ends around three months of age. The best thing you can do is find ways to cope:

- Try feeding your baby before he starts to cry. When he cries for food, he may be gulping down air before a feeding.
- If you are breastfeeding, consider eliminating milk products from your own diet. Your baby may be sensitive to traces of cow's milk in your milk. Talk with your doctor before you make such a change in your diet and then keep him up to date, letting him know if it's working.
- Burp the baby before switching breasts or at the end of a bottle feeding. For more on burping, see page 176 in the chapter on nutrition.
- Put a hot water bottle on his tummy for a few seconds. (Make sure it is not too hot. For added safety, wrap it in a towel.)
- Offer chamomile tea weakened with boiled (then cooled) water.
- Put your baby in his car seat and drive around town in your car.
- Run the dryer, the dishwasher, the vacuum, or other appliance that makes a loud humming noise.
- Put your baby in a Snugli and take a walk.
- Make sure feeding time is a quiet time. Unplug the phone, close the door, dim the lights, and breastfeed in peace.
- Try placing the baby, stomach down, over the inside of your forearm, legs straddled over your arm, chest and head resting on your open palm. This gives even pressure on the tummy and feels good to some babies. You can stand up and, with your other arm for added support, rock the baby slowly back and forth in this position. (See illustration.)

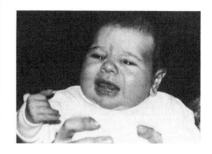

A Doctor's Thoughts
"The crying of colic usually stops at three months but there's no law that says it has to. I once had a mother call me at midnight, just as her baby turned three months, to ask why he hadn't stopped crying yet."—Dr. Alvin Eden, Chairman, Department of Pediatrics, Wyckoff Heights Medical Center, and Associate Clinical Professor of Pediatrics, New York Hospital—Cornell Medical Center

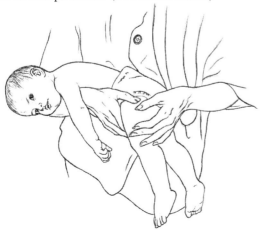

The football hold, with baby held tummy-down over your forearm, is often especially comforting to a fussy baby.

A baby may feel most comfortable tummy down across your lap.

Prevent Child Abuse

If you are having a lot of trouble dealing with your newborn's crying and are beginning to feel out of control, call for help. 1-800-4-A-CHILD is a toll-free child abuse hotline staffed by trained therapists who can help talk you through things and give referrals for help in your area.

- Place the baby stomach down across your legs. With one hand on baby's back, gently rock baby from side to side with your legs. (See illustration.)
- Buy a stuffed animal that has a recorded heartbeat sound or a tape of sounds from the womb. Some parents find these familiar womb noises calm babies.
- Swaddle the baby. See page 57.
- Try giving a baby massage. See page 58.
- If you have a baby swing, try putting the baby in it for a few minutes. (If the baby is at least six weeks.)
- If you are formula feeding, talk to your pediatrician about switching formulas or returning to full-time breastfeeding where possible. (Colic is less common in breastfed babies.)
- Give the baby a warm bath.
- Offer a pacifier, if this is something your baby is comforted by.
- Put the baby down. Babies can get overstimulated and over-handled. He may just need some rest!
- Step outside with your baby. The fresh air on his cheeks and change of scene may startle him into silence. There's a chance it'll help him to calm down.
- Play music. Some babies respond positively to the beat of the radio, or even MTV. Dancing with your baby in your arms sometimes adds to the calming effect for baby.
- Take a break. If you think colic is tough on your baby, take a look at the way it has been making *you* feel! There's no reason why both you and your husband have to stand there helplessly watching a baby with colic. Take turns. One of you can go to a movie or out for a walk before returning to relieve the other one for a similar respite. Babysitters and other relatives can help give you time off too. Don't feel guilty. You need time to regain your sanity. That way, you'll return ready to cope again.
- Check with your doctor to reassure yourself that there is no underlying physical cause for the colic. The pediatrician may also offer some tried and true colic busters of his own.

DIAPER RASH

Delicate newborn skin can easily develop a rash. The diaper area is especially sensitive because feces and urine are extremely irritating to the skin. Diaper rash happens, at one time or another, to most babies and is no reflection on your mothering skills. You will recognize diaper rash as a redness on all or part of the diaper area. The baby may or may not act uncomfortable.

To minimize the irritation and help clear it up, expose your baby's bottom to air. A perfect time to do this may be after the bath, as he lies (already dried) on a towel in a warm room. Or, you can take your time at each diaper change to allow some air to get on the baby before you put on a new diaper. Change your baby frequently, to avoid skin contact with the irritant. Make sure you clean in all the folds where dirt can hide. A rash may benefit from a special cream. Ask your pediatrician for a favorite brand name or type. In severe cases, a prescription cream may be ordered.

When in Doubt, Switch
If you are using disposable diapers, you might try switching to cloth diapers for a few days and see if this helps to clear up the rash. If you are already using cloth ones, make sure you are changing frequently and that you are not using rubber pants.

BABY CARRIER OR STROLLER?

Up until now, you may have carried your baby in a front carrier strapped to your chest on outings. This can be a great way to go: baby loves the closeness and the rocking; you're free to use your hands. As your baby gains weight and you go out more often, however, you may elect to push rather than tote that weight. Also, you may feel it's time for baby to see something of the world besides your chest. If you haven't already purchased a stroller, this may be a good time to do so. Now that you have baby, you'll be a better consumer as you shop for the right carriage. Switching baby from front carrier to stroller may take a little adjusting. Used to the close confines of the carrier, your baby may at first object to this freewheeling mode of transportation. To retain that snug feeling for baby, you might want to use some rolled receiving blankets around the head. A padded stroller seat insert may also help make her feel more cozy. For more information on purchasing a stroller, see page 10.

PLAYTIME

All work and no play make Mom and Dad pretty dull. You'll want to spend time playing with your baby, shaking rattles for her, showing her interesting toys, smiling at her, and talking to her. Place your baby over your shoulder and show her some of the sights: blinking lights on a Christmas tree, her own face in the mirror. Place her on her back and dangle a toy in front of her. Your baby

will play along for quite a few minutes, smiling, cooing, kicking arms and legs. Or place your baby tummy down and hold a toy a few inches out in front of her. Slowly raise the toy up in the air, encouraging her to keep the toy in sight.

Babies also need a break from playtime, however, and may suddenly turn away from you during play. This is your signal that baby needs some quiet time. She is still very young and lots of new stimuli can cause sensory overload. She needs some quiet time to assimilate all she has seen and heard. Babies will also turn away from a toy when they have had enough. Take your cue from your baby—removing toys from view when she wants no part of them, allowing her the time to enjoy the ones she seems to be most interested in.

You Are Baby's Favorite Toy
Although some babies can play "alone" for a short period of time—watching something of interest dangling from a mobile, for example—play should be interactive and reactive. You'll want to be a part of it. For now, you are baby's number one playmate, and as you talk, laugh, and present the toys to your baby, you are adding the social and linguistic elements that only you can bring to playtime.

TOYS FOR THE SECOND MONTH

Toys should be matched to your baby's age and skills. A toy that excites a ten-month-old might frustrate a two-month-old. Furthermore, a toy designed for an older child may be dangerous for a younger one, sometimes in ways that might not be immediately apparent to you. There's no need to surround your baby with toys. A few interesting toys are a lot more appealing than a whole crib full of stuff. For a baby under two months, choose a toy that not only has visual appeal but makes an interesting sound. A rattle is good because it combines visual appeal with moving parts that tinkle or rattle. You want to make sure that if the baby manages to bat this toy, it will give a positive reward, either by moving in an interesting way, changing color, or making a sound. Choose a toy with unusual shapes, contours, and feel: for example, a stuffed cube with different material on each side. For in-the-crib fun, try a mobile or crib gym strung across the crib with rings and colorful objects to look at.

HAPPY BABY'S HIT PARADE

Here's a roundup of what's high on this month's hit list of what makes baby happy:

- Sucking on fingers or pacifier
- Seeing your face
- An attractive rattle
- Being held
- The sound of your voice
- Feeding time
- Going for a drive in the car
- Hearing music

CHAPTER 8
✦ Your Baby's Third Month ✦

Yicon might want to view the third month as the top of the hill you've been trying to climb ever since the baby was born. By now, your baby should be crying a little less and sleeping a little longer. He is much more aware and alert to his surroundings. You've fallen into, if not a routine, at least a pattern. You get up every morning knowing what you can expect from your day. You and your baby are both energetic enough to go on outings, join mother and baby groups, play together. You may also be returning to work. Feeding times should now be a pleasure instead of a chore. In short, life has stabilized a bit. There are still many more changes in store for you and your baby, of course. This chapter will cover some of your baby's newfound skills, including batting at toys, following you with his eyes, gurgling and chuckling, and more.

✦　✦　✦

WHEN TO CALL THE PEDIATRICIAN

Unless there is a particular problem or reason for seeing your pediatrician, you will not need to do so this month. The next well-baby visit is scheduled for when your baby is about four months old. After that, the schedule of well-baby visits is months six, nine, and twelve. Because of the space in between checkups, make sure you use office time well by covering upcoming milestones with your pediatrician. Always look ahead to issues that might come up between visits. For example, at your next visit (the four-month checkup), you'll want to discuss the introduction of solids since this is something you'll probably want to start before the sixth month.

This month, if any questions or concerns do arise, make sure to call your pediatrician. Even though there is no scheduled visit, there

An End to Colic?

By three months of age, you can expect an end to the nonstop crying that may have characterized your first months with your baby. No one is quite sure why it comes to an end then. It may just be that your baby's systems have matured enough for him to handle the outside world well now. Some babies, however, will continue their problem crying into the fourth month.

A Doctor's Opinion

"In general, I think parents hesitate to call the pediatrician. I tell them, 'If you're worried, please call me. If you get home after your visit and realize you forgot to ask me something, call. Leave the message that it's not an emergency, so I can call when I have time to talk."—Dr. Modena Wilson, Director, Division of General Pediatrics, Johns Hopkins Children's Center

may be a need to chat about a particular issue or problem of interest to you. If it is not an emergency, try to call during calling hours or regular office hours, so your doctor has the chance to give the proper time and attention to your questions. If it is an emergency, do not hesitate to call anytime. After hours, you will usually get a phone service, which can, in turn, contact your doctor and have him or her call you back. See page 97 for more information on phoning your pediatrician and obtaining over-the-phone diagnoses.

From time to time, review with your pediatrician the signs and symptoms that warrant a call to the doctor. For very young infants, be on the lookout for:

- A baby who won't eat
- A baby who is sleeping all the time
- A baby with a fever
- A baby who is not wetting her diapers frequently
- A baby that doesn't seem "right" to you

I'm sorry to bother you again, Doctor, she seems to be all better, and she did cough only once or twice today, but the second time she coughed it made a funny little noise, you know, like a whistle, and it did only last a second, and as I say, she hasn't coughed again all day, but I was a teeny bit worried, so I thought I'd better call you, to see if you thought it might be anything (the cough, that is), because it's better to be safe than sorry, but, really, she's fine, but I thought I'd better check anyway, and, of course, I can bring her right over there if you think it sounds serious, but she is just fine, there was only that funny cough...

SIPRESS

MUSCLE CONTROL

Your baby is developing more control over his own movements. By the end of the third or fourth month, he can hold up both head and chest when in a tummy-down position. You can support your three-month-old in a sitting position, and although the head may bob a bit, your baby is now better able to help hold this position. The hands uncurl and are open for swatting and batting at toys. Sometimes, your baby will be able to reach for an object or even grab at it. More likely, he will close his fist before he can get his hands on it. Babies at this age can usually bring both hands together, and delight in seeing their own hands perform "tricks" like this one.

VISION

Your baby will now follow the track of a toy from one side of his body all the way to the other side. He can concentrate on a toy whether it is close up or even if he notes it far away. He perceives the difference between objects that are near to him and those that are farther away. He delights in watching his own hands and feet. He is now able to look at things while still doing something else, such as sucking or moving. By now, your baby can probably see colors just as well as you do.

GURGLING AND CHUCKLING

Last month brought cooing sounds. This month, your baby will continue to coo but will likely add to his repertoire with some throaty gurgles and even some chuckles. This is not quite a laugh-out-loud sound yet. Your baby can also whimper, which may not seem like much to cheer about, but it does beat all-out crying. Your baby can now use that whimper to show annoyance, mild discomfort, or frustration and doesn't need to launch into the scream that was previously his only means of communication. In fact, over the course of the third month, crying spells decrease and life with baby generally gets quieter.

Color Preference
Most babies seem particularly interested in bright colors, with red and blue being favorites. Remember this when purchasing toys.

LEARNING

It is not just your imagination: your baby is starting to seem comfortable with certain routines. As you sit down in your favorite

Your Baby Is Unique
No two babies develop the same way or at the same time. Although it is interesting to read in books like this one what milestones and skills you can expect at certain months, you must not hold your baby too rigidly to these markers. It is the nature of parents to worry about these things, but slow development usually has nothing to do with poor parenting skills or a problem with your baby. Slow or fast teething, talking, rolling, crawling, and so on are determined by a number of factors, from inheritance to baby's own physical size, weight, and personality. Variations in development and learning are great in normal, healthy babies.

A Doctor's Thoughts
"Some of the same sleep behavior which may be seen as a problem in one family is not seen as a problem in another. It is not just the behavior but the parents' response to it."—Dr. Thomas Anders, Professor of Psychiatry, University of California, Davis Medical Center

chair for feeding, your baby starts to settle in for the feeding he now knows is coming. When you hold him or he sees your face, he may stop crying. He recognizes your voice, smiles at you, and tries to engage you in conversation or play. When you say goodbye and leave, he may cry in a way that he would not for others. It is believed that by now he is beginning to recognize all the different family members.

When at play, he will repeat an action that brings pleasure. For example, if he shakes a rattle and likes the swirling colors and tinkling sound, he will try to shake it again. It is not entirely clear whether he understands that there is a connection between his actions and the pleasant sound and colors, but he's getting there. His memory does not extend to objects that have been removed from his view. So far, out of sight is still out of mind. Even if he happens to move his own hand to a place where he can no longer see it, he will forget his interest in it and will not search to see where it has gone to.

SLEEPING

Yes, sleep (or lack thereof) is still a major issue in the third month—and often beyond. According to one source, sleep problems are the most common complaint aired at pediatric visits by parents with children under two. Many of these infants disrupt their own (and their parents') sleep enough to cause the parents to seek professional assistance for the problem. After two or three months of waking during the night, you may not feel quite so desperate . . . yet. Then again, you may already be teetering close to the edge of insanity!

Some babies (and their lucky parents) are now sleeping through the night. Most babies, however, will still cry when they wake up during the night. During the third month babies are taking in more food, and the length of time between feedings is stretching so sleep times should lengthen too. There is a tremendous variation in sleep requirements, however. Some babies seem to sleep all the time, while others are much more wakeful.

Interestingly, all young babies wake up during the night, but some never let you know about it. One study that videotaped sleeping infants at three weeks and three months of age, noted that sleeping infants do wake up one or more times briefly during the night. Some parents remain blissfully unaware of these awakenings while others are invariably called cribside. At three weeks of age, almost all the babies in the study woke their parents when they woke up. But by three months of age, half of these babies would wake momentarily and then put themselves back to sleep. Why are some babies able to return to sleep while others feel the need to call the cavalry? Researchers believe that some babies are simply "self-soothers." Parents can encourage self-soothing techniques by allowing babies to use a sleep aid such as a pacifier or finger sucking. Self-soothers are usually put into their cribs awake and learn to put themselves to sleep. This is a pattern that they are then able to repeat in the middle of the night when they awaken alone in their cribs. Infants who are put into their cribs already asleep may awaken later and be unable to put themselves back to sleep without that same stimuli (your rocking and cuddling or breastfeeding) that got them to sleep in the first place.

If you feel your baby is having problems staying asleep at night, you may have to do some experimenting to find out what works best in your family. Try putting the baby in her crib while she is still awake to help her learn how to get to sleep on her own. Try waiting a few minutes before rushing to her crib in the middle of the night. Perhaps she'll put herself back to sleep. For more ideas, see page 111.

THE FAMILY BED

Is the family bed an option for you? This is the norm in many cultures and may provide the infant with the comforting (and sleep-inducing) knowledge that you're there. On the positive side, you don't need to get out of bed and walk down a cold hallway in the dark to get to your baby for a feeding. Advocates of the family bed say it's much more restful just to roll over and breastfeed, while drifting back to sleep. Other parents find the idea of a family bed too intrusive and prefer to retreat to their own private space at night, *sans* baby. They worry about the appropriateness of the family bed and wonder about the effect on the child. Those who use the family bed say there are many other rooms in the house which can be used for private grown-up time (and sex) when desired. No one can tell you what is right for you. You will have to decide for yourself, based on your baby, your spouse, and your lifestyle.

Are Girls Better Sleepers?
In a sleep study involving twenty-one babies from three weeks through eight months of age, and published in the October 1992 issue of *Pediatrics*, seven babies were identified as problem sleepers at the age of eight months. An interesting (and unexplained) finding: All of the problem sleepers were boys! The study could not draw any conclusions about this footnote but perhaps more studies will follow.

A Doctor's Opinion
"I think the family bed is wonderful as long as the parent can take it. There are very cogent arguments for cosleeping. The problem is when and for how long. I think from birth until nine months, under the right circumstances, it's great—as long as it's for the child's comfort and not for the parent's (for example, a single parent who simply wants the company in bed or parents who want a child in between them because they don't want to talk to each other)."—Dr. Thomas Anders, Professor of Psychiatry, University of California, Davis Medical Center

Smoke Alarm

Make sure that your home is equipped with working smoke alarms. You should have one alarm on every floor of your house.

✦

Face-to-Face

When you play with or talk to your baby, be sure to hold him so he looks right into your whole face. He won't enjoy your profile nearly so much. In fact, studies show that a profile only confuses babies.

SAFETY TIPS FOR THE THIRD MONTH

The more active and involved in the outside world your baby becomes, the more cautious you have to be about his safety. Here are a few things to keep in mind:

1. Offer large toys that can be mouthed without being swallowed.
2. Make sure toys have no small parts that can break off.
3. Avoid stuffed animals or dolls that have button eyes or other loose parts, which can be pulled off.
4. Never leave the baby unattended on an elevated surface. It's possible for your baby to surprise you and roll over.
5. Your baby is still too young for pillows, which could smother him in his crib.
6. Your baby is starting to reach for things, so keep sharp objects, small objects, and hot objects and those with strings out of his reach.

✦ ✦ ✦

PLAYTIME

Your baby is becoming an increasingly interested partner in play. When you talk to him, he will coo back at you. When you smile, he will smile back. When he sees you, he can get all-over happy, with his whole body moving about to show how he feels. He is becoming more social and actively seeks out his playtime with you, encouraging you by responding so readily to your face, your singing, your words. Babies learn through play, so make sure you provide enough stimulating toys and take the time to interact one on one with your baby during playtime. Playing with toys encourages language skills, social skills, and the understanding of basic ideas such as cause and effect.

TOYS FOR THE THIRD MONTH

Look for toys that appeal to his increasingly refined visual abilities: colorful beads in a clear casing, rattles, plastic mirrors, or other shiny, eye-catching toys. Take advantage of his desire to grab at toys by offering rubber rings and colorful toys he can grasp. The object should not be too big or too heavy for little hands. You want to reward his successful attempts at targeting, reaching, and obtaining the toy. Look for toys that "feel" good and sound good, too, such as a stuffed animal with a bell inside.

HAPPY BABY'S HIT PARADE

High on this month's list of what puts a smile on baby's face:

- Watching his own hands and feet
- Kicking his legs in the air
- Batting at a toy you hold up for him
- Reaching for and possibly even grabbing a toy
- Staring at his own face in the mirror
- "Conversing" with you face to face
- Playing with crib gym

A Doctor's Thoughts
"It's not as though you can take out a game and play it with a baby. The key is to hold them and talk to them and make faces and tickle them and make them laugh. That's what playtime with a young baby is about."
—Dr. Alvin N. Eden, Chairman, Department of Pediatrics, Wyckoff Heights Medical Center, Brooklyn

CHAPTER 9

✤ Your Baby's Fourth Month ✤

During the first year, every month brings with it new delights and the unfolding of new skills. It is almost as though your baby is growing right before your very eyes, knowing and doing a little more today than she did yesterday. The fourth month can seem particularly full of changes. With the first three months of real infancy behind you, the fourth month is the beginning of babyhood. This month can bring with it any number of exciting new behaviors, possibly including the ability to roll onto one side, and the sound of real laughter. This chapter will cover the latest in baby's language and developmental skills, her social coming-out, appropriate toys, and more.

✤   ✤   ✤

THE FOURTH-MONTH CHECKUP

By this time, you and your pediatrician know each other. Your doctor has some idea of your baby's personality and growth rate. When you bring your baby in at the end of the fourth month for a visit, expect lots of questions about how your baby is sleeping and eating, whether or not he or she has tried to roll over, and so on. Your doctor may do a complete and thorough exam of your baby's developmental progress or he or she may depend more on observation of the baby during the visit and your comments and questions. If your doctor had noticed anything of concern at the last visit, such as a hip problem, this will surely be looked at again. A specialist may be suggested if there is a particular health problem outside the realm of the pediatrician.

At this visit, your baby will face another round of shots. Review with your pediatrician your baby's reaction (if any) from the shots given at two months. Your baby will receive the DTP (diphtheria, tetanus,

Find the Information You Need
Babies develop at different rates. If by the end of the fourth month, your baby is up to something not covered in this chapter (teething, rolling over, or starting solids, for example), just use the index at the back of the book to find the information you need to know now.

Weigh-in

At the end of the fourth month, the average baby weighs about 13 to 14 pounds and is about $24^1\!/_2$ inches in length. He appears more babylike, with a rounded head, plump cheeks, and even dimples on his knees.

✦

Working Up an Appetite

All this exercise may make baby hungrier than usual. If you are breastfeeding, your body will naturally keep up with the demands of an active, growing baby. If you are bottle feeding, you'll be able to follow your baby's cues and offer more formula as necessary. For more on the nutritional needs of your baby, see Chapter 18, "Feeding in the First Year."

and pertussis) as well as the oral polio vaccine. You can expect a certain amount of local pain or tenderness at the site of the injection, as well as some mild crankiness or fever. Your doctor may suggest offering Tylenol every four hours after the shot. At this visit, your child may also get the HIB vaccine, depending on which brand of the vaccine your doctor has been using (see page 69 for more on the HIB vaccine).

Since you may not be seeing the doctor again until the sixth month, the two of you will have to take a look ahead at what's to come and try to go over a few issues in advance of their occurrence. Your pediatrician will surely discuss the introduction to solid foods with you. Doctors differ in their opinions, but most will advise trying a few spoonfuls of mashed banana or rice cereal sometime between now and the next visit.

MUSCLE CONTROL

Although every baby is different, by the end of this month your baby will probably be steady enough to sit up with support and hold her head erect. Babies at this age often like to be pulled to a supported sit. Most babies will achieve good control of the neck muscles this month. When she's on her tummy, she can now lift her head and chest, possibly even lifting herself up onto straight arms. Lie down on the floor in front of her and do what she does. She'll enjoy seeing your face down at her level and it will make her work harder at trying to maintain this position. Your baby may try some other new tricks while in the tummy-down position. She may arch her back and extend her arms and legs to rock in an airplanelike position. If "flying" isn't enough, she may opt for some real movement: by rolling from her tummy to her side. Some babies will flip all the way over onto their backs. Others won't try any rolls until much later. When it comes to using her hands, your baby is probably becoming more adept but is still using her whole hand to grasp things, as though she were wearing invisible mittens. (Over the next few months, she'll eventually learn the more accurate thumb and forefinger grasp.) She will reach for objects of interest but may not make her mark.

You will notice your baby playing with her own hands during this stage of development. This "play" will eventually teach her how to effectively reach for an object she desires. For now, you may want to encourage her hand play practice by holding a toy above the middle of her chest, allowing her to grab at it with both hands or arms.

VISION

By now, what you can see, she can see. She tracks objects smoothly and can see things far away. Her eyes adjust now to various distances. Your baby can now use her good vision to get really good information about the environment around her. You will see her take a giant step forward in learning in the coming months, in part due to this ability to see well.

LAUGHING AND BABBLING

Last month brought you gurgling and chuckling. This month, language takes one step ahead. For many babies, gurgling and cooing become babbling, with strings of syllable sounds. Your baby may even make an occasional vowel sound mixed with a consonant, such as *ah-goo*. No matter where she is in language development, your baby loves it when you talk to her. She will try to repeat the sounds you make, or at the very least, the tone of your voice. She will smile and coo delightedly as you make a fuss over the sound of her delightful little voice.

One of the real high points of this month's development is the all-out laugh. You may not always know what causes it (does she have the same sense of humor you do?) and you can't always bring it about, but it's always a pleasure to hear. If there are older siblings in the house, they can often get the biggest laughs. Big brothers and sisters love to play to an appreciative audience and will stand there making funny faces and sounds until baby laughs. The baby probably won't tire too easily of this game. She can now sometimes spend as much as an hour socializing before she needs or wants a break.

LEARNING

Your baby is becoming a discriminating fellow these days: he knows your voice and face from others, he knows the difference between people and things, and he prefers faces to patterns. He plays with his hands and is beginning to realize that they are attached

Late Laughing
Perhaps your baby's funny bone is hard to tickle. Some "serious" babies may laugh later than the fourth month. Don't worry about the timing of the first laugh. Just enjoy it when you hear it.

Safety Tip
A pacifier should never be hung or tied around baby's neck. A baby could strangle on such a cord.

An Expert's Opinion
"My philosophy is that kids have an instinctive need to suck, which goes beyond sucking for nutrition. Up until age three, I consider sucking behavior to be no big deal. Personally, though, I would encourage pacifier use over the thumb. I find that, down the road, it's easier to discontinue the pacifier than the thumb."—Dr. Frank J. Courts, Chairman, Department of Pediatric Dentistry, University of Florida

to him. He is developing definite tastes. He may prefer one toy to another, for example. He is beginning to be aware of himself as a separate being, distinct from the world around him and the other objects in it. You may notice that he is able to recognize himself or you in the mirror. When he sees that you are preparing to feed him (sitting down with him in a chair, unbuttoning your blouse, for example), he may stop crying in anticipation. He is able to wait now for what he expects will come next.

THUMB SUCKING AND PACIFIER USE

By four months, the thumb sucking or pacifier use you thought was cute the first three months may start to appear as a bad habit. This is not the time to try to "break him" of a practice he clearly enjoys. Sucking on fingers or a pacifier is a natural and comforting thing for a baby to do. In fact, it may become more comforting for him now if teething has begun (see page 101). This is the time babies become *more* likely to put things (including their fingers) into their mouths, not less likely. The thumb can be a part of play for them, a soother and a comfort to the gums.

Some parents prefer to encourage the pacifier over the thumb, arguing that the pacifier is something that can be taken away. While this is true, any parent of an avid pacifier user will tell you that removing a beloved pacifier is not so easy as it may sound. It may be as hard for a young child to voluntarily give it up as it is for him to quit sucking his thumb. Of course, the pacifier can be physically removed while the thumb cannot be. In any case, if you are patient (and there's no reason why you shouldn't be), both thumb sucking and pacifier use usually play themselves out during the first three to four years of life, without your having to take any active steps to discourage it. Thumb sucking throughout these years is not likely to damage the teeth, nor is it a sign of emotional instability.

INTERRUPTED FEEDINGS

As your baby becomes more social, he begins to take his time at meals, stopping now and then to coo at you or look around. Some new mothers panic and try to turn baby's attention back to the task at hand. Don't worry. Your baby will still get the nutrition he needs . . . but more than just his tummy warrants attention these days.

Think about your own meals. Do you sit down to dinner, wolf down every bite, then leap from the table? More likely, you enjoy sitting down to a leisurely dinner, which is also a social occasion, allowing you time to chat with your family, look over your mail, listen to music. Your baby wants the same things from his meal now. Feeding times can take a little longer because of his newfound interests, but they can be just as satisfying, if not more so, for both mother and baby.

SAFETY TIPS FOR THE FOURTH MONTH

Continue to pay careful attention to the toys you select and play with. Make sure there are no loose or small parts that can come off. Remember that your baby may now be capable of putting things into her mouth, so beware of any items your baby could choke on. If your baby is still using a pacifier, hand it to her. Do not hang it around her neck on a cord, as this can get tangled and cause choking. Do not place your baby's crib, carriage, or infant seat within reach of any cords (whether a drapery cord or a lamp cord) or electrical sockets. Never leave your baby unattended, even though she may seem to be happily playing alone. Babies at this age can sometimes inch forward or roll over and could suffer a nasty fall if unattended.

PLAYTIME

You and your baby will benefit from lots of unstructured fun time together, when you can show her a toy, make faces at her, coo back at her, even read her a book. It is never too early to read to your child. The sound of your voice and the expressions on your face will enchant her. Hearing the same book over and over may become a comfort. For a first book, choose a short rhyme or opt for a book with bright, primary colors and simple text. Playtime also means exercise time for some young moms who take their babies along to special mom and tot exercise classes.

You already know how much your baby enjoys toys with sounds. Now that your baby is getting older, however, she'll be able to have more fun with sounds. Sit your child in your lap. Hold a bell up above her and to one side, and then jingle it, to encourage your child to turn and locate the sound. This type of play encourages her to use her awareness of the sound and combine it with muscle coordination and control as she turns to locate it.

A Note

Injury, not disease, is the biggest threat to a child's health. Injury is the leading cause of hospitalization in children and the first year is statistically one of the most dangerous. Apart from auto accidents, the greatest dangers facing babies under age one include drowning, suffocation and strangulation, falls and burns. Safety needs change quickly as your child grows and becomes more independent. Try to keep one step ahead, with safety in mind.

✤

Toy Talk

For more information, send for the free brochure "Which Toy for Which Child" (from birth to age five), Office of Information and Public Affairs, Product Safety Commission, Washington, DC 20207. Or get a copy of "The TMA (Toy Manufacturers of America) Guide to Toys and Play" by writing to: Toy Booklet, P.O. Box 866, Madison Square Station, New York, NY 10159-0866, or by calling 1-800-851-9955.

Young babies love a crib gym or floor gym and will look at or even bat the interesting shapes hanging above them.

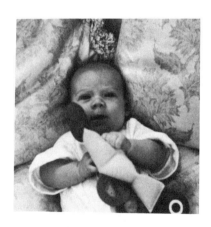

TOYS FOR THE FOURTH MONTH

Brightly colored ball (she'll have fun watching it roll away).

Squeak toy.

Activity gym (complete with items to bat and rings to grasp as baby lies below).

Music box (for listening and looking, but not handling . . . a plus if it includes a moving picture or a revolving toy).

Activity mat (brightly colored washable quilt with mirror, soft book, squeaky toy, and more sewn in for fun).

Big piece of patterned cloth or colorful blanket, which a baby can get both hands on, grasp at, pull on, and turn to see colors and shapes changing.

Colorful large animal rattle that attaches to the wrist.

Oversized stuffed animal (choose one almost the size of your baby but make sure it's extremely soft so it can fit nicely in between baby's outstretched arms and be hugged).

HAPPY BABY'S HIT PARADE

This month's favorite things include:

• Playing with her own hand as though it's a toy
• Bath time (splashing, kicking, and grabbing at bath toys are all part of the fun)
• Listening to music
• Batting, feeling, grabbing at toys
• Holding on to an object
• Mouthing objects
• Smacking her lips

CHAPTER 10

✦ Your Baby's Fifth Month ✦

Already your baby is into the fifth month—"talking" and smiling and getting everyone's attention! This is a chubby, happy month, full of lots of forward strides in language sounds, physical activity, and more.

✦   ✦   ✦

PEDIATRIC CARE BY PHONE

Although there is no formal checkup this month, you should, of course, call the pediatrician if you have a particular concern or if your baby is sick. Over the coming months, you will find that the telephone call is an important part of your baby's general health care. Pediatricians often diagnose and prescribe over the phone, so it is important to know how and when to call, and what to say.

A routine, nonemergency call should preferably be made during routine calling hours. A more important call regarding an ill baby should be made anytime the problem arises. It helps if you have taken the baby's temperature and have your baby nearby when you make the call in case your pediatrician asks a question that demands a closer look at a rash or listening to a baby's chest, etc. If your baby has been in someone's else care all day, it also helps to have that person nearby to answer questions you may not know the answer to. Try to be as prepared as possible to give all the information you have. If there's time, jot it down before calling. Your pediatrician will need to know the symptoms and when they began, any fever and how it has responded to Tylenol, and your insight into the child's general well-being (looks very sick, or not acting sick, and so on). If you are calling about diarrhea, you should also be prepared to report on the color and consistency and number of stools in the last twelve hours, how much the infant is drinking, and whether there are signs of dehydration (dry lips, sunken eyes, no tears). If you are calling about a head injury, your doctor will want to know if

Pediatrics by Phone
According to an April 1992 article in *Pediatrics,* 12 to 28 percent of primary medical care is handled over the phone! This means that you and your doctor need to have good phone skills to effectively communicate about your child's health. If, after hanging up, you continue to worry or feel that your pediatrician did not listen to your recitation of all the symptoms, or if your child seems ill or worsens, call the pediatrician again. Don't be embarrassed to be your child's advocate. You need to trust your own instincts if you believe your child needs medical attention. If necessary, you can bring your child to an emergency room for diagnosis and/or treatment.

your child ever lost consciousness, whether he cried right away and for how long, whether he has fallen asleep and if you are able to wake him without trouble, how he is acting and whether there are any other injuries involved such as bumps or cuts. Basically, your doctor will lead you through the phone call by asking questions. If it is something the doctor can handle over the phone, he or she will do so. If not, you may be asked to bring the child into the office or to the emergency room.

Whenever instructions are given, make sure to write them down, and if possible, read them back to the pediatrician. Often, you may be given dosage instructions for over-the-counter medications. It's imperative that you record this information accurately and follow it carefully. Over-the-counter cough syrups and other cold medicines usually do not have dosage information for children under two on their labels. If not used as prescribed by your doctor, these seemingly benevolent cough and cold medicines can be dangerous.

MUSCLE CONTROL

Holding skills are improving, as your baby plays with toys and learns to hang on to them. Possibly happening this month: transferring objects from hand to hand. You place a toy in your baby's right hand. He looks at it with interest awhile, then shifts it to his left. A small move, but an exciting step forward.

Your baby will probably also start to make lots of precrawling movements. He may inch forward. He loves to kick and wiggle and seems ready to motor ahead, if only he knew how. He may even be able to push up onto his hands and knees and rock. These are all beginning crawl movements. Your baby must not be left alone on a changing table or bed, now that he has these new talents.

Besides enjoying it if you pull them to a sit, many babies like to be pulled to a stand. They will extend their legs and push their feet against the surface—whether the floor or your lap. Some babies prefer this position to a sit. Of course, they cannot stand alone and should not be asked to perform this "trick" if they have tired of it.

ROLLING OVER

Some babies will roll over by this age. Others may not do so until next month or later. You may not see it happen the first few times. You may put your baby down in his crib on his stomach and return to find him on his back. Or you may lay her on her back only to find she has flipped to her side or tummy. Because most babies can push themselves up onto their arms, some can take it one step further by rolling over from stomach to back. They may roll the other way with vigorous kicking that swings them over. They may even surprise themselves with their newfound trick. Make sure the surprise is not an unpleasant one—never leave a baby unattended on a bed or changing table, as they may suddenly roll off the edge.

Some babies, owing to extra weight or a lack of interest in the sport, will not flip over at this stage. If you wish, you can help your baby learn to roll over through play:

1. Place your baby on her back on a carpeted floor.
2. Hold a toy she likes about six inches above her.
3. Once she has it in sight, slowly move it to one side so she has to roll onto her side to keep track of it.

Your baby may or may not be interested in this game. Take your cue from her.

WEIGHT GAIN

Weight gain is slowing down as motor activity picks up. He still needs plenty of nourishment from the breast or bottle, given his active lifestyle. By now, he may already have doubled his birth weight.

LANGUAGE

Your baby learns more and more about the sounds of language as you continue to engage her in conversation. During playtime, your child is rewarded for the sounds she makes and the ones she imitates simply by your own delight in her and continued play. It appears that babies enter the world with some innate concept of the structure and sounds of language. A five-month-old baby, for example, can already hear the difference between two very similar sounds, *bah* and *gah*. While this might not seem monumental, it does prove that even very young infants are able to perceive and discriminate speech sounds, in spite of their very limited experience with hearing and making them.

A Doctor's Thoughts
"Rolling over is a milestone. Being able to roll from tummy to back or back to tummy greatly enlarges the amount of environment that the baby is in control of. If you can flip over, you can see a whole other scene."—Dr. Mary Howell, Assistant Clinical Professor of Pediatrics, Harvard Medical School

A Doctor's Thoughts
"Babies are absolutely accurate barometers of what's good for them. If it makes your baby laugh or look attentively, it's good. When they're happy, shoulders, arms, and hips wiggle. If your baby turns away and whimpers, the game has gone on too long."—Dr. Mary Howell, Assistant Clinical Professor of Pediatrics, Harvard Medical School

Well before babies are able to use words to describe things or feelings, they use sounds, stares, and body language to get their messages across to family members. A four-month-old baby will look with great interest at something he likes, and will turn his head away from it when he has tired of examining it. Your baby may look directly at a toy with his eyes and grunt slightly, as if to say, "Give me that." Crying, of course, remains an expressive part of his language, but he now has so much more in his repertoire that he doesn't always need to fall back on a scream to get what he wants. The more time you spend conversing with your baby and playing together, the better you will be able to understand your baby's "language" and "read" his needs.

LEARNING

Your baby is becoming a pretty savvy member of the household. She will turn to look at the person talking in the room. She may even stop crying just because she has heard the sound of your voice or even your footsteps. If she has more than one primary caretaker, she will recognize the sights and sounds of this person as well. As she comes to recognize people and things, she may begin to form an attachment to a favorite toy or blanket just as she forms an attachment to her primary caregivers.

She knows how to get your attention with smiles and playful noises. She is even busy imitating movements she sees other people make. You're also likely to know about it now if you do something that annoys her—such as remove a favorite toy from her line of sight.

Learning is what baby's life is all about right now. Everything she does, from rolling over to watching you cross the room to listening to the dog bark, teaches her things about her environment. Early stimulation (exciting things to look at, people to talk to, walks to go on, etc.) helps your baby to develop.

SLEEPING

Night waking continues to be common in many children during the fifth month. Studies have found various reasons for continued night waking that range from an infant's particular temperament to family stress to breastfeeding. One thing that many experts believe is tied to night waking is the tendency of parents to rock or feed baby to sleep and then put him to bed already asleep. A study published in April 1992 *Pediatrics* tested this hypothesis and concluded, "While separating parent and child prior to the child's completely falling asleep reduces night waking among infants, it also reduces parental sleeplessness. This may increase parental energy and satisfaction with their infant, thereby improving the parent-child relationship." Not all parents are comfortable with the idea of putting an infant to bed awake, however. You will need to parent your child based on your own instincts and feelings. If night waking is an issue of concern to you, speak with your pediatrician and consider the many alternatives available to you as a family. See pages 86–87 and 111 for more on sleep habits and for information on the family bed.

TEETHING

Long before any teeth actually break the surface and show themselves, you may notice signs of teething. One noticeable symptom: a lot of extra drooling. You may even need to use a bib to help protect your baby's clothing from getting soaked! Drooling may be accompanied by some loose mucousy spitups or loose stools and diaper rash. (Full-blown diarrhea, of course, can be dangerous and should not be ignored as a simple side effect of teething. Some parents insist that a low-grade fever and irritability also accompany teething. Most pediatricians would probably prefer to be the judge of that, however, so call the doctor if your child has a fever rather than simply chalking it up to teething. Studies have not been able to document a clear tie between teething and gastrointestinal discomforts or fever.

A teething baby will constantly place her fingers (if not her whole fist) into her mouth to relieve the uncomfortable tingling or aching that can accompany teething. They are driven to chew on things more than ever now. If your baby is having trouble teething, she may act cranky during the day or wake up during the night. If your child pulls on her ear or appears to experience ear pain, however, do not write this off as a teething symptom. A child who has ear pain should be seen by a pediatrician, to make sure it isn't an ear infection. In general, discomfort from teething can range from mild to moderate, depending on your child.

In some children, a new tooth may push so hard against the gums

Five-Month-Old Math Whiz? Some researchers now believe that children as young as five months old understand the basics of math, just as they seem to have a propensity for learning language. In a study published by developmental psychologists in the journal *Nature*, and reported in an August 27, 1992, *New York Times* article, babies were presented with simple math problems. Researchers showed babies, for example, one Mickey Mouse figurine, which they would then hide behind a screen. They would add one more figurine while baby was watching and then lift the screen to reveal either 2 (the correct answer) or 3 (the incorrect answer). Babies stared longer at the incorrect answer, indicating that it did not meet their expectations. (Babies stare longer at something that is surprising than they do at something familiar or expected.) Thus, they concluded infants can recognize simple numbers and math.

Prenatal Tooth Development
Even before a baby is born, teeth begin to form below the surface of the gums—as early as the sixth week of pregnancy. Future dental health can be affected by the mother's prenatal diet or exposure to drugs or other factors. For example, if you lived in an area with fluoridated water during your pregnancy, your baby will probably reap the benefits with more cavity-resistant teeth today.

✛

Don't Serve Minors
Some parents opt for an age-old remedy—scotch or bourbon on the gums. Do not rub alcohol on your baby's gums. It won't relieve your baby's pain and could be dangerous. Even small amounts of alcohol can be harmful to a young child's system.

that it causes a blood blister to appear. You may notice a purplish black bump on the gums. This is not a discolored tooth. Known as an eruption cyst or hematoma, it should be left alone. It will disappear on its own and the baby tooth finally will emerge by itself sometime later.

Some ideas for teething relief and chewing satisfaction:

- Offer your little one a clean, cold wet washcloth to suck and chew on.
- Freeze a bagel or offer a hard, stale one for good gnawing fun. Make sure your baby doesn't manage to break a piece off, as she could choke on it.
- Buy a plastic teething ring and refrigerate it for added soothing relief.
- Rub her bottom gums with your thumb.
- Apply a teething solution which numbs the gums.
- Offer a big fat carrot, dipped in ice water. Make sure she doesn't break a piece off.
- Give her rubber or plastic toys that are easy to hold and easy to chomp on. One favorite is a plastic hand and foot set, complete with fingers and toes that make a satisfying rubbery squeak as baby rubs them across the gums. Make sure the plastic toy you offer will withstand chewing. Avoid toys with sharp edges or toys which might break easily.

STARTING SOLID FOODS

Very few babies actually need solids at this age, but many will be offered something by the end of this month. Although there is no real reason to rush this milestone, the fifth or sixth month can be a good time to begin to offer a small taste of solids (a teaspoonful or so at a time) to your baby. Later, your baby will be a lot more opinionated—and a lot more likely to turn down solids if he isn't used to them. Nutritionally, iron-containing foods are appropriately offered at six months, when iron stores are diminished. Developmentally, a baby is ready to chew at about 6 months. Talk with your pediatrician and start off slowly, following your baby's cues. See page 179 in Chapter 18, "Feeding in the First Year" for more on starting solids.

SAFETY TIPS FOR THE FIFTH MONTH

Mobiles should be removed from cribs, as should crib gyms that are strung across a crib. Babies who can push up on hands, or possibly on hands and knees, run the risk of getting tangled in these hanging crib toys. Your baby may be spending some of his playtime on the floor. Make sure carpets are clean and small objects are off the floor. Keep cords out of reach. Cover unused electrical outlets with plastic safety caps. She can't get to them yet, but it's a good idea to always remain a step ahead of baby's abilities when it comes to safety. Since teething may be under way, offer only toys that can be safely chewed—no hard, plastic or brittle parts or small pieces. At this age, you can expect that everything within reach is likely to end up in the mouth.

PLAYTIME

Besides quiet conversation and animated toy play, you may want to add dancing to your list of playtime activities. For many moms of hard-to-soothe babies, dancing to music with a baby in your arms may already be second nature. Happy babies love this active game too. An added benefit: moms get a little needed exercise while they're at it! As usual, follow your baby's cues when choosing music, volume, and dance pace.

Your baby's attention span gets a little longer each month. Play conversations will become longer as well. You say something to your baby, she says something back to you, you say it back to her. Your baby is trying to imitate you and is delighted when you imitate her as well. Playtime is pleasurable for both mother and baby.

Now that two-handed play is so much fun, offer your baby a block for each hand and watch while he compares them and maybe even bangs them together. Dropping them is fun for baby too! As you sit with your baby at the dinner table, you may notice this is the perfect position for many interesting games: from slapping the table to playing with a napkin or a spoon. Just be careful that plates of hot foods and sharp utensils are not in front of him as well.

Of course, babies, with their unique personalities, all respond to playtime differently. Some are more fun-loving than others; some laugh more easily. Different toys and sounds and colors attract different children. You may have an irritable, hard-to-comfort baby who

Time's Up!
Give your baby the right to say, "That's enough!" When conversing with baby, be sensitive to her cues. If she starts to break eye contact and look or turn away, this is a sign that she is fatigued and the game, or conversation, should come to an end.

Baby Club
This can be a good month to join a play group with other moms and babies. Your little one will probably enjoy the chance to see and hear other babies in action. They will look at other babies with interest, make sounds at them, and even reach out to touch. Besides being nice for them, it's nice for you. For more on how to find or start a mother-baby group, see page 280.

It's not THUMBSUCKING I'm worried about...

demands a lot of your attention. Or you may be raising an unusually quiet child who doesn't ask for much stimulation. Try to engage this baby as much as you might a more demanding one. It is simply in your baby's nature to be quiet—she will still enjoy playtime.

TOYS FOR THE FIFTH MONTH

Smooth plastic nesting cups
Soft blocks in primary colors
Unbreakable plastic mirror
Large wiffle balls (the holes can be perfect for little fingers to grab on to)
Squeeze toy
Rubber rings (to hold on to and transfer from hand to hand)
Records, CDs, or tapes played for her listening enjoyment
Heavy cardboard or cloth book
Plastic book for bathtime or teething
Clear plastic pad filled with water and floating objects inside
Stuffed musical toy animal

HAPPY BABY'S HIT PARADE

- Going for a drive in the car.
- Repeating your sounds.
- Looking at himself in the mirror.
- Seeing other babies' faces in picture books.
- "Playing" with other babies (they like to look, watch, and touch).
- Being whispered to (a baby may even stop fussing to try to hear what you have to say).
- Playing with his feet.
- Doing push-ups (lifting his chest off the floor with arms extended).
- Pulling your hair, nose, cheek (whatever's handy!).

CHAPTER 11

✛ Your Baby's Sixth Month ✛

Here you are, almost halfway through the first year, well into a relationship that is beginning to feel natural. It's hard to remember a time when you didn't have a baby to care for and delight in. Your baby is truly blossoming into a little person. As she approaches the halfway mark in the first year, she begins the exploratory stage. All the skills of the first six months are coming together now for baby, making it that much easier for her to enjoy and explore the world around her. She can reach for some of the objects she wants and get them for herself; she can probably wave, shake and pound, feel, chew and taste everything in reach. She can probably roll over if she wants to. She can hold her own bottle and may even try to feed herself with the help of one new tooth. Perhaps nicest of all is her newest (or soon to be newest) skill: learning to sit up alone. Once this skill develops far enough, she will be able to use her hands to explore toys while sitting—a real treat for your baby and the beginning of independence!

✛   ✛   ✛

THE SIXTH-MONTH CHECKUP

At the end of this month, it's time for another visit to the pediatrician, more measurements (length, weight, head circumference) and another round of immunizations. Some high-risk children may also be screened for exposure to lead at this age. Lead is a widespread environmental toxin, which can cause serious health problems in exposed children.

Your pediatrician will probably also stick a finger into your baby's mouth to check for swollen gums or erupting teeth. As your doctor examines your baby and talks with you, he or she is also checking

your baby's development. Some doctors check for specific developmental milestones by performing "tests" (pulling your baby to a sit, etc.), while others will rely more on their own observations and a report from you. This is the time for you to discuss any eating or sleeping questions you might have. You will also want to review the list of any possible reactions your child might have from the immunizations and how they should be treated. If you are back at work and have taken time off for this checkup, make sure your caregiver comes along. If your child is in day care, tell your pediatrician and discuss any concerns or questions you may have about your day-care situation.

LANGUAGE DEVELOPMENT

Babies continue to listen to every word you say and may soon reward you with a first "word" like "mama" or "dada." At this point, however, it is unlikely that they associate these words with the real thing. They are simply using the sounds. *Ba, ma, da, pa,* and *ga* may be repeated and strung together in a babbling conversation that sometimes sounds remarkably as if the baby is saying something. This is because your baby is sometimes able to imitate the tone and pitch, the rise and fall of the human voice that you normally hear in a conversation. During this period of intense language development in the first year, it is important to talk to your baby. Speak slowly and in simple sentences. Use words to describe every action as you do it: "Here's the dog. The dog is going out now. Bye-bye, doggie." Your child will watch a scene like this played out over and over with great interest. You may even want to single out words that have great meaning for your baby—words like cup, car, Daddy, ball, book. If your baby attempts to make a sound, repeat it. If it's close to the name for the item in your hand, hold it up and repeat again. Babies love the attention and smiles that go along with these little language classes. They love hearing you repeat their sounds. Repetition is fun for babies! Try repeating a favorite rhyme or short song every day and watch the delighted reaction in your child! Take the time to point things out to the child from the world around him, looking up to show him birds and planes, looking around to show him cars and animals. Babies also begin to distinguish emotions by the tone of voice in the sixth and seventh months. Your baby may be able to use his own voice to signal displeasure or joy.

CREEPING

When lying on her tummy, your baby may be able to do a modified pushup, lifting most of her torso off the ground. She may even be able to push herself around a bit, perhaps spinning herself around to face many new directions. Watch her pivot to get to a new toy! It is unlikely that she will be able to get her tummy completely off the ground as she does this, but there are, of course, some babies who will get themselves up on their knees and are advancing toward crawling at this age. Even if your baby is able to get herself up on all fours this month or next, she probably won't go anywhere just yet. Forward (or backward) crawling movements usually come later, although the exact timing depends on your baby.

Your baby likes it if you get down on your tummy and face her. With you down on her level, she may try harder to keep the pushup position. You may also try putting an appealing toy just to the right or left of her and watch her try to scoot over and reach it. If baby needs a rest, but still wants to play with floor toys, sit up with your legs extended and crossed to make a slight incline. Place your baby's chest across your lap on your legs, allowing arms to dangle down in front for free play with toys on the floor. (See illustration.)

For early floor play, prop baby over your own outstretched legs (or use a wedge-shaped cushion) with an interesting toy in sight.

SITTING UP

Learning to sit up is a major leap for baby, allowing him to play and enjoy his world from a new perspective. Once a sitter, the baby need no longer always depend on your lap or a baby seat. He commands his own stage once he sits alone and you can enjoy watching him from across the floor with a new perspective yourself. A baby does not simply learn to sit all in one day. This is a maneuver he has been practicing for the past couple of months, as back muscle strength increased. Sitting without support is usually accomplished anywhere between five and eight months of age. At first, you may notice that your baby sits slumped over. It may be only a moment before he topples to one side. Little by little the baby learns to use his arms to help keep himself in a seated position a little longer. Next, he is able to take away his hands and achieve a balance. Once back muscles are strong enough and balance is good enough, the baby can stop using his arms as balancing mechanisms and start using

Don't Run Off!
Even though your baby looks much more independent now, sitting up (maybe even with her toys in hand), she still needs her favorite playmate: you. And staying close by has another benefit: it keeps baby safe. Now that she can sit, reach, and topple, your baby may be able to get into a few unforeseen positions where danger may lurk.

Time to Sit
As with all developmental milestones, this one may be reached earlier by some babies and later by others. Your baby may sit up as early as four months or as late as eight or nine, and still be within the "normal" range.

The beginning sitter tends to slump and may topple over.

Soon back muscles become stronger and your baby will learn to balance himself in an erect sitting position.

them for play and communication. The sitting position encourages your child to begin the mastery of fine motor skills. Seated, he can concentrate on playing with the toys you leave in front of him.

To encourage sitting up while your baby is still a novice sitter, place your baby in a balanced sitting position in front of you, between your outstretched legs. Start out by supporting him with your hands. Once he is focused forward and feels steady, loosen your hold on him to allow your baby to try to balance himself. As baby gets more proficient, you can back away, but leave him surrounded with some soft pillows to cushion the fall when baby inevitably topples to the side or the back.

THE FIRST TOOTH

Although a baby's teeth actually begin to form under the surface of the gums before birth, the first tooth does not usually appear until six to seven months of age. There is a wide variation of normal, however. Some babies are actually born with a tooth while others are twelve months old when that first tooth erupts. As long as a first tooth appears sometime during the first year, there should be no cause for concern.

The bottom central incisors will almost always be the first teeth to appear in your baby's mouth. These are the middle two teeth on the bottom. By the end of the first year, most babies will have six to eight teeth, usually two to four on top, and four on the bottom. The toothless grin you've been admiring for the first half of the year is disappearing. It's an exciting (but sometimes also a troublesome) time. Your baby may experience some discomfort as these new teeth push and turn and slide their way into place through the sensitive gums. (See the section on teething, p. 101.) With all your attention focused on your baby's pearly whites, you may notice some imperfections. It is not unusual for the teeth to grow in slightly crooked, turned sideways, or with spaces between them. Spaces may actually be a plus: they allow more space for the second teeth to come through without crowding. Your pediatric dentist may keep an eye on crowding or other problems to see if they eventually correct themselves or not.

Once these new little teeth start appearing, you'll want to take good care of them. Although it's true that these teeth will be replaced, they serve important functions. Clean, healthy teeth are necessary to baby's happiness, well-being, and general development. Primary teeth play a role in the development of speech and obviously help your child to eat. Although your child may not be aware of appearance yet, by two or three he will be—and a pretty smile will be a part of that! Furthermore, cavities hurt and missing teeth can end up causing orthodontic problems as other teeth drift over to fill the empty space. For all these reasons and more, then, it is important to help your child keep his teeth healthy and in place.

DROOLING

With teething and teeth comes drooling. With drooling occasionally comes some minor problems. Wet shirts can be changed but raw red chins have to be lived with! If you notice a red rash developing around your baby's mouth and chin, redouble your efforts to wipe away excess drool. (Pat it with some absorbent cotton—don't rub!) A little Vaseline or other skin cream recommended by your pediatrician may help as well. Drooling may sometimes be accompanied by loose stools and mild diaper rash. Be careful not to ignore real diarrhea, however. If stools are not only loose but frequent, call your doctor. For more on the common discomforts of teething, see page 101.

CLEANING TEETH

It is not too soon to begin cleaning your baby's new teeth. You may prefer to use just a piece of gauze wrapped around your finger. Just wet the gauze with a little water. Place the infant in your lap with his head facing you. Wipe the teeth with your finger. Tooth decay is caused by plaque, a sticky film on the teeth. By wiping the teeth with gauze, you help to wipe away the bacteria, acids, and plaque that can hurt your baby's teeth. With many very small and soft toothbrushes on the market, it is perfectly appropriate to use a toothbrush to clean your baby's teeth. Doing so early on may help your baby to get used to the idea of the brush and to the routine of having you clean the teeth with one. This may help prevent brushing battles later in life. Toothpaste isn't necessary yet but can be used. If you use toothpaste, apply it yourself, placing no more than a pea-size drop

A Look Ahead
Baby teeth remain until around age six years, when they start to fall out and are replaced by permanent teeth. The average adult has thirty-two permanent teeth.

✢

A Mother's Reflections
"I was afraid I might have to stop breastfeeding when he got teeth, but I didn't. He did bite me once or twice, but when I yelped and pulled away, he seemed surprised and after that he didn't repeat it. For the most part, he took feeding times seriously and seemed inclined to use his time for sucking, not playing around with his new teeth!"

A Doctor's Thoughts

"Babies this age are very interested in mirror images. Strap an unbreakable plastic mirror to the inside of the crib. When the baby wakes up in the morning, he can amuse himself for a while just looking in the mirror."
—*Dr. Gary Freed, Assistant Professor of Pediatrics and Public Health Policy, University of North Carolina at Chapel Hill*

on the brush. Do not let your child play with the tube. In fact, swallowing too much fluoridated toothpaste can eventually cause a problem known as fluorosis, in which the teeth enamel can become discolored.

FLUORIDE

Fluoride helps to strengthen the teeth and make the enamel more resistant to decay. Formula is not made with fluoridated water. Breastfed babies do not get much fluoride through mother's breast milk. Should your baby receive supplements? Discuss this with your doctor. If your baby drinks water from a fluoridated drinking water source, or uses a fluoridated toothpaste, he probably won't need supplements. (You can contact your local water department to find out whether and how much fluoridation is in the water.) If your baby receives no fluoride from the water or does not drink water, the answer may be yes, but many doctors are being conservative about fluoride supplements today. There have been cases of overfluoridation, which can lead to discolored teeth.

EARLY WAKING

By now, your baby may be sleeping through the night. Unfortunately, sleeping through the night may not be what you'd always dreamed it would be. Your baby may bed down at ten and wake at five, for example. This can seem as much like torture as her previous schedule of waking at three and then going back to sleep till seven. You might start out by trying to keep her up a little later at night, in the hopes that she'll sleep longer in the morning. If you have a determined early riser in the house, make sure you keep her room dark with heavy, drawn curtains. Even the weak light at daybreak can wake some babies. You might even consider moving her crib to a quieter, darker room. Be aware of what might be waking her. Is it hunger or is it possible that, because she's on the street side of the house, she hears the early morning noises of garbage trucks? If she's just looking for company or activity, a few toys placed in the crib the night before may help her to entertain herself quietly for a half hour or so while you continue to sleep. (Make sure all toys are crib safe.)

NIGHT WAKING

It is not unusual to have a baby who still wakes during the night for food or company. Knowing that other moms have the same problem you do may not offer you much comfort on your second trip to the nursery since midnight, however. The problem is not likely to be that your baby is hungry or in distress. The problem is more likely to be that your baby doesn't know how to put himself back to sleep without your help. He may need your breast, his pacifier, or just a warm body nearby. Some families opt for the family bed, so that the baby doesn't have to go without human companionship at night and may stay asleep till morning. See page 87 for more on the family bed. Other parents prefer to gradually encourage baby to sleep alone.

Start by examining your baby's going-to-sleep pattern. Does he always fall asleep at the breast? or while being rocked in your arms? Your baby may be asking you to replay this scene for him every time he wakes up. Try putting him in his crib while he's sleepy but still awake, and see if he lets himself drift off without you. Getting a baby to learn this new trick may involve some crying (possibly not only from the baby but from you as well!). Various experts have suggestions ranging from the cold turkey "letting him cry himself to sleep" approach to other less radical methods, including going in to offer comfort but not food. Another method: going in to check on baby so baby knows you're still around but no feeding, no picking up, no back rub, no pacifier. You might go in after five minutes of crying, then leave and wait ten minutes before returning. Obviously, some babies are more stubborn than others about this sudden change of behavior on your part, and the first couple of nights can be tough to get through. Still, the fact that you repeatedly go in to see and talk to your baby helps you as a parent to get through it. (Somehow it's worse to listen to the screaming from behind a closed door while you imagine the worst and fear the baby thinks himself abandoned!)

Clearly, this is your baby and your life—so the best way to deal with sleep patterns and problems often comes from you. If you cannot stand the thought of letting baby cry it out, don't push yourself into this method. (In fact, in the first few months of life, cries should most definitely be answered.) If you find the family bed works for you, use it. If sleeping in the same room with your baby seems to placate him, try it. If your partner is willing to put the child to bed and answer nighttime calls, let him. (Sometimes certain sleep difficulties are

---

The Night Owl Club

According to one large-scale study, by five months of age, 50 percent of the babies studied were sleeping through the night. The other half were still waking up. By nine months, 90 percent of the babies were sleeping, leaving only 10 percent in the night owl club.

✠

Mothers' Reflections

"After many sleepless months, everyone suggested I let my baby cry it out. Out of desperation, I gave it a try. After a heart-wrenching hour of nonstop screaming, he finally threw up and I had to go in to change him . . . needless to say, I couldn't imagine going through that again!"

✠

"My firstborn did not sleep through the night until he was almost two! I did nothing different (that I know of) the second time around and ended up with a daughter who began sleeping through the night at the age of six weeks! Go figure."

specific to baby's relationship with Mom and may disappear if someone else takes over at night.) If you think you can hang in there until your baby learns to sleep through the night on his own without any pressure from you, ride it out. If you are exhausted and miserable, however, it's only fair that you try to change your baby's night-waking behavior. Working it out on your own, with help from books, friends, and your pediatrician, you may eventually come to the best solution for your household. Don't expect to repeat the same sleep prescription from one child to another, though. What works like a charm for one baby may not work for another. You may just have to go with the flow and try to find your own way down this dark corridor of nights with baby!

SAFETY TIPS FOR THE SIXTH MONTH

With creeping and crawling coming up, start thinking ahead by placing stair guards or gates at the tops of steps. Lock cabinets containing dangerous household items, use safety netting on landings to prevent baby from slipping between banisters. Be sure the crib is lowered now that baby might be sitting up and in anticipation of a pull to stand. If your baby can sit, you might want to use a special baby seat for the bath. This helps keep a slippery, active baby in place as you wash him. Remember, these are not safety devices. Never leave baby unattended near water. (See photo on page 113.)

If your baby uses a walker occasionally, you must be especially vigilant. Anecdotally, there have been many cases of accidents occurring with walker use and the American Academy of Pediatrics does not favor their use. Keep a child in a walker away from steps and doorways and out of the dangerous areas of the house. Be careful that your child doesn't pick up too much speed and crash into furniture. Better yet, most pediatricians would advise you not to use a walker at all.

PLAYTIME

It may look like play to you, but for baby this is business. As your baby goes through the day, she learns from everything she sees, tastes, and touches. The carpet is soft, the water is hot, the TV is loud. She plays with a cup in the bath and sees water spill out of it. Another cup with tiny holes in the bottom does not hold the water at all. She kicks with her legs in the tub and Mom gets splashed with water. She grabs and pulls her brother's hair and finds out not only about hair but about brother's reaction! By now, your baby may not only be able to hold a toy in one hand, but she may be able to bring it closer or farther from her face, and pass it from one hand to the other. This allows her new ways to look at and examine the item from all directions. Babies this age seem endlessly interested in everything around them. Playtime is a time to encourage this interest, by letting baby explore freely (within the bounds of safety, of course). At this stage, your baby may begin to enjoy peek-a-boo and pat-a-cake and itsy-bitsy spider, although she won't be an active participant until sometime later.

TOYS FOR THE SIXTH MONTH

Now that she can sit up and focus, as well as move toys from hand to mouth, you'll want to offer toys that fit the bill:

Teething rings
Plastic toys that can be chewed on
Bright pictures on the walls
Squeak toys
Toys that make noise when you shake them
Toys with finger holes for easy grabbing
Unbreakable plastic mirrors
Rag doll or soft cuddly toy
Activity board (little windows to open, buttons to press and squeak, and so on)
Blocks
A ball to roll while sitting up

A Doctor's Opinion
"Playtime is always important, no matter what the age of the baby. Everyone needs to play—even grown-ups. Around this age, babies enjoy social play with interactive games like pat-a-cake."—Dr. Gary Freed, Assistant Professor of Pediatrics and Public Health Policy, University of North Carolina at Chapel Hill

Many babies love being pulled to a stand on your lap.

HAPPY BABY'S HIT PARADE

- Passing toys from hand to hand
- Dropping toys on the floor and watching you pick them up
- Feeding herself
- Hearing nursery rhymes and songs, especially if accompanied by clapping and finger play
- Being pulled to standing in your lap
- Playing in a baby bouncer
- Playing with and banging spoons

CHAPTER 12

✤ Your Baby's Seventh Month ✤

Your baby is already starting to seem . . . grown up! It's hard to believe that he was once so little that his head barely peeked out over the top of the Snugli, that your floppy little newborn probably now sits up, babbles, and passes toys from one hand to another. The seven-month-old is fun-loving and active. The only thing that may spoil some of his fun is the continued discomfort of teething or the frustration of not being able to do everything he sets his sights on! During the seventh month, your baby will refine some of the skills that were being worked on last month: sitting better and for longer periods, and even pushing himself up into a sitting position from the floor. Your baby will still rake things toward himself with a thumb and all four fingers, but the pincer grasp (thumb and forefinger) is not far away. Crawling—or the beginnings of it—may be under way.

✤   ✤   ✤

BOOKS

A baby at this age delights in all aspects of books: holding them, chewing on them, looking at the pictures, hearing the words as you read them. The children's section of any bookstore is brimming with appropriate material for your baby. Good first books include plastic books with bright primary sentences and simple phrases or rhymes. These can go into the bath. They are also easy for baby to hold because they are so light and good to chew and drool on. Fabric books

also fit easily into little hands and can be not just read but grabbed, felt, and hugged. Board books, which are printed on thick cardboard pages, are also appealing. Choose one with bright primary colors and simple language. Some simply identify the picture with one word, a good choice for reinforcing the names of some of the objects already familiar to your baby: bottle, crib, kitty, and so on. Books that use big bold photos instead of drawings also get baby's attention, especially if they include photos of babies his own age making interesting faces. Many books also take a hands-on approach to reading and encourage the baby to "pat the bunny" or "feel the terry-cloth towel." Many babies will enjoy stroking these things with your help. Books provide your child with a lasting toy. These same books can often still provide entertainment at ages one, two, and even three. Even if your baby doesn't want to do much more than chew on the book, introducing him to books opens up the strong possibility that in the months and years to come he will be a lover of books, language, and reading. It offers you a chance to sit with your baby and talk about pictures, words, actions, feelings, and colors.

MUSIC

Babies love to bounce, wiggle, and shake—often to the beat of music. Music seems to strike a primal chord in all humans—from the rhythmic beat of the heart babies hear in the womb to the lullabies you begin singing them in their first few weeks of life. Now is the time to let your baby play with sounds—jingling bells, banging spoons, babbling to the beat. Play with the types of music you offer to your baby. If you love Anita Baker, play that. There is no rule that says babies have to listen to baby songs. On the other hand, many nursery rhymes set to music and traditional lullabies do seem to have universal appeal. With so many babies being born each year, there is a wonderful assortment of good music for children as close by as your nearest record store (or supermarket). Some babies enjoy listening to the same tape over and over, delighting in the familiarity of the tunes.

LEFT-HANDED OR RIGHT-HANDED

It is impossible to tell yet whether your child will favor his left hand or his right hand. For now, encourage him to use either or both to get what he wants. Your baby may remain ambidextrous for most of the first year. Or he may begin to show a preference for one side right away. Some babies show a preference for one side only to switch to the other side a few months later. Do not be premature in predicting left- or right-handedness. If, however, you see an early preference, you can take your cue from this. For example, you might offer toys to either side when your baby is in a good mood, but when he's tiring, offer toys to the side he seems most likely to get. Do not be concerned about a potential leftie. There would probably be a lot more of them in the world if they hadn't been discouraged from using their left hands as a baby. It is no longer fashionable (or advisable) to force a baby into right-handedness.

SECURITY BLANKETS

Around now you may start to see an attachment to a special item. You may first notice it when you try to put baby to bed without her usual blanket, or leave a room that has a favorite teddy still sitting on the floor. For whatever reason, your child has attached to this specific object because it offers "comfort." Of course, you cannot make your child become attached to a particular item—or any item for that matter. Even if the small brown teddy is more convenient for you to tote, your child may declare his devotion to a big pink rhino instead. Some children, of course, are content without any special object—whether *you'd* like them to have a "lovie" or not!

The more independent your baby becomes, the more likely she may be to feel the need for a security object. While independence is fun, it is also scary and new and the security blanket or stuffed animal offers constancy and unconditional comfort. When baby is faced with a new babysitter, a dark room, a frustrating moment, or an unexpected visitor, the security object spells relief. It can be awfully cute to see your baby cuddling up with this special item and it can make new situations, like an overnight trip or a family vacation in a hotel, a lot easier to get through.

A "lovie" has its downside too. Assuming your child becomes more and more attached to it over the next one or two years, you

---

Left-handed News
Although the number of left-handers born in America may be as high as 25% by some accounts, the number of adults who end up using their left hand seems to be about 12%. (This discrepancy is probably due to the fact that left-handedness used to be discouraged.) Wisdom has it that left-handed folk may be better at tennis, baseball, and even blackjack dealing! On the down side, however, egg beaters, scissors, and manual pencil sharpeners—often made with the right-hander in mind—can be a source of frustration!

A Mother's Reflections
"I never particularly encouraged or discouraged a security object. Of three children, only one attached to an item—a blanket. She was also the same one who fell in love with her pacifier. The other two never had any love object—not a pacifier, not a stuffed animal or blanket."

The Carry-on Bag

You'll know best what your baby needs, but here are some suggestions:

- Enough diapers for the entire flight, plus the time to and from the airport.
- A change or two of clothes.
- A bib.
- Plenty of baby wipes for diaper changes and for cleaning hands and faces.
- Some favorite small toys.
- A receiving blanket (can be spread on the floor at your feet for a play period or used a myriad of other ways!).
- Diaper rash cream.
- Plastic bags for dirty laundry, leaky bottles, etc.
- A changing pad.
- Jarred baby food, snacks, and beverages, depending on your baby's age.
- Liquid Tylenol, saline nose drops, or other items your doctor has recommended for possible use on the trip.

often find yourself scrambling to find it when it's lost, drying tears when a little friend or sibling dares to pick it up, sneaking it away to wash it, and having a major panic attack if you forget to bring it with you on a trip. It may not be a bad idea to allow the security object to be carried in the house only—not outside or off to the supermarket or playgroup. This cuts down not only on the possibility of its getting lost, but also the perceived need for having it in all situations.

TAKING A TRIP WITH BABY

Of course, you can take a trip with your baby anytime after your own gynecologist and pediatrician give you the okay. Some parents start traveling with infants as young as one month. If you are planning a trip, consider your options. By car, you have the benefit of being able to bring all kinds of baby paraphernalia with you. This can make you feel more secure (even if your baby doesn't really need it all). When traveling by car, always use a car seat. It's the law. See page 11 on choosing and using a car safety seat.

By plane, you'll have to travel a little lighter, but you will get there faster. Small children are usually fine on plane rides. Make sure to breastfeed or bottle-feed on take-off and landing, to help reduce any ear discomfort. Airlines allow you to hold a child under two in your lap. There has been much discussion recently about the safety of this. After all, we use car seats in cars, why not in airplanes? If you can afford to buy an extra seat, you may feel more comfortable doing so. Or ask the airline to try to put you next to an empty seat, assuming the flight is not fully booked, so you can set the car seat up there. Make sure your car seat is labeled for airplane travel, especially if it's a hand-me-down. Bring along the car seat and use it in the airline seat. This helps to keep your child confined, out of trouble, safe, and off your lap for a more comfortable flight.

Trains provide another good method of baby travel. Babies often enjoy the passing scenery and the rhythm of a train. In fact, it puts many babies right to sleep. Trains also have the benefit of snack cars and room to walk and stretch your legs (and maybe even your baby's).

Think about what you need to have with you. A lightweight umbrella-style stroller is going to be a lot easier to fold, store, and maneuver than a bigger bulkier model. A front carrier may be ideal with a young baby and leaves both hands free for dealing with luggage and tickets. Likewise, a baby-carrier backpack may be the perfect solution for a baby seven months and up.

LIKES AND DISLIKES

Your baby is a discriminating shopper now—looking for the toy, food, and type of stimulation that suits him best. He may love a rubber pig and consistently ignore a stuffed bunny. He may think the sudden noise of a sneeze is a real hoot but the humming or clanking noise of an elevator is scary. He may delight in ripping up old magazines and ignore the new book you bought. Within reason, you'll want to respect your baby's opinions. Of course, next month they may change entirely!

TOYS FOR THE SEVENTH MONTH

Toys with wheels, so your baby can make them move
Plastic donut rings on a stand or other stacking toy
Activity board

HAPPY BABY'S HIT PARADE

Playing with other babies
Bouncing in a baby bouncer
"Swimming" in a pool with a parent (stay in the shallow end, where you can stand, and think of it as a big bathtub)
Playing pat-a-cake and peek-a-boo
Being bounced gently on your knee

CHAPTER 13

✤ Your Baby's Eighth Month ✤

You are now the mother of a busy, active baby who sits without support and is ready for physical action. From this playful position, he can examine toys, feed himself, and play games. Sitting is great fun but not always enough—your baby may even be trying his hand (and knees) at creeping and crawling this month. Once he takes off, you become the mother of a baby on the go. Your parenting style will have to change with your baby's new skills. With the excitement of movement come the dangers of independence and you'll need to be on your guard, ensuring your baby's safety as he explores. The eighth month can bring many happy surprises, including a possible first "word" and lots of laughter and fun.

✤   ✤   ✤

CREEPING, SCOOTING, OR CRAWLING

Throughout the eighth month, the buzzword is motion. Your baby loves to move and daily pushes his physical abilities a little further. He may or may not try to crawl yet, but he will surely be moving in some direction in some fashion. Some babies will pivot on their tummies, enabling them to reach around in all directions. Some can even drag themselves around with their arms, while remaining on their tummies. This is often called "creeping." Some sit on their bottoms and scoot themselves forward, bouncing along on their buttocks until they get where they want to go. Those babies who get themselves into a hands-and-knees crawl position may go forward, or they may go backward at first. The backward crawl is attributed to the fact that baby's upper body is still stronger than the legs. (As Jean-Jacques Rousseau once said, "There is a period of life when we

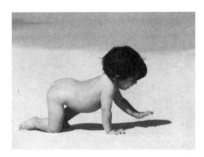

A Mother's Reflections

"My mother says that as a baby I never crawled, but that I suddenly walked at ten months. She says it was typical of my personality—I just watched and waited and then stood up and did it. I had no interest in getting from here to there on my hands and knees."

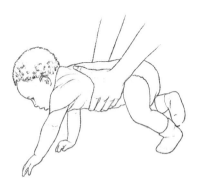

To help a baby eager to crawl, you can lift baby onto his hands and knees while firmly supporting back and rib cage, allowing baby to get his balance.

go backward as we advance." Perhaps he was talking about 8-month-olds!) She may crawl gracefully on two knees and two hands, or she may "scoot" along by using one knee and dragging the other leg behind. Crawling isn't accomplished the same way, or at the same time, in any two babies. Some are up on their hands and knees and tearing around your house by six months, while others crawl at nine months. Still other babies appear to skip the crawling stage altogether and often will walk early instead. For the most part, you'll just have to leave the style of movement up to your baby.

You can encourage creeping and crawling, however, by trying some of the following things (as long as your baby is willing and able):

1. Allow your baby lots of time down on the floor with toys around him. (Do not continually keep him confined in a seat, baby bouncer, or playpen.)
2. Place a favorite item a little out of his reach. This way he is encouraged to move toward it and rewarded for his efforts once he reaches his prize.
3. If he's up on his hands and knees but seems to need a little help getting started, place the palms of your hands flat against the soles of his feet and let him push against you. (Do not push your child forward. Just let him use your hands as leverage.)
4. If your child gets up on her hands and knees but then tends to cave in and sit on her feet, you can help her to get her balance this way: Place her tummy-down with an interesting toy about a foot in front of her. Lifting her up onto her hands and knees, support her in that position while gently rocking her back and forth. (See illustration.) This enables her to feel her weight alternately on her arms and legs and may help strengthen the muscles in the thighs that support her weight in a crawl position. Gradually, try to loosen your hold on her so that she can learn to balance by herself.
5. Put your child in a sitting position. Place an interesting toy in front of her and then drag it forward, encouraging her to reach forward until she shifts into a crawling position.

STANDING WITH SUPPORT

Although it depends on your baby, some will begin to stand with your help around now. As you hold them in an upright position, they bounce down, putting a little weight on their legs, and testing the waters for actual standing skills coming up in the next few months. Some babies enjoy baby bouncers if they are interested in supported standing. It provides them with a new view from their suddenly vertical position. Baby bouncers hang from door frames and allow the baby to push off the floor with his feet and bounce. He can also play with putting a little weight on his legs each time. Baby bouncers are certainly not necessary. Babies will learn to stand on their own, as long as they are given ample opportunity to do so.

WALKERS

Many parents want to buy walkers for babies who are too young to walk but appear interested in movement. Walkers can seem fun for a baby, but they are not essential to your baby's physical development and can be very dangerous. Babies often thrill to the upright position and sudden freedom of movement as they whiz around a room. With their curiosity and wide-ranging movement, however, come many obvious safety concerns. It is difficult to protect your baby from stairways, rug edges that can trip him up, dangerous objects on tabletops that are now suddenly in reach, and so on. Remember, not only can he reach for more trouble in a walker, but he has both hands free with which to grab it. For these reasons the American Academy of Pediatrics is working with consumer groups to ban the sale of walkers, which have been associated with injury and even death.

CLINGING

As the second half of baby's first year continues to unfold, he becomes more and more mobile and, therefore, more and more independent. Independence for the baby is exciting but it is also scary. You may notice clingy, fussy behavior beginning just at the moment you thought your baby was growing more mature and less dependent on you. The truth is: he needs you now more than ever. His own ability to scoot or crawl away from you frightens him. He, therefore, may protest more strenuously when you walk away from

Walker Safety Tips

If, in spite of pediatricians' warnings, you use a walker, be as vigilant as possible. Never use a walker near steps or in a split-level room. Put guards in front of heaters, radiators, and fireplaces. Reassess each room from the height of a walker. Remove tablecloths as they can be easily tugged off tables, taking the contents with them. Never leave a baby in a walker unattended—even for a second. Put plastic covers on all electric outlets.

✦

Jewel Thief

Look out! Your baby thinks that everything within reach is for the taking these days. Necklaces and earrings are often the first to go! Babies have a surprisingly strong grab-and-pull approach now and it can be hard to get their little clenched fists off your things . . . so for now, avoid flashy jewelry, dangly earrings, or long necklaces.

Doctors' Opinions

"I don't recommend walkers for two reasons. The first is safety. There are tons of case reports of kids going down steps, out doors, or crashing into furniture or people. Second, children who use walkers for more than an hour a day seem to walk later. Walkers teach them to walk incorrectly. To make the walker move, they must stand on tiptoe and lean forward. Try this same movement without the walker and you fall over. Whenever I see an otherwise normal child who is delayed in walking I always ask about how much time is spent in a walker."—Dr. Gary Freed, Assistant Professor of Pediatrics and Health Policy Administration, University of North Carolina at Chapel Hill.

✦

"Your baby's wishes should be honored. Let him warm up slowly to new people. Don't push him into a situation too quickly. If you wait, gradually his curiosity will overcome his stranger anxiety."—Dr. Max Kahn, Clinical Associate Professor, New York University Medical School

him, or leave him with a sitter. This clingy behavior may or may not come at the same time as stranger anxiety (see below), which can make it even harder for you to easily leave your baby and go out. It can even make it hard to take your baby to a playgroup or a pediatrician visit. He may decide to remain in your lap and bury his head in your shoulder. New experiences and people can be overwhelming right now. Rather than close yourself up in your house, adapt to your baby's insecurity. Keep him close, let him stay in your lap, ask Grandma not to rush in for an immediate kiss. In short: Give your baby time to look around and get his bearings before he gets involved. Do things gradually and slowly. Have a new person sit an arm's length away and talk to you rather than to the baby. This allows the baby plenty of time to eye the stranger and watch this person in action with you first.

In order to encourage your baby to explore freely, he has to be sure that you are a constant in his life. If he crawls away, he likes to know that, when he turns around, you are still sitting in the same place watching him. If you are out of the house, he expects, and deserves, the same type of devoted attention from his babysitter. When you return home, you may find him fussy with you and clingier than ever. This is not because he is "mad" at you for leaving or because he "likes the babysitter better than you." It's just the tension between his new independent self and his old dependent self. The only way you can bolster his self-esteem and foster his increased independence is by allowing him to fuss and cling—make a fuss over him and cuddle right back. Shoving him away will only make him more fearful of losing you, thereby making matters worse.

STRANGER ANXIETY

For the first four to six months of life, many babies seem pretty happy no matter whose arms they find themselves in. This can make having relatives and friends over easy and fun. Some time after that, however—anywhere from seven months to nine months—most babies become suspicious (even downright unfriendly) when "strangers" appear. When you take her out for a walk and an unknown person comes by to tickle, talk, or coo at your baby, you may notice your baby's instant withdrawal from the situation. Strangers may be treated warily now. (Other babies continue to be perfectly happy with strangers until much later.) If your baby is shy or scared, respect your baby's feelings and stem the tide of well-meaning but unwanted advances. Try to move her along quickly with a brief nod to the person who's trying to talk to her. Or simply say, "Strangers make her nervous." If she's in your arms, simply holding her tightly and keeping her an arm's length away can help make her feel more secure in the situation.

Unfortunately, sometimes the person who appears as a stranger to your baby may be anything but a stranger to you. The "stranger" may even be your own mother! You cannot reason with a baby in the throes of stranger anxiety. This is a normal stage, one that some children pass through quickly while others take more time. This sudden "unfriendly" behavior does not mean your child is a social misfit or an insecure person. In fact, it is a sign of your baby's emotional and social growth. She is aware of the differences among people and is selective. If your baby is unhappy about the stranger before you, it is not a good idea to force that person on her. (Sometimes, however, this may be necessary in the case of a trusted but occasional babysitter if you have an important event you need to attend.) It's best to try to respect her wishes and keep her securely in your arms. Let her get used to the "stranger" first from a distance, rather than immediately thrusting her into Grandma's open arms. Grandma might sit nearby and talk to you and baby, or offer baby a toy, to give the baby time to get comfortable.

SEPARATION ANXIETY

Around six to eight months, you may notice that your baby starts to cry whenever he sees you leave the room. This separation anxiety can also be seen with the babysitter or Dad, depending on who has been spending the most amount of time with baby lately. As your baby matures and continually sees his parents and babysitter come and go, he soon starts to realize that you will return. Although you want to respect your baby's feelings, this doesn't mean that you must remain glued to his side—just that you can expect a certain amount of tearful goodbyes before he figures out that Mommy always comes back to him later.

Doctors' Thoughts
"The baby is not really anxious about Mom leaving the room. It is her unavailability which upsets him. Even if she simply busies herself in another part of the room, he becomes upset."
—Dr. Michael Lewis, Professor of Pediatrics, Psychology and Psychiatry, Robert Wood Johnson Medical Center

✛

"You can play hide-and-seek with your baby as a fun way to give him the idea that people leave and come back."—Dr. Max Kahn, Clinical Associate Professor of Pediatrics, New York University Medical School

NAPPING

Your baby may be napping one or two times a day. As he becomes more physically active, you might expect him to be more tired, but instead of adding naps, he's probably dropping them. There are just too many interesting things to be done during the day now and he fights sleep to have time to do them. You may be facing one afternoon nap a day now. Since he is now a bit more independent (he might sit up at your feet playing with spoons while you empty the dishwasher), you can usually get the same amount of things done even though he's not sleeping as much during the day. Usually, the morning nap is the first to get dropped. The benefit may be longer sleeps at night. For parents who have long wrestled with a baby who wakes at night, this month may at last provide some relief. The worst of teething may be over, the frustration of not being mobile is passing, and daytime naps are less frequent: this can all add up to a baby who sleeps through the night.

BOTTLE MOUTH (NURSING CARIES)

Putting your child to sleep with a bottle may seem like a benign thing to do, but it can have disastrous results for those new teeth. Milk in a sleepy baby's mouth tends to pool, giving teeth a sugar bath that hastens decay. Sometimes, the decay is so bad that teeth must be removed. You can offer a bottle at bedtime, but make sure that you take it away once your baby stops actively sucking and swallowing. Active swallowing helps to rinse the teeth with saliva and keep them protected from the sugar in formula or juice. If your baby needs to suck on something to fall asleep, try a bottle of plain water or a pacifier instead. During the day, do not allow your baby to have a continual bottle for nonstop sipping. This can cause dental caries as well. Apparently, it also possible for nursing caries to occur in a breastfed baby, if you allow your baby to nurse on and off all night long (something which may be more likely to happen if the baby sleeps in bed with you at night). Be aware that this high-frequency nursing can cause dental caries, and change your behavior accordingly. Do not, however, give up breastfeeding, which has many medical, dental, and emotional benefits!

FINGER FOODS

You may already have been feeding your baby for a couple of months now (see Chapter 18). You're probably settling into a routine of three meals a day. Why not try to introduce some finger foods at these meals? Your baby may or may not be wild about the idea of a spoonful of mush going into his mouth, but almost all babies seem to like to feed themselves just as Mommy and Daddy do. By this month or next, you can start to offer a few finger foods that baby may enjoy (if not eating) at least playing with! The basic rule of thumb of early finger foods is that they must be soft enough to be gummed, rather than chewed. That new little tooth or two that may have erupted last month or is about to erupt this month won't be too much help in chewing tough foods. Rule number two: Your baby should be fed finger foods only when sitting up in his high chair or other seat and you are watching him eat it. Offer only a little at a time.

Of course, for now, finger foods will only round out his diet. You will still have to shovel the rest in with a spoon. Down the road, however, your baby will be able to get more and more of the meal into his mouth by himself. As each new finger food is introduced, pay careful attention to how your baby handles it. If he tends to get large pieces in his mouth or doesn't chew long enough before swallowing, change the size, consistency, or type of food you offer. Or, wait and try again when he's older. Safety is the first consideration here—not nutrition (he gets what he needs most from breast milk, formula, and the pureed solids you offer on a spoon).

DIRT AND GERMS

With your baby spending so much time down on the floor, you may start wondering about all the dirt, dust, and germs he might encounter "down there" hidden in your deep shag rug (not to mention the ones he ingests when he finds a dropped piece of food and pops it into his mouth). Luckily, babies are pretty resilient little creatures who can handle a little bit of all of the above. Needless to say, however, it is important to try to keep the carpet as clean as you can by vacuuming often. Vacuuming actually helps to save your child

Early Finger Foods to Try
Soft, skinned cooked apple in cubes or mashed
Well-cooked white potatoes, mashed
Stale bagel (feels good on gums too!)
Banana slices (remove strings and seeds)
Hunk of French bread (make sure he doesn't get a pasty wad of it in his mouth at one time)
Cottage cheese
Cheerios
Canned peaches
Teething biscuit, Arrowroot cookie, or other cracker that dissolves in the mouth
Little bits of pasta

Finger Foods to Avoid
NO Nuts
NO Popcorn
NO Hot dogs
NO Chunks of raw, hard fruits or vegetables
NO Foods that need actual chewing (all foods must be able to be gummed into a swallowable paste)

Carry a Spare

An eight-month-old is bound to drop a lot of what you offer him—and then cry to get it back. It's a good idea to have an extra pacifier, extra Cheerios, or other food with you just in case.

from something much worse than dust and dirt: tiny objects that inevitably end up on the carpet (a penny, a hard crumb, a straight pin, a paper clip, a button, a dead fly?) and next find their way into baby's hands, or worse—baby's mouth.

Outside, your baby will also enjoy being down on the ground, into the dirt and action of the playground. Even if your baby doesn't crawl yet, she will still get into plenty of dirt by sitting there digging with her hands in the ground, yanking up clumps of grass. If your baby is a crawler, it's hard to stop her now, so it's best to go with the flow. Expect grass stains on the overalls, filthy hands, a diaper full of sand and dirty socks. Of course, you can keep her clean and pressed, strapped into her stroller watching the excitement from the sidelines—but you'd be depriving her of what every baby needs: a chance to explore, experiment, and discover. Naturally you need to use your good sense and make sure the area she's playing in is relatively sanitary and safe. Beyond that, however, you'll just have to relax a little and carry a big box of baby wipes.

INTEREST IN GENITALIA

It is natural for babies (especially boys) to touch their own genitalia, and to enjoy doing so. Babies take great pleasure in discovering their own bodies, whether it's their own hands and feet or more private parts. Erections do occur in infancy . . . often spontaneously. Sexual feelings in a baby are normal and healthy and to be expected. There's no need to make a big deal out of any of this or to try to stop your baby from touching himself. In fact, pushing baby's hand away may send an early signal that this is a "bad" part of the body. Instead, try to encourage a positive view of the human body. Allow your child to explore. Use the proper words when referring to these areas: words like "penis" and "vagina" should be used in the same way we'd tell a baby the words "eyes," "ears," and "nose."

SAFETY TIPS FOR THE EIGHTH MONTH

As you probably have already come to realize, as your baby becomes more mobile, you have to be more vigilant about potential household dangers. Whether he's moving around the house on his hands and knees or just spinning about on his tummy, your home becomes more exciting and more dangerous. You can't stop your baby from growing, moving about, and exploring. You can take precautions to safeguard him from the potential dangers in every house. Now is the time to lock doors and cabinets where dangerous tools or chemicals or drugs are stored (if you haven't done so already). Breakables should be removed from low-lying areas (coffee tables, bookshelves). Drapery cords should be tied back (you should have done this in the baby's room). Keep house plants out of baby's reach. See the sidebar for a list of particularly dangerous plants. Keep the number of the poison control center on your phone. Have syrup of ipecac in the house, to be given under instruction of the poison control center or your doctor only.

TOYS FOR THE EIGHTH MONTH

Interconnected rings, to pull, teethe on, twirl
Objects of different sizes, shapes, and colors to feel and compare
A ball
Large wooden beads
Blocks in a box or plastic jar
Paper cups and wooden spoons
Empty box for filling up and emptying

HAPPY BABY'S HIT PARADE

- Being pulled up to a stand
- Clapping
- Picking things up off the floor
- Making a mess (pulling books off shelves, clothes out of drawers)
- Ripping up a magazine
- Movement, whether it's inching along on his tummy, scooting, or crawling around on the floor

Common Poisonous Plants
castor bean, avocado leaves, water hemlock, oleander, rosary pea, autumn crocus, azalea, elephant ear, buttercup, foxglove, cherry twigs and foliage, mistletoe, iris, jimsonweed, lantana camara, larkspur, lily-of-the-valley, daffodil, hyacinth, pokeweed, English ivy, tulip, yew, philodendron, dieffenbachia. This list is not complete. There are at least 700 species of plants in North America that can cause death or illness. Parts of plants can differ in toxicity (the fruit or stalk may be edible but the leaves toxic). Parents should use caution and not allow children to put plants into their mouths. Call your local poison control center immediately if your child has eaten a plant. The poison control center can also give you a more complete list of poisonous plants in your area, as well as a list of *non*-toxic plants (such as petunias and violets).

CHAPTER 14

✢ Your Baby's Ninth Month ✢

Your baby is becoming a real show-stopper now, and loves being the center of attention, moving easily from his stomach to a sit, and may be even pulling himself to standing. In this wonderful upright position, your baby suddenly seems like a real little girl or boy. In some ways, your baby isn't much of a "baby" anymore. Far from helpless, he will let you know what he wants by grunting and pointing, and complain if you take a toy away too soon. Objects that interest him can be scooped up and examined. Games are fun and mama/dada chatting continues. As your baby moves through the ninth month, you will see his delight and confidence in all he can do rising steadily.

✢   ✢   ✢

THE NINTH-MONTH CHECKUP

Make an appointment with the pediatrician for the end of this month. Your pediatrician will be wowed by how mature your baby has become since the last visit. As part of that maturity, your baby may now act a little wary of the pediatrician. If stranger anxiety is high, you may be able to keep her in your lap for some parts of the checkup. Unfortunately, the HepB immunization may be given at this visit, so the ouch of a shot may have to add to baby's fussiness. (Some doctors also recommend a TB test at this visit or possibly a blood test to check for anemia and/or lead exposure.) The usual checks will be made: length, weight, and head circumference, to make sure your baby's first-year growth is progressing normally. Developmental assessments will be made either by direct examination or by talking to you about baby's newest physical and mental skills. Pediatricians are also able to observe a great deal on their own as they focus on and handle your baby. As your baby begins or moves

A Doctor's Thoughts
"Eight and nine months are fascinating moments in a child's life. Powerful reflex systems give way to the growth and development of powerful cognitive capabilities. The child's behavior is now governed by learned behaviors."—Dr. Michael Lewis, Professor of Pediatrics, Psychiatry and Psychology, Robert Wood Johnson Medical School

What's Your Baby's Major?
For every child who talks at nine months, there's another one who doesn't say a word until twelve months or even later. These children are making sounds but they're often too busy doing other things (like walking and climbing) to be bothered much with conversation. For a baby, the first year might be likened to college: you can't major in everything at once. Some babies concentrate on the language arts and have a repertoire of words by one year, even though they can't yet walk, while others major in phys ed and walk confidently at ten months but don't talk until fourteen months.

ahead with eating solids, your pediatrician may have recommendations for age-appropriate foods. Let your doctor know if there have been any reactions to foods previously introduced. You might also get some advice about introducing the cup. (At this age it would be more of a novelty than a way to get milk.) Recommendations for vitamin or iron supplements may be discussed.

PULLING TO A STAND

Your baby may pull himself up to a stand position anywhere between now and the end of the first year. (A few babies do it even earlier, a few even later.) If your baby is interested in going vertical, he will be doing everything he can to get up on his own two feet these days. He may crawl over to a chair and "climb" the leg in an effort to get himself pulled up to a standing position. If he can, he'll pull himself to stand on anything available (couch, table, even people's legs!), so move unstable furniture out of the way. His legs will soon be able to support his full weight. For now, though, most babies need some extra help from you or a nearby chair or low table. Until your baby becomes a pro, you should be right behind him, guarding his backside, just in case he loses his balance. Once he's up, an interesting toy placed on the seat of the chair can help him balance by getting him to lean forward with interest. As he gets more adventurous, you won't be able to snatch him from a fall every time. A few unexpected flops aren't likely to hurt anyone.

The only thing that can sometimes spoil the pleasures of standing up is finding a way to get down. Not every baby realizes that bending is a necessary part of getting back down to the floor. Some babies demand help with this maneuver (even if it means calling you in the middle of the night), while others press on alone and often come thudding back down to the floor. In the beginning, it's a good idea to help your child down, showing him how to bend at the knees or the waist.

FIRST WORDS?

There are so many firsts during the first year, but one of the most rewarding is to hear your baby say "mama." Of course, the first word is often "dada" instead, which many moms count as unfair; it's just that the "da" sound is easier for many babies to say than the "ma" sound. First words grow out of these language sounds. One day his "dadadadada" singsong sounds more like "dada." The sound may sometimes be directed at you or Dad, but you may also hear "dada" when he's nowhere around. Rather than assume she's just practicing her "da" sounds, reinforce the meaning of the word by answering your baby. "Dada's at work," or better yet: "Dada's watching TV. Let's go find him." This will help her to sort the sound "dada" out from all other sounds and will eventually come to mean "father" to her. Parents usually know better than anyone else whether or not their baby is attaching a certain word to a certain object. You may even be a pretty good judge of whether she understands what she's saying or she's just babbling. Each child develops his own rudimentary language that only his parents can understand. For example, "nana" (from "banana") may become your child's word for all food. It may be another child's word for the grandma who takes care of him every day. Only you would know this. There is no dictionary of baby sounds which an outsider could use. When you leave your baby with a sitter who's unfamiliar with him, you might mention some of these words or make a list of them, so she knows when your baby is talking about the dog (daw) or calling for her bottle (ba).

FREEWHEELIN' FUN

Now that your infant can sit up so well and enjoys outings, you might want to take a bike ride together. This is a terrific way to get some exercise while your child gets some fresh air and enjoys a view of the world around him. Kids normally love riding with their parents. You want to be as careful about safety on a bicycle as you are in the car, however. Install a child seat on your bike. The seat should come with its own safety belt and be installed according to the manufacturer's instructions. Bike helmets must be worn by infants, no matter how unlikely you think a fall will be. You should wear one also. In 1991 alone, 196,000 head injuries were reported to be due to bicycle accidents. Still, fewer than 2 percent of children under the age of fifteen reportedly wear helmets when they ride. Make sure your child is protected. The association he makes now between bikes and helmets sends an important message that will hopefully encourage helmet use as he grows and encourage the helmet habit throughout his bike-riding days.

A Breath of Fresh Air
The town of Greenfield, California, now requires developers of new housing to furnish each house with two new bicycles, as an antipollution measure! Next time, why not consider taking a tip from Greenfield and donning your safety helmets to bike to the beach or to the corner store instead of getting in the car to drive there!

With the pincer grasp, the baby can use thumb and forefinger to pick up small objects.

PINCER GRASP

Sometime in the ninth or tenth month, you may begin to notice your baby picking up small items in a refined manner—with the thumb and forefinger only. Known as the pincer grasp, this opens up a whole new world of small-object exploration. It also helps your baby to become a more expert self-feeder. Prior to the pincer grasp, your baby had to rake things toward herself and handled objects as though she were wearing mittens. All the fingers had to be involved. Hand skills in general are becoming more purposeful and effective. Your baby will even open her hand to the shape and size of the objects he is reaching for. Once obtained, she will probably pass it from hand to hand to feel and examine it. Unfortunately, she cannot always let go of it when she wants to. For some reason, opening her hand to drop it takes more effort than reaching for and closing her hand over the item.

SELF-FEEDING

A baby's delight in being able to feed himself ranks right up there with being able to play with toys. For some babies, it just doesn't taste so good on a spoon as it does on their own fingers! A simple cheese toast can be fingered, flipped over, bitten into, or the cheese can be sucked off the top. For suggestions on what to offer, see "Early Finger Foods to Try" (page 127). Don't worry if your baby still has no teeth. Self-feeding can still be a sport for your baby. (The one or two tiny teeth other babies have really don't help much anyway.) Choose only foods that can be gummed. Let them get into some spoon foods with their fingers too, if they so desire. Fingers can be great for dipping into baby applesauce.

Besides using their own hands, babies often enjoy mastering the spoon as well. Give your baby one spoon for self-feeding and keep one for yourself. He may tap it, wave it, bite it, or actually use it to eat. In between his messy mouthfuls, you may be able to scoop a little in with your own spoon. Don't worry if he decides to eat his applesauce before or even at the same time as his chicken and beets.

The greater independence you allow him now, the sooner this experience with self-feeding will pay off. The trick is to sit back, relax, and expect a mess. Babies are simply not tidy eaters, and anything you do to try to force them to be neat at this stage will only spoil the fun of eating. If you are relaxed and encourage your baby to enjoy his food, he will grow up knowing that eating is a pleasurable thing. Self-feeding helps your baby become the master of what he needs. Little people know how much they should eat. Forcing a baby to finish something isn't good for him now . . . or in the long run. It is not likely that your baby will eat too little, as long as you continue to present good, nutritionally balanced foods for him to sample.

SUGARY FOODS

From the time your baby can hold a cracker, you may have the urge to also introduce your baby to the finer things in life: cookies and candies. As an adult, though, you know that these little treats come with a price. With a long life of Halloween candies and birthday cakes ahead of him, you would be doing your baby a real favor to keep refined sugars at bay a little longer. There is certainly no reason for offering refined sugars to a baby, but there are a number of reasons not to do so. Introducing sugary foods at an early age may encourage your child's "sweet tooth" and lead him right up the path toward his first (unnecessary) cavity. You may be helping to create a habit that is hard to break in later life (look at yourself struggling with weight and good nutrition—wouldn't it be easier if cakes and other goodies weren't so appealing to you?). Check the labels on baby food jars to make sure sugar hasn't been added. When making your own foods for baby, leave the sugar in the cabinet. Many tasty treats can be made without sugar.

HAIR CARE

The first haircut is still a ways off, but hair care goes on every day. Up until now you may have just been rinsing with soap and water. If your baby has a pretty good head of hair now, baby shampoo may be in order. Obviously, you need to use only a little bit at a time. You should continue to brush out the hair after the bath (even if there isn't much of it). This helps to increase circulation of the scalp. Continue to use a very soft baby brush. If you have a girl, you may have the urge to fuss with her hair. This is probably more bother to the baby than it's worth, but tiny barrettes can be purchased for baby-fine hair. Parents who want to dress up a girl with little or no hair may

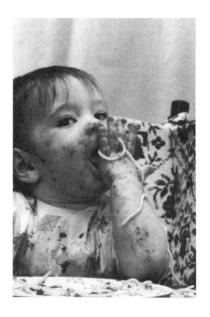

Stool Changes
As your baby's food repertoire grows, the diapers you change may contain some surprises. As your baby eats more solids, you may notice a change in the smell. You may also see signs of the food you offered earlier—red from some beets, a whole pea, sandy-looking grit from the Cheerios he ate, and so on. This is perfectly normal. Babies don't always get everything well chewed or well digested. If you see something you don't think is normal, call your doctor.

Spare the Change
Changing the normal night-time pattern—by taking an overnight trip or placing baby to bed in a new room in your house—can upset his delicate sense of routine and has been known to cause some temporary sleep problems.

✦

A Doctor's Thoughts
"If your baby is still having sleep problems, and you are thinking about letting him cry it out, this may be your last chance to do this. It's easier for a baby to fall asleep while lying down and crying than it is for him to fall asleep while standing up and screaming 'Mommy'."
—*Dr. Max Kahn, Clinical Associate Professor, New York University Medical School*

opt for a thin cloth-covered elastic headband with lace or bows. Of course, as every parent knows, babies are beautiful totally unadorned. Hairlessness is not uncommon in babies under a year and is nothing to be concerned about.

BEDTIME

You might notice you are starting to have trouble getting your baby to go to sleep at night. Now that he is so busy and active during the day, he may fight sleep. Even though he may be tired, he may be too wound up to drift off. He is also objecting to your absence as you say good night and close the door to his room. The clingy behavior you may have noticed this month or last underlines baby's fear of losing you. When you are out of sight, he does not yet realize that you are still nearby or that you will surely come back. This disquieting view of his world may make him more resistant than usual to bedtime.

Babies at this age are already comforted by having a certain bedtime ritual: a bath, changing into pajamas, a drink, a book, a song. Bedtime is not sprung on them all at once—all these things lead up to it. Sticking with a bedtime routine may help your baby to get in the mood for sleep. A blankie or other security object can also help (although you can't make your baby attach to one). Once you have departed, the baby still has his cuddly to cling to. (See page 117 for more on comfort objects.)

If bedtime rituals and security blankets don't do the trick, you may want to try some of the sleep suggestions on page 111. As described there, returning to the room to comfort your little one (without picking him up or feeding him) may be the only way you can convince him that you are nearby but also that you're serious about bedtime.

PLAYTIME

Your baby is full of fun; he demands playtime and wide open spaces in which to have a good time. Get down on the floor with your crawler. Challenge him to a race. Babies love to imitate your sounds and actions and they think it endlessly funny when you mimic *them*. Place a toy on a non-glass tabletop where he pulls up, encouraging him to stand there for a moment and play with it. Your baby will find toys of his own design as well as the conventional store-bought variety. Hand him a spoon and it becomes a toy. Leave the broom out and it's a toy too. A garden hose with a little water dribbling out can provide good fun on and off throughout a summer's day! Toy play can take on new conversational dimensions as your child babbles to his toys. Join in the fun by talking to your child about his toys. If you have other children, get them involved in baby's playtime too. Babies this age love to have an audience—the more the merrier. They try to entertain and love to be entertained by the older siblings.

SAFETY TIPS FOR THE NINTH MONTH

Don't forget that when you take your baby visiting at other people's houses, your host may not be so well prepared for your baby's active curiosity as you are. It may be a good idea to carry some extra electric outlet caps and cupboard latches or locks with you in your diaper bag. This way you can baby-proof wherever you go!

TOYS FOR THE NINTH MONTH

Nesting cups
Soft blocks
Stacking toys
Foam or cloth ball
Play plastic mirror
Dolls

Baby Swipes
The better she gets at reaching and grabbing, the more often she'll want to enjoy the fun of the sport. Anything in front of her is fair game, so be extra careful about what's in baby's reach—your earrings, a necklace, a china dinner plate, a glass of water on the table—all might be swiped, some with disastrous results.

A Mother's Reflections
A Mother's Reflections
"Nothing's more fun for Lawrence than having his three-year-old sister get down on her hands and knees and crawl with him. The two of them just laugh and laugh."

Playtime Is Learning Time
A baby who is playing is a baby who is learning. Around this age, you can encourage some new learning experiences through your games. For example, if you place a toy your baby has been playing with on a blanket or place mat, he will try to get it back. If it is out of his reach, he may tug on the corner of the blanket or mat to pull it closer. With this success comes the understanding that he can use one thing to get another.

HAPPY BABY'S HIT PARADE

High on baby's list of really fun things to do this month are:

• Banging two blocks together
• Stacking games
• Peek-a-boo
• Listening to music and clapping along
• Waving bye-bye
• Crawling (maybe even with one toy still clenched in his hand)
• Getting himself from a sitting position to a crawl and back again
• Swinging in a baby swing at the park

CHAPTER 15

✦ Your Baby's Tenth Month ✦

Y ou and your baby are headed into the last "trimester" of the first year. Both of you are moving into high gear—your baby, with his increasing physical prowess, and you, with your increasing confidence in the role of Mom and the nonstop job of watching and chasing an active, curious baby. Your baby will make many strides during the tenth month—whether pulling to stand, crawling, climbing, cruising along the furniture, or even standing alone for a second. Even though it seems like he's the one doing all the work, you're probably the one who's exhausted! Here is a guide to some of what you can expect during the tenth month.

✦ ✦ ✦

CRUISING

If your baby was pulling up to a stand and leaning on furniture last month, this month he'll probably try to move himself along the furniture or from piece to piece. It's called cruising, a delightful way to describe your baby's latest living-room safari. As your baby becomes more adventurous, he may let go with one or both hands for a second before grabbing on to the next stable surface. If it all becomes too much for him, he'll simply sink to the floor and try again later. Once cruising is part of his abilities, your baby has a far-ranging reach. Put him down in one part of the room and he can now navigate his way to another part of the room. On these little voyages, he is picking up the skills he needs to stand alone and eventually to walk.

Babies enjoy cruising along the furniture before they learn to walk alone.

A Doctor's Thoughts

"A child can see a lot from sitting, but the entire world opens up to the child when he becomes mobile. There is an enormous sense of exploration. Now your house is no longer yours. He's going to get into your room and into trouble. From a child's point of view, the world is a toy."—Dr. Michael Lewis, Professor, Pediatrics, Psychiatry and Psychology, Robert Wood Johnson Medical Center

✦

Toe to Toe

For a baby, going barefoot is a lot more fun than even the fanciest shoes. Just as they love to play with their hands, babies love to play with their feet and toes too. You can join in the fun with an old favorite: "This Little Piggy." Just in case you forgot how it goes, here it is:

This little piggy went to market,
This little piggy stayed home,
This little piggy ate roast beef,
This little piggy had none,
And this little piggy went . . .
Wee wee wee wee, all the way home!

FEET

As you begin to see your baby in an upright position, you may notice that the feet appear flat. This is a normal appearance during the first couple of years. As a baby walks on his feet and loses baby fat, the arches will become apparent.

Bare feet are best for your baby until walking is well established. In the meantime, for dress up, you can put your baby's feet in fancy socks and booties, although he may pull them off faster than you can get them on. Some parents are anxious to buy the "first shoes." If you must give in to this desire, do not buy real walker shoes. Choose lightweight footwear—nothing stiff, hard, or heavy. (See page 152 for information on how to buy the first shoes.) Make sure the shoes don't restrict or confine the feet. Little feet grow fast and need room. Too-small shoes (or even socks for that matter) can retard normal growth patterns. Shoes do not make learning to walk any easier for baby. In fact, it is probably easier for a baby to learn in his bare feet—he can feel the floor, get his balance, and get a grip. Unless you're dressing baby up for a special occasion, it's best to leave off the shoes until your baby reaches an age when he can walk without support.

MESSY BABIES

Getting to know the world is sometimes a messy business. Babies end up with food on their faces and down their shirts when they eat. They smear mud on their clothes. They try to eat sand at the beach. They leave strewn toys in their wake. Having a baby in the house means constant cleanup and pickup work. It isn't fun and often cleaning doesn't seem worth it. Minutes later, the toys you put in the basket arc out again. Of course, you'll have to find your own way of coping with the mess of children (messes don't end with the first year—they can get worse as children get older). As your baby's toy collection grows, invest in some boxes and baskets for toy storage. Low-lying shelves can be built, allowing baby access to piles of books, early puzzles, and some toys. If you're a very organized person with a place for everything and a need to have everything in its place, make sure your sitter knows this. It will save both of you a lot of frustration if you show her where everything belongs and let her know that you expect to find it back there again after it has been used. If you are less of a stickler, forget about sorting toys into their proper homes and use a large basket as a catch-all instead. Cleaning up once a day (at the end) can be a lot less annoying than trying to clean up all day, shoveling against a tide of ten-month-old curiosity and activity.

BABY'S BODY LANGUAGE

Your baby may be forming a word or two that you can understand, but most of her communication remains nonverbal. Long before your baby can put together a sentence, she will use powerful facial expressions and body language to get her message across. She might lick her lips at the sight of you preparing food, melt into you when she's relaxed, look away when she's had enough of something, stiffen when she's unhappy, squirm to get out of your arms, and so on. Most parents instinctively respond to these cues. A ten-month-old sitting on the floor may tug on your pant leg and raise her arms straight up in the air. Clearly, she is saying "Pick me up," and so Mom usually does. She may also raise her arms when she wants to invite you to play. Her whole face lights up and she extends her arms wide in a greeting, as if to say, "Hi Mom! Come join me!"

Around nine or ten months of age, your baby adds an important piece of body language to her overall vocabulary: the point. When your baby points at something, you can follow with your eyes to discover the very item she wants or is interested in! Your baby understands your point now too. Prior to this understanding, she would stare at your finger instead of the thing you were pointing at. All body language is a precursor to verbal communication, but the point is closely linked to language development. Child development experts consider the point to be a symbol. Once the child understands that symbols stand for something, they naturally progress to the understanding that certain words (sound symbols) also stand for things.

HEAD BANGING

Some babies comfort themselves by cuddling with a teddy bear, pulling on an ear, or rocking on all fours. Unfortunately, some babies also "comfort" themselves with a much noisier and, to parents, more disturbing habit: head banging. When put in the crib at night, these babies rock themselves on all fours, while banging their head against the end of the crib. The head banging for the baby is supposedly a

A Mother's Reflections
"He's getting into everything these days. He climbs out of the stroller, he knocks glass bottles to the floor in stores. One day in the store, he even reached out and took a small toy and put it in his stroller when I wasn't looking. I didn't find it until after we'd gotten home! He reaches for pens, forks, wires, dirt. He wants whatever he really shouldn't have. I hate to say 'No!'—so I'm always taking things away."

When to Call the Pediatrician
Happily, head banging is not usually violent enough to actually hurt your baby. If he is bruising himself or you see other unusual or unhappy behavior, contact your pediatrician and fill the doctor in on the details.

way of rhythmically comforting himself and relieving the tensions of the day (maybe even the tingling of teething too). Babies seem to pick up and discard this habit by themselves and at their own pace.

Although often benign, head banging is not the norm. If the baby seems otherwise healthy and happy, it is probably nothing to worry about. If you think the head banging is associated with a particular area of stress for your baby (a new sitter, frustration with mastering a new physical skill like standing), do your best during the day to ease the tension. A little extra time in the morning with the sitter while you're still there, for example, may help. Encouraging the physical play that leads to success at crawling, standing, or walking can also reduce the baby stress that may be causing head banging. If you see other disturbing behavior that leads you to believe your baby is unhappy, however, talk to your pediatrician.

HAIR PULLING/TEETH GRINDING/ EAR TUGGING

It is not unusual for a baby to develop a physical habit like hair pulling that comforts him. Sometimes, this habit grows out of a pleasant sensation associated with nursing. He may have stroked your hair while nursing or pulled at his own ear as he ate. Now, in moments of insecurity, he tries to recreate for himself those happy days.

Many parents are surprised that there is stress or tension in the life of a child under age one, but the truth is that there is some. It makes sense if you really think about it: First, they have little control over their environment (they are picked up and placed in a high chair, a toy is removed, another is offered, and so on); second, they have limited means of expressing themselves verbally; third, they are trying to learn challenging new physical feats every day. Add to this an inability to understand the permanency of objects (this understanding will come sometime in the beginning of the second year) and you have a picture of baby stress. Maybe it's not so bad as what you experience on April 14 every year, but it's there all the same.

Occasional, nonviolent hair twirling and pulling is nothing to worry about. If it soothes your baby, let it be.

Teeth grinding (often done in sleep) sounds bad but is not likely to cause any dental problems in a child. The surfaces of the baby teeth are fairly flat, so the teeth slide easily and grinding does not cause the mouth to open. Teeth grinding may or may not be linked to tension. No one knows why some children grind teeth in the night. For now, it's best just to ignore it and wait for it to stop on its own. If you have any questions about this or other habits, ask your pediatrician.

NEWFOUND FEARS

With newfound independence often come newfound fears. Suddenly, the elevator, an escalator, the vacuum cleaner, or the bathtub drain are scary. Trying to make a young child realize that his fears are "silly" will not help. For now, you'll have to respect his fears by holding him close in the elevator, or turning off the vacuum cleaner. Forcing him to do something frightening to him will only make the problem worse. You might encourage him to take control of his own fears by letting him press the elevator buttons or turn the vacuum on and off with your help. Be gentle and sympathetic and your child will outgrow these irrational fears on her own.

TOYS FOR THE TENTH MONTH

Plastic keys
Toy telephone
Small push car
Soft balls
Books
Basket or box of small toys (to empty and fill)

Safety Tips
It is natural for a baby to have fears. The more he explores, the more he realizes the world can be a dangerous place. Help him to learn about the true dangers in his environment. When your baby is near the oven or stove say, "Hot! Ouch!" to help him begin to learn the meaning of these words.

✛

A Doctor's Thoughts
"It's as though nature said, 'Before you can have the keys, you've got to learn to drive.' So, some sense comes in but babies only have a little sense and they're mobile, so nature thinks, 'If you don't want him to wander too far away, make him fearful.' This is the bipolar nature of the child's relationship to the world around him: a desire to explore and create new experiences combined with a need for safety."—Dr. Michael Lewis, Professor, Pediatrics, Psychiatry and Psychology, Robert Wood Johnson Medical Center

Babies often love to walk along supported by your hands.

Back Savers

If one of your baby's favorite activities involves dropping a toy and watching you pick it up, try these back-saving suggestions:

1. Have a bag of toys nearby so you can replace one dropped item with an-other instead of always having to retrieve the first.

2. Tie an interesting object to the high chair. At lunch, when he plays with it and tosses it overboard, you'll be able to fetch it back by pulling on the string.

3. Involve an older child in the game. You may tire easily of "pick up," but a three-to-five-year-old may find it as funny to play as the baby!

HAPPY BABY'S HIT PARADE

- Crawling over obstacles, like pillows, strewn on the floor
- Crawling up stairs (with Mom right behind)
- Picking up small objects
- Bath time
- Cruising
- Watching older children
- Hugging
- Offering parent a bit of his food or drink from bottle
- Tapping, clapping, or banging out rhythms
- Dropping things just to see them fall

CHAPTER 16

✦ Your Baby's Eleventh Month ✦

This month brings continued, seemingly nonstop action. At seven o'clock, he's having breakfast, feeding himself a pancake and some sliced fruit. At eight, he's "walking" all over the kitchen, while noisily pushing a chair as support. At nine, he's trying to climb up the shelves of a bookcase. At ten, he's on the terrace, playing with the garden hose; at eleven, he's pulling his clothes out of the drawers and pouring the apple juice out of his cup; at twelve, he's eating some scrambled egg yolk but most of it is ending up on the floor or down his diapers; at one, he takes a nap . . . and your day is just half over! Your baby's eleventh month is full of crawling, climbing, touching, investigative fun. A child in his eleventh month is a doer—maybe even a talker, too.

✦   ✦   ✦

STANDING ALONE

Once balance and strength develop, your child may be able to hold himself in a standing position for a few seconds. You may first notice this ability while he's cruising, or simply standing with the support of a chair. While playing with a toy or moving from couch to table, he may briefly let go of his support and remain upright. Skills like this do not come with age alone. Your child is not likely to master one skill until an earlier skill which leads up to it is not only accomplished but mastered. A child who has been pulling to standing or standing with support may be ready to stand alone this month. Another child may still be trying to master the pull to stand. There is no rush. Children will naturally come to acquire all the physical, emotional, and mental skills life demands at their own pace.

Even if he is not yet standing alone, he may by now have figured out how to get himself back down to the floor from a standing position.

Barefoot Safety
As your baby pulls to stand, cruises, stands alone, or takes his first steps indoors, let him do it barefoot. Shoes can interfere with the balance and traction he needs. Socks can be slippery and lead to falls. If it's cold, put your child in socks with special nonslip soles.

MORE FIRST WORDS

As you talk to your baby during the day, you are, without even realizing it, teaching him to talk. Babies are expert listeners. They hear the sounds and the intonations in your speech. From your child's perspective, language is beautiful to listen to and fun to play with. He enjoys imitating sounds and playing with the tone and volume of his own voice. (This sometimes means shouting for a fun effect.) Your child may suddenly amuse you with whole speeches made up of an incomprehensible gibberish that sounds amazingly like real language.

Typical first words will include items most important to his world: mama, dada, block, book, car, cracker, and so on. Toward the end of the first year or the beginning of the second, language may also become something which helps a child to get what he wants. As your baby begins to associate words with objects, he sees the power of language. For example, when he says "cracker," you probably go get one for him.

Parental conversations, encouragement, and word repetition all help baby to form the words for things in his environment. You can support a baby's natural love of language by playing word games, reading books, and pointing out everyday objects. As you dress your baby, you can show him shirt, shoes, and pants. When he eats, tell him the names of the foods. When you go out together, point out the cars, the dogs, the trees. Of course, you cannot "train" your child to speak. He will do so in his own good time. Sometimes, no matter how much talking you do, your child is not ready with first words until well after his first birthday or even close to his second birthday. As long as he is listening appropriately and making speech sounds, this developmental range is normal.

UNDERSTANDING LANGUAGE

It is likely that your baby understands a lot more of what you say to him than what is reflected in his own speech. If you ask your baby a question, you will often get an answer, although not necessarily a verbal one. (See the section on body language, page 141.) "Do you want your bottle?" or "Let's go to the store!" are familiar statements usually met with positive responses by baby. If you ask, "Where's Teddy?" he may look for his bear. Babies toward the end of the first year also understand words like "no," "hot," and "stop." Although they won't always comply, these are important words for baby's safety and often are heeded. Don't depend on the power of speech alone to deter your baby from danger, however. Often, you need to accompany the word "no" with a physical restraint (holding his hand or removing him from a dangerous spot).

MENTAL SKILLS

It's easy to see what baby is doing physically. It can be harder to know what's going on in baby's mind. Developments there are just as dramatic and startling. You can see the growth and changes in understanding as you observe your baby at play. He may already understand that objects have permanence. In other words, the toy you hide under a blanket is still there and worth looking for. The toys closed in the cupboard are just behind the door, and knowing this, he crawls to it or even bangs on it. Previously, anything that you removed from baby's line of sight was literally out of his mind. It would no longer exist for him. Your baby is developing a larger memory of things now, and is able to keep a mental picture in his head. For this reason, you may notice that stranger anxiety and clingy behavior is on the decline. Your baby is starting to realize that, when you leave the room, you still exist and will return.

Other new mental abilities include the realization that a small cup fits into a bigger one, that some things fit together like a key in a lock. You will see your child examining the sizes and shapes of toys and noting the differences.

A sense of self begins to emerge now. As he moves through his environment by crawling or scooting or even walking, he gains a new perspective on himself and sees himself in relation to the world around him.

FUSSY EATERS

Not all babies happily eat every nutritionally balanced thing put in front of them. If you start fighting about food now, it is a battle you'll be waging until you send your child off to college. Instead, back off and let your baby be your guide. If you continue to offer nutritionally balanced foods, it's a good bet that she will somehow get a smattering of these into her system. Remember, too, that the milk she drinks is

A
"

eating *o.*
ness. This is normal. —*D.*
Max Kahn, Clinical Associate Professor of Pediatrics, New York University School of Medicine

✦

Not Feeling Well
A loss of appetite can sometimes signal an illness. If you notice a sudden lapse in appetite, especially if it's combined with other symptoms such as a lack of energy, call your doctor. Your baby may be coming down with something.

✦

Mouth Trauma
It's not unusual for babies learning to walk to fall and cut a lip or bump a tooth. The mouth is a very vascular area, which means that you can expect it to bleed a lot when injured. Seek attention if the bleeding doesn't stop quickly or if the tooth appears to have moved or is sensitive to pressure.

...though most tumbles
... not serious, you may
...eventually encounter a cut
or fall that needs emergency
treatment. To prepare for
this possibility:

- Have a well-stocked first-
  aid kit, complete with antibiotic cream and band-
  ages, accessible.
- Have a book on first aid in
  the house.
- Have phone numbers of
  pediatrician, poison control, fire, police, and
  ambulance posted in a
  convenient spot (if not
  programmed into your
  phone's memory).
- Know the route to the
  nearest emergency room
  or, if convenient, pediatric
  emergency room.
- Make sure your sitter
  knows what you know:
  emergency numbers and
  emergency room loca-
  tions. Don't go out without
  leaving a number where
  you can be reached. Leave
  a general letter of consent
  in the house that autho-
  rizes your sitter to get
  emergency medical attention for your child (to
  avoid possible entangle-
  ments on admission).

still a very important part of her diet and most nutrition still comes from this source. The solids only help to round out their diets. Babies who are fussy eaters won't fade away. If you have a fussy eater, relax. Some days your baby may refuse lunch. The next day, she may gobble up everything in sight. Figure that over the course of a week, the entire meal plan will have evened itself out. If there's a food she loves (be it strained, mashed lentils or plain old bananas), indulge her preference. She will change when she's ready. (Keep offering alter-nate foods at meals in case she wants to dabble in something new.) Allow her to self-feed if she's interested.

ACCIDENTS

With an increasing need to get up, get out, and do things, but not always with the common sense or physical wherewithal to do them, babies this age are set up for falls, bumps, and bruises. Accidents will happen the first year. The threat of baby getting hurt certainly keeps you on the edge of your seat, but doesn't seem to faze your active child. Little boo-boos become a fact of life for her as she keeps on trying to crawl, climb, stand, cruise, or walk. The important thing is to try to make her world as safe as possible for her, and keep her under constant supervision, while still allowing her to explore and make her own mistakes. If you try to keep your baby out of every potentially dangerous situation (not possible unless you live in a padded cell), she won't get the chance to do anything for herself. Children learn through doing. Teaching them to be overcautious or even fearful will hurt their development. When accidents happen, quickly assess the situation. If you see it was just a little flop, don't rush in with panicked expressions of sympathy. Hang back a mo-ment and let your baby collect herself and go on. If you fuss and squeal over every tumble, you will eventually have a child who does the same. If you must say something, "Oops" is preferable to "Oh no!"

SAFETY TIPS FOR THE END OF
THE FIRST YEAR

1. Remove the crib bumpers and large stuffed animals, which might otherwise be used to help baby climb out of crib.
2. Make sure your baby is securely strapped into his high chair

or stroller, to ensure that he won't try to stand up or climb out. Never leave him unattended.

3. Beware of what baby might try to climb on—open dresser drawers, bookcase shelves, television stands. Be vigilant and on guard so you can get him down before he's up.

4. Even though he may seem stable and busy with toys, do not leave a baby sitting alone in the bath.

5. Set the crib mattress in the lowest possible position, if you haven't already done so.

6. Make windows safe with window guards. An open window can be an open invitation to disaster.

7. Take all breakables off low tables where baby cruises.

TOYS FOR THE ELEVENTH MONTH

Ride-on car with high bar for pushing (no pedals)
Rocking horse with secure basket seat
Shopping basket
Large nesting cups
Toy food, toy dishes
Hats for dress-up
Wooden workbench
Picture books with pictures of everyday items

Safety Awareness
The month of September every year has been named Baby Safety Awareness Month by the U.S. Consumer Product Safety Commission and the Juvenile Products Manufacturers Association.

HAPPY BABY'S HIT PARADE

• Helping around the house: dusting with his own cloth, watering the plants, putting potatoes in a bin, putting tennis balls back in a can.
• Eating "grown-up" foods
• Self-feeding
• Cruising
• Having parents "walk" him around by holding his hands
• Finding a toy hidden under a cloth

CHAPTER 17
✤ Your Baby's Twelfth Month ✤

On the fringe of toddlerhood, your baby and you are about to enter a whole new realm. As the first year draws to a close, you may even mourn a bit for the loss of babyhood. Your child is growing up. The first birthday seems like a graduation of sorts: you and your one-year-old have made it through a year full of changes and wonder, excitement and frustrations.

✤   ✤   ✤

THE TWELFTH-MONTH CHECKUP

This checkup will be similar to other months. At the end of the first year, your baby will be weighed and measured and given a physical exam. A HepB shot may be given at this visit if it wasn't done at nine months. No other immunizations are needed unless you missed one before. A tuberculin (TB) test will probably be administered now. You will be asked to "read" it after forty-eight and seventy-two hours by looking for redness or swelling at the site. The TB test has no side effects. A more accurate test for tuberculosis is now available and may be used in high-risk areas, such as inner cities. It is called the PPD (pure protein derivative) and also needs to be "read" by the parent or pediatrician. If your child hasn't already been tested for exposure to lead, it may be suggested now. The American Academy of Pediatricians has recommended that initial screening for lead exposure be done between nine and twelve months.

At this checkup, you and your pediatrician will also be able to discuss any developmental milestones that may have been passed since the last visit. This is the time to ask if you have concerns about your baby's ability to pull to a stand, cruise, walk, talk, self-feed, sleep through the night, play games. You may also wish to discuss the introduction of new foods: When can you offer whole milk, egg whites, certain meats?

Just Checking
Once your baby begins to walk, your pediatrician will be on the lookout for any possible problems with weak ankles, bowlegs, or knock-knees during the second year. He will let you know if anything seems out of the ordinary or appears to need correction.

A Doctor's Thoughts
*"Most parents have the idea
that the baby will walk on his
first birthday. Most walk anytime between ten and fourteen
months. I've seen some very cautious babies who wouldn't walk
until eighteen months and I was
convinced, and convinced their
parents, that their baby was
fine."—Dr. Barbara Fran-
kowski, Assistant Professor of
Pediatrics, College of Medicine,
University of Vermont*

Perfect Fit
To check the fit of your
child's shoes, have her stand
up. Press your finger down
at the tip of the shoe to determine where your child's
toes are. There should be
about half a thumbnail's
space between your child's
toes and the end of the
shoe. The act of walking
presses the toes farther up
into the top of the shoe.
Now check the width by running your fingers along the
sides of the shoe top. The
width should appear com-
fortable. Get reasonably
priced shoes so that you
won't feel bad throwing
them away in a month. Then
you can buy shoes that fit
better.

WALKING/NOT WALKING

Your little one may be ready to take that first step away from you
this month. Or this momentous milestone may be months away.
Whether or not your baby is walking depends on your baby: how
much she wants to walk, how happy she is crawling, how intimidated
she is by falls, how heavy she is, and so on. A baby who is walking this
month is one who was successfully standing and cruising last month.
During the physical activities of the last few months, your baby's legs,
balance, and will to walk were all being strengthened. The first steps
will be small ones and falls will be frequent. You and your partner can
kneel down close together, allowing your baby to take a few small
steps in between before "falling" into your arms. Early walkers may
look bowlegged or knock-kneed. Toes may turn in or out, as baby
tries to get his balance. The stance may be wide-based, with feet far
apart. As he continues to walk, his feet gradually turn back toward a
more parallel position. One thing that bothers parents is the way
babies this age tend to walk on their toes. They get all excited and
tense up their muscles. In the beginning, this is normal. If it persists,
discuss it with your pediatrician.

SHOES

Shoes are not necessary until walking is well established. Even
then, they are more necessary outdoors than indoors, for obvious
safety reasons. Young walkers benefit from going barefoot, as it
encourages them to use their developing foot and leg muscles fully.
Constantly encasing the foot in a shoe may actually cause the foot
muscles to relax and the arch may not develop as it should, resulting
in flat feet.

When buying the first pair of shoes, opt for a semisoft sole. Hard
soles prevent a child's foot from moving. Go to a store where they are
familiar with fitting young children for shoes. The shoes must not be
too tight or too big. Your child needs room at the toe (young feet
grow fast) but you should not see the heel slipping out of the shoe.
High-top shoes are often a better fit than low shoes and tend to stay
on a baby's fat foot more easily.

THE FIRST VISIT TO THE DENTIST

Sometime between twelve and eighteen months, your child should make his first visit to a dentist. You can take your child to your own dentist for a checkup or you can arrange to see a pediatric dentist. A general dentist may or may not feel comfortable working on your child. If you want to take your child to your regular dentist, ask first if he sees young children in his practice. Some general dentists are interested in seeing young children and may do a great job for your whole family. Having the entire family cared for by the same dentist can be convenient.

If your dentist does not usually see very young children, he may refer you to a pediatric dentist. (Even if he is willing to provide dental care for your child, you may prefer using a pediatric dentist.) A pediatric dentist is trained not only in dentistry but also in child behavior, so he is familiar with the likes, dislikes, fears, and attention span of young children. The pediatric dentist may be more likely to have an office set up for children—with toys and child-friendly decor.

By making the first appointment for a routine checkup, you allow your child to meet a dentist for the first time in a nonthreatening, nonpainful situation. Don't wait until you have an unpleasant reason (tooth pain) for calling a dentist. At the first visit, you will probably be asked to sit in the dentist chair with the child in your lap. The dentist will want to take a look inside your child's mouth, to count and view the teeth and examine the mouth and jaws. He may show you how to clean the child's teeth with gauze or his first small toothbrush. The dentist will also discuss some general dental hygiene issues with you. You will probably be warned about the dangers of offering sticky sweets or putting a child to sleep with a bottle. (See the section on bottle mouth, page 126.) The whole visit probably won't take more than fifteen minutes.

SHARING

You may join with other moms, babysitters, and babies for routine playtimes. Children at this age do enjoy playing alongside other children, but they don't always interact. In other words, they may

Good Vibes

No matter how you might feel about going to the dentist, it's important to present a positive outlook to your child. Don't make a big deal about the visit. Try to remain calm and cheery. A one-year-old can feel your tension as you hold him. Be matter-of-fact about the visit, telling your child that a dentist is someone who helps you take care of your teeth. And remember, things will likely be better for your child than they were for you growing up. We know a lot more today about how to prevent cavities, and if you follow the rules of good dental hygiene, your child may be one of the lucky ones who never has to experience a drill.

A Doctor's Thoughts

"Twelve months is not too early to see a dentist. This is a good time to begin a preventative program. Dentistry is not all drilling and filling these days. It is a process of educating the parent and child to achieve the best dental health."—Dr. Frank J. Courts, Chairman, Pediatric Dentistry, University of Florida

A Doctor's Thoughts
"At this age, they will sit next to each other and play but they won't really share. In large day-care centers, however, where whole groups of one-year-olds play together, the idea of taking turns is enforced out of necessity. It's a difficult concept for a one-year-old, but the adult can structure the environment so that sharing takes place."—Dr. Barbara Frankowski, Assistant Professor of Pediatrics, College of Medicine, University of Vermont

watch another child with interest and happily play with a toy telephone while another child sits alongside banging on a tool bench. A child under age one, however, has no concept of "sharing," and however embarrassing this fact might be to the polite moms and caregivers looking on, it is too soon to force the issue. One-year-olds are natural grabbers and keepers. They are not likely to give up a toy unless they are through with it, or have been distracted by something better. You are not likely to see any true "generosity" until your child is two and a half years old or, typically, even older. Even then, it is something that must be learned gradually and cannot be forced upon the child. If you're constantly taking things away from your child, insisting that she "share" them with a friend, you'll only make her more determined. At this age, your job is simply to make sure that a tug-of-war does not end up with one child being hit over the head with a hard toy and that there are as few tears spilled as possible. It is often possible to get one child interested in something else by removing her from the action and showing her a toy in another part of the room. It also helps to look for similar toys, so that if your child has a ball that is being coveted by another, you can hand over a second ball.

BITING

You may have already been bitten by your child while he was teething. Children under one sometimes bite a shoulder or a chin, just as they would any hard surface, to relieve the tingle of teething. This is obviously not an angry or aggressive bite, and one you may have largely (and rightly) ignored. As your child gets older, however, he may sometimes bite out of anger. It may be hard for you to believe that your angelic child is capable of such aggression, but it happens. Children are human—they sometimes have the need to strike out and don't know yet that such behavior is entirely unacceptable. An angry child may bite without thinking. You may be the one bitten, or a playmate or sibling may be the object of his aggression. Be on the lookout for such behavior. Other parents (naturally) will get particularly upset if their child is bitten by yours.

You may be lucky enough to be able to pull yourself away from his jaws just in time or to quickly remove your child from a play situation in which he was just about to bite. If you don't manage to prevent a bite, immediately tell your child "No Biting!" and put her down abruptly or remove her momentarily from the play area. She'll soon get the idea that no one likes being bitten. Biting must be stopped as soon as it starts. Biting back, which some parents advocate, is not a good idea. Although it may surprise your child and make him realize that biting hurts, it may also lead him to believe that biting is acceptable and he'll keep it up.

YOUR GIRL: SUGAR AND SPICE?

Boys and girls are different—no one can argue about that. Are these differences genetic or do we contribute to them after our children are born? Do we as parents and does society at large tend to unreasonably amplify those differences? We may never know the full answer to the nature vs. nurture questions that have plagued psychiatrists, sociologists, and feminists over time. One thing we do know, however: As women and men become more equal in the workplace and on the home front, we want to pass on what we've learned to our daughters so that they won't be hampered by anyone's stereotypical ideas of their capabilities.

During the first year of life, however, you may have already noticed an easy tendency to define your daughter in terms of her sex. You may be overly protective of her "soft fragility" or more worried about her looks, clothes, and hair. You may have caught yourself saying she's a "typical girl" and referring to her behavior as flirtatious or catty, manipulative or sweet. Without realizing it, you may perceive her actions in terms of typically feminine behaviors and preferences. Perhaps "feminine" characteristics are common in our little girls, but we should not make blanket generalizations. You may have a girl who's loud and aggressive, not shy and demure. To shake things up a bit more, your loud, aggressive girl may love Barbies while the shy and demure girl may turn out to be a terrific athlete. The important thing is to realize that little girls come in all sizes and shapes, with different interests and strengths and personal style. You'll need to see her as an individual first in order to give her the room she needs to grow into who she really wants to be.

A Doctor's Thoughts

"The minute parents know the sex of the baby—whether prenatally or at the birth—they start treating them differently and have different expectations."—Dr. Barbara Frankowski, Assistant Professor of Pediatrics, College of Medicine, University of Vermont

A Mother's Reflections

"I wanted my daughter to have toys that weren't just for girls, so I bought her a tool kit. Next thing, I look over and see her using the screwdriver as a lipstick!"

Sexist Toys

A recent talking doll met with public outcry when it was discovered that one of the things she wanted to chat about was how much she hated math class! The offending sentence was later removed from her programmed repertoire.

YOUR BOY: PUPPY DOG TAILS?

Are boys really bolder and more aggressive? Are they tougher? Do they have different needs? We may never know whether boys are simply born the way they are, or whether we mold them to fit our idea of "maleness." This is a conundrum that may never be answered to everyone's satisfaction by scientific literature. It may be one that you can't answer either, even if you are bringing up both boys and girls. For now, look at your own behavior from time to time. Are you already treating your baby boy differently than you would have treated a baby girl—offering trucks and hammers, rather than stuffed animals and crayons? When he fusses to get out of his stroller, do you allow him to get out and walk along holding on to it? When his sister was the same age and fussed, did you instead take her out and carry her? Do you unconsciously expect your boy to be physically active and strong? Thinking it over, you may conclude that these are the right choices for your child, or you may decide you are laying down a framework of gender stereotypes. The important thing is to be open to the individual difference your little boy displays. No one can tell you what your son's interests, likes, and dislikes will be. He needs the room to find out for himself, with your help.

TV SHOWS AND VIDEOS

By the age of one, your child may enjoy a child's program on TV or a short children's video. If you decide to let her watch something, sit alongside her and add your comments and hugs. This will make what can be a passive experience a more interactive one for baby. The TV is not a babysitter, although it may give you time to pick up the room while your child is busy watching. Do not leave the room, however, thinking that your child is safely engaged. Your child may lose interest and wander off, and into trouble. Some won't watch for more than a few minutes anyway. As your child becomes older and the desire for TV becomes a larger part of her life, you may want to set limits or rules. If you think you will want to restrict TV watching later, it may be best not to start at all at this point in her life.

Although it's tempting to allow your child to sit beside you as you watch grown-up TV shows and videos at night, this becomes less appropriate as your child gets older. Although it's true that a five-month-old would have no idea what's happening, a one-year-old already understands a lot more than he can let on. It's probably time to start being selective and allowing him to view child-friendly programs only.

CRIB OR BED?

Although it's perfectly fine to leave your child in a crib well into the second year, some parents consider a bed at age one, especially if they already know there's a new baby on the way. The crib has its benefits: It is a safe, confined place that your baby is used to. Assuming he cannot climb out, it can offer you greater piece of mind. Once in a bed, your child can obviously get up after you have put her to sleep for the night. Once she wakes up, rather than having to alert you that she wants to get out of her crib, she can quietly get herself up—something that has its pluses and minuses. Make sure there isn't anything dangerous out that she can get into.

If your child is already able to climb out of the crib, the bed may be the safest alternative. You'll have a number of options when choosing a bed: some catalogs offer a way to convert your crib mattress into a junior bed. Stores also sell low-to-the-ground, junior beds with mattresses. Or you can place a regular twin mattress on the floor. Lastly, you can use a regular twin bed with a guardrail (or, later, without it if you have a child who doesn't fall out of bed). Your baby will probably still crave the security of a closed-in space, so put the bed up against a wall and use an approved safety side bar for a more enclosed safer space. Try to make the switch sound exciting, so your baby doesn't miss her crib. Choosing appealing sheets or bedspread can add to the fun for your child.

"NO!" BABY'S NEW WORD

Heading into the second year is a headstrong toddler who realizes the instant power of the word "no." If your child is a big talker, he may already have discovered this important word. You do not suddenly have a "bad" baby. You have a very normal child who needs to exert some control over the people and things around him. One very effective way to assert one's independence is by saying "no." Within reason, allow him some of the control and independence he seeks.

Transitions

Try putting the crib mattress on the floor and letting your baby sleep on that for a while before you go out and get a real bed. If there is room, you can leave the crib up a few more days, until you both feel comfortable with the new bedding arrangements. Then, as part of the ongoing festivities, you might let him "help" you take the crib apart, to avoid the feeling that it suddenly disappeared when he wasn't looking.

In the "No"

Hearing your baby say "no," you may suddenly become more aware of how often you yourself say the word. Perhaps it's time to start trying alternatives that your baby can understand, like "hot" or "sharp"—short reasons for not touching rather than a one-word "no."

At this early age, however, the word "no" may or may not mean "no." You may sometimes hear it even as you hand him the very item he just indicated wanting. Stay in good humor and try to do your best to circumnavigate this contrary behavior. The "no's" will continue during the second year and you will be quite happy to see them go as you make your way out the other side of the "terrible twos." Until then, allow him his no's when you can, avoid them if possible, and insist on your own way when you must.

THE FIRST BIRTHDAY PARTY

You may have a secret desire to rent out Madison Square Garden, hire a marching band, have pony rides and thousands of helium balloons to mark the big number 1! You are right in believing that turning one is a monumental achievement, but your one-year-old will not be expecting such fanfare. For the first birthday, the guest list is up to you—you might have your whole playgroup plus their parents and some of your relatives over for a big party. Or you can celebrate quietly with just the family. Too much excitement can be tiring for a one-year-old—all the presents, the cake, the people, the noise. If you do a large party, try to keep it fairly short (one to one and a half hours), and have the children's needs in mind. Avoid overloading the table with sweets and instead offer many toddler-friendly finger foods. Have a safe play area available for the children, with appropriate toys out for their use. If there are a lot of presents to be opened, let your child be your guide. After a few are opened, you may start to see a glassy-eyed look that says, "This is all too much for me." Put the rest away to be opened later. Don't expect her to stop and appreciate the presents either. Ripping open the packages will offer more fun than playing with the toys just now.

SAFETY TIPS FOR THE TWELFTH MONTH

With your child on the move, you must baby-proof your house on a whole other level. You must be on your guard for accidental poisonings. More than 1 million American children under age six are

A Doctor's Thoughts
"Parents need to be realistic. Some parents will keep all their little knickknacks out and say 'He'll just have to learn not to touch them.' That's unrealistic. Baby-proofing makes life easier for everyone."—Dr. Barbara Frankowski, Assistant Professor of Pediatrics, College of Medicine, University of Vermont

poisoned each year. The peak age for poisonings is twenty-four months. Here's how to protect your child:

1. Remove poisonous plants from the house and yard or devise ways to keep your child away from these plants. (See page 129 for a list of some common poisonous plants or ask your local Poison Control Center for a list.)

2. Keep syrup of ipecac in your home. Use only as instructed by a Poison Control Center.

3. Know the number of the Poison Control Center (look in the white pages) and keep it near the phone.

4. Make sure all medicines are stored out of reach of children and that they all have child-proof caps. Throw away all outdated medicines.

5. Keep household cleansers and other toxic substances out of reach of children. Use child-proof locks on cabinets that hold these items.

6. Make sure these same precautions are taken at the babysitter's house, the day-care center, or Grandma's house.

7. Use back burners and turn pot handles in toward the center of the stove, so nothing can be inadvertently knocked over onto little heads.

8. Keep the toilet lid down and buckets empty of water. One-year-olds are still top-heavy and can fall into a toilet or bucket and may be unable to get out.

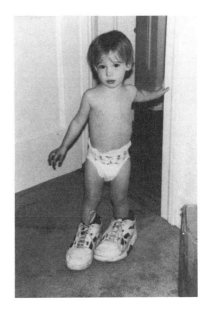

TOYS FOR THE TWELFTH MONTH

Hats, grown-ups' shoes, and more for dress-up and pretend
Toy vacuum cleaners and lawn mowers and corn poppers
Books that tell stories
Dolls
Duplo blocks
Pull toy on wheels (with a string for pulling; never leave child unattended)
Push toys (cars, trucks, animals on wheels)
Toy telephone
Simple shape sorter
Easy-to-play musical toy
Riding toys

The Littlest Consumers
They don't even have their driver's licenses yet, but the country's littlest consumers have helped create the most popular car in America! Take a look: Number of Ford Tauruses sold in 1991: 299,700
Number of Honda Accords sold in 1991: 399,300
Number of Little Tikes Cozy Coupes sold in 1991: 500,000!

A sturdy, nontippable pushcart can offer a little extra security (and fun) for the beginning walker who's already fairly steady on his feet.

HAPPY BABY'S HIT PARADE

High on your baby's list of activities this month include:

- Going for a walk with the help of a pushcart.
- Climbing up steps (with you right behind)
- Going down a small slide
- Going to the park
- Pretend play (acting out talking on the phone, shopping, eating)
- Feeding self
- Water play with close supervision

CHAPTER 18

✤ Feeding in the First Year ✤

Within minutes of your baby's birth, she will be looking to you for sustenance. As a fetus, she never felt a hunger pain or had to worry about her next meal. Now she is wholly dependent upon you to provide. This tiny person, so seemingly fragile at birth, will double her weight in the first five months and triple her weight by her first birthday. She will soon be able to astound you with physical feats, from lifting her own head, to sitting up and crawling. Where does she get the fuel to do all this growing and changing? During the first year, her major nutritional source is breast milk or formula, with some solids rounding out the picture in the second half of the year.

Use this chapter as a companion to the month-by-month baby guide (Chapters 6 through 17), dipping in and out of it to get the information you need on everything from the basics of breastfeeding and some common concerns and questions about it, to the basics of bottle feeding, through questions about vitamin supplementation for babies and adverse food reactions and allergies.

✤   ✤   ✤

BREASTFEEDING MADE SIMPLE

Happily, breastfeeding already *is* quite simple. In most cases, a mother naturally offers her breast and the infant instinctively latches on to suck, stops when he has drained that breast, completes his meal on the other side, and finishes a happy and pleasantly full baby. The breasts do not need any special preparation, nor do you *necessarily* need instruction. Being a new mother and a new breastfeeder, however, can engender feelings of uncertainty. Countless questions float through your mind: Am I doing this right? Did the baby get

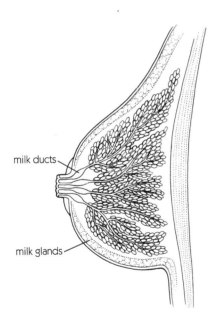

milk ducts

milk glands

Milk glands produce the milk that is
released into the milk ducts, eventually
leading to the nipple.

enough milk? Why are my nipples sore? He just ate but wants more
. . . should I feed him again? More than instruction, the average
mother needs reassurance: it's likely that you are already doing
everything right. With that in mind, here are the answers to the most
common questions:

Q: *When should I start nursing?*
A: The sooner you start, the better. If all systems are go, it's wise to
put the baby to your breast within thirty minutes after birth. Babies
are often very alert and have a strong sucking reflex right after birth,
so this is the best time to begin. Breastfeeding is easier to learn with a
cooperative baby who's ready to suck. The earliest milk your breasts
produce is known as colostrum. Some women mistakenly feel that
this is not "real" milk and therefore the baby is not getting what he
needs. In fact, colostrum is the perfect first food for your baby and is
full of the protective antibodies your baby needs. It also helps him to
produce his first bowel movement, known as meconium.

Q: *How do I get the baby interested?*
A: Just touching the baby's cheek with your breast or finger will
cause your newborn to instinctively turn toward the cheek that you
touched, helping the baby find the breast. Just minutes old, with
their earnest and serious-faced search for the nipple, newborns can't
help but immediately endear themselves to their mothers. It is amazing that newborns come with the knowledge that there is anything to
search for at all. Considering that for nine months all their nutritional needs were met without any work on their part, this willingness to work for the first meal is pretty close to miraculous. Some
babies may seem a little lazy at first, worn out from their trip through
the birth canal. Continue to offer them the breast even if they only
suck and doze, suck and doze at first.

Q: *How do I know the baby has latched on right?*
A: The infant should have the entire nipple and some of the areola
in his mouth. You can achieve this by guiding your breast toward his
mouth and placing your nipple well back in his mouth when he
opens it. When you look down at your baby, you should see that his
lips are splayed out so the bottom lip is flat out around the bottom of
the nipple and some of the areola and the top lip is splayed out to
cover the top of the nipple and some of the areola (see illustration).

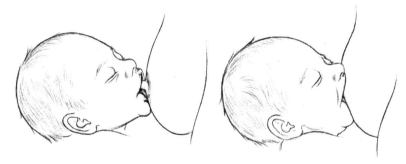

Make sure your baby's mouth is open to its widest so you can guide in the nipple and as much of the areola as possible.

When the baby is latched on correctly, the lips are splayed out over much of the areola.

It depends on the size of the baby's mouth how much of the areola he is able to cover. If you think he didn't latch on quite right, slide your index finger between your breast and the baby's mouth to break the suction and try again. When the baby is in place, you may want to gently press down on your breast just under the baby's nose to make a little extra breathing room for the baby.

Q: *Why switch sides during a feeding?*
A: Usually, mothers offer both breasts at feedings. This ensures that both breasts produce adequate amounts of milk. Draining both breasts equally also helps to reduce nipple soreness and to prevent problems with blocked ducts or infections. To switch sides, slip a finger in between your breast and the baby's mouth to break the suction. Pulling the baby off without breaking the suction can hurt your nipples. Then switch the baby to the other breast and encourage him to begin eating again. It's a good idea to begin the next feeding on the breast you last left off on. This way you alternate the lead breast, which usually gets the benefit of a hungrier baby.

Q: *How long should a feeding last?*
A: There's no reason to time yourself or to feel you have to conform to a certain time chart. Your baby may drain both breasts in as little as ten minutes or he may suck for up to twenty minutes. Babies nurse at different rates and some continue to suck for pleasure long after they have finished the actual meal. Let the baby stay at your breast until he appears relatively satisfied, and sucking movements are stopping. Then, burp the baby and switch sides. Nurse for an additional ten minutes or more on that side, or until sucking and swallowing movements stop.

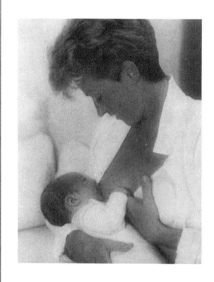

Forget-Me-Not
To remember which breast you left off on, use a ring. When you switch sides during a feed, switch the ring from one hand to the other. Next time, start breastfeeding on the side with the ring.

Dad's Influence
Not surprisingly, women whose partners support breastfeeding and believe it's good for babies are more likely to breastfeed their babies than those whose partners are against it, according to one study by Dr. Gary Freed and others. (*Pediatrics*, August 1992)

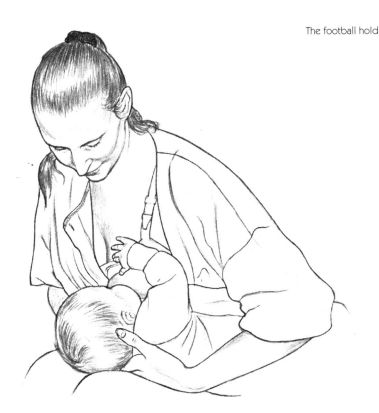
The football hold

Q: *What if he falls asleep before he has finished eating?*
A: It can be aggravating (and uncomfortable) if your baby falls asleep at one breast and won't wake up to feed on the opposite breast. Although you may be reluctant to do it, there's no harm in waking the baby up to finish a feeding. (After all, this baby isn't going to give a second thought to waking you up at all hours in the coming months!) Unwrapping the baby may help to wake him up enough to finish eating, as does a gentle tap on the bottom of the foot, or rubbing the baby's back. Sometimes just moving the baby to burp him wakes him up. If you have a very sleepy baby and this is a constant problem, you might even start out with the baby unwrapped so he doesn't get too snug and cozy. Just drape a blanket over the two of you. As the baby gets a little older, he'll be a lot less sleepy and this won't be so much of a challenge.

BREASTFEEDING POSITIONS

The best way to hold your infant during a feeding is the way that makes you and your baby (and your back) feel most comfortable. It's

The cradle position is a natural for breastfeeding.

The side-lying position

good to try a number of different positions to see what's easiest for you. Also, switching positions from time to time helps ensure that your breasts will be evenly drained and, as such, may help prevent blocked ducts from occurring. Changing positions also decreases your chances of getting sore nipples. By putting the baby's mouth over different parts of the areola, the stress of sucking does not always occur in the same place. Here are the three most comfortable breastfeeding positions:

Sitting Up: Put some pillows behind your back for support if you are in bed or sit well back in a comfortable chair. Cradle the infant in your arms. A pillow in your lap underneath the infant can help get him a little closer to you and may make breastfeeding more comfortable. Pull him close until his mouth can reach your nipple. When sitting in a chair, it can help your back if your feet are up on a low stool. A chair with arms is also a plus, as it can help you support the weight of the baby and take the strain off your lower back. (See illustration on page 164.)

Football Hold: To use a "football hold," cup the baby's head in your hand and hold the baby to your breast, with his legs under your arm and to your side. (See illustration on page 164.)

Side-lying Position: Lie on your side in bed with some pillows behind your back and head for support. Your knees should be slightly bent to take strain off your lower back. Place the infant alongside you, turned on his side, facing your breast. If you like, you can also cup one hand around the baby's back or the back of his head to keep him comfortable at the breast. (See illustration above.)

A Nurse's Thoughts

"The emotional impact of having a baby and being tired, combined with the change in your relationship with your husband, and with your other children—all of these can be factors, outside of the breastfeeding itself, that may make you feel as though you're constantly nursing."—Linda J. Kobokovich, R.N.C., M.Sc.N., Clinical Nurse Specialist, the Birthing Pavilion, Dartmouth Hitchcock Medical Center

✦

Finger Sucking

Your baby may discover that his own fingers make a lovely pacifier once the breast has been taken away. Sucking right after a feeding should not be interpreted as a sign that the baby did not get enough to eat from you. Sucking is such a pleasant sensation for the baby that he learns to reproduce these good feelings by himself. Don't worry . . . if it's hunger that's driving him, your baby will let you know!

CONSTANT NURSING

You may be wondering, "Why does he want to eat again when I just fed him?" During the early days, it can indeed seem like you're nursing all the time! Let's say you nursed at ten o'clock for twenty minutes. Your newborn baby will probably be ready to eat again at twelve, only about an hour and a half after you last fed him. This is perfectly normal in the early days. Be sure you drink plenty of liquids.

Frequent nursing is a blessing in disguise. It helps to stimulate good milk production and establish successful breastfeeding. A baby who nurses six to twelve times a day in the early months is normal. This is not a sign that your baby needs more food than you can provide. It is a sign of an active, healthy baby. Don't compare your breastfed baby with a friend's bottle-fed baby. Breastfed babies tend to eat more frequently than bottle-fed babies because human milk is more quickly and easily digested. Especially in the first two or three days when you have colostrum instead of milk, you may feel like the baby is sucking all the time. There isn't a lot of volume in those first three days, but colostrum does offer a lot of calories and immune system benefits. Within just a few weeks' time, you should begin to see a more comfortable routine emerging. Most breastfeeding difficulties have resolved themselves by this time. (Frequent feedings can sometimes cause sore nipples. If this is true in your case, see page 168 for more information.)

ENOUGH MILK

Some mothers worry that they do not have "enough milk." They may not be sure their babies are getting what they need. Rest assured that your breasts will automatically produce the right amount for your baby. If your baby is hungry and stays at the breast longer or eats more frequently, your breasts will increase production of milk to meet the demands. If you ever feel as if you are not providing enough to satisfy your baby, the trick is to nurse more frequently to increase your supply of milk (supplementing with a bottle will only decrease your milk supply). As long as your baby continues to grow well over the coming weeks and months, you can assume that he is getting enough milk. You can also gauge the amount that goes in by the amount that comes out. If your newborn averages about six wet diapers a day and has regular bowel movements (see page 60 for information on newborn bowel movements), he is taking in plenty of your milk.

DEMAND FEEDING vs. SCHEDULED FEEDING

At one time, it was considered important to keep an infant on strictly scheduled feedings, usually three to four hours apart. Opinions then changed and women began feeding their babies "on demand" (that is, whenever the baby appeared to be hungry). It seems safe to say that demand feeding works very well in the early weeks and helps to establish a good milk supply. There is really no reason not to use demand feeding. As your baby gets older and life becomes more complicated, however, it is up to you whether you want to continue demand feeding or make an attempt to adhere to a loose feeding schedule. Of course, some babies will naturally create a schedule of their own over the first three months. Stay flexible, however. A baby's feelings of hunger and need for nutrition can change periodically due to growth spurts and you may have to return to more frequent feedings to bolster your milk supply.

If you are returning to work but wish to continue breastfeeding, this situation demands more active scheduling of feedings. See page 285 in Chapter 31, "Returning to Work," for more information.

VITAMIN SUPPLEMENTS

A vitamin D supplement is usually recommended since this is not found in breast milk. Some pediatricians, however, find that regular, indirect exposure to the sun when the baby is outside on walks offers more than enough vitamin D.

Full-term babies may be born with enough iron reserves to last until they begin solid foods containing iron at around six months of age. Iron supplements may also be offered to exclusively breastfed babies. Furthermore, some iron is passed to the newborn through the breast milk. Some recent research, however, seems to indicate that iron reserves are depleted by four months. Still, iron deficiency is rare in the breastfed infant. Your pediatrician may decide to recommend iron supplementation for your exclusively breastfed infant from the fourth month of life just to be sure.

Breast Size
Breast size has no relation to the amount of milk you can produce.

A Mother's Reflections
"One great benefit to breastfeeding is how quickly it can calm a baby down. If he's upset or bumped himself, putting him to the breast immediately distracts him, and stops the crying. It's also a great pacifier if you have to make an important phone call. No one will ever know there's a baby in the room with you!"

Refusing the Breast

If for some reason your exclusively breastfed baby is refusing the breast, tell your pediatrician. There may be an underlying health problem such as an earache, a stuffy nose, thrush (an irritating fungal infection of the mouth), or teething difficulties that is making sucking difficult for her.

Fluoride, which has been found to strengthen teeth and prevent decay, is not passed through breast milk and is sometimes offered by pediatricians as a supplement. If the water in your community is fluoridated, and your baby drinks water, no further fluoride supplements would be advised, however. For more on fluoride, see page 110.

It is up to you and your doctor to decide whether any of these supplements might benefit your particular baby.

BREASTFEEDING PROBLEMS

Inverted Nipples: Even if your nipples are inverted, your breasts will still produce adequate amounts of milk. The problem is: how to get your baby to latch on. There is no reason not to try breastfeeding, if that is what you want to do. Place the baby's mouth over the inverted nipple and much of the areola. Some babies will manage to latch on without a problem. As they suck at the breast, inverted nipples are drawn out. If, however, your baby continues to have trouble latching on or you are becoming worried or frustrated, talk to a lactation expert or consider a switch to bottles.

Sore, Cracked Nipples: Although newborns are surprisingly strong suckers and some soreness is natural during the first few days of breastfeeding, breastfeeding should not hurt. If it does, it is probably a sign that the baby has latched on wrong. Break the seal with your finger and correct the baby's position. Remember, he should take all of the nipple and much of the areola in his mouth, with his lips splayed open around the breast. Take care, also, to vary your breastfeeding positions (see pages 164–165). Sometimes, even with all the proper techniques in place, there is still some nipple soreness. Some babies (affectionately known as barracudas) have an unusually strong suck. Or perhaps you have unusually sensitive breasts. Your breasts will adapt soon, however.

If nipples do start to crack or become very sore, you may need to feed your baby only from the good breast for a while and express milk from the sore one while it heals (see the section on hand expression on page 171). There is no need to use any creams or ointments except as advised by your physician. Wiping a little of your own breast milk around the nipple and then leaving it to air-dry for ten minutes or so is usually the best medicine. Speak with your pediatrician or a lactation consultant if you need more advice about proper positioning or latching on during breastfeeding. Try varying your breastfeeding positions, from sitting up to lying down, from a cradle hold to a football hold. See pages 164–165. This way, the infant won't constantly be sucking on the exact same tender spot.

Breast Engorgement: Characterized by a feeling of fullness and hardness, breast engorgement is very common in the early days. It can be relieved by frequent nursing. (If you are *not* breastfeeding and engorgement occurs due to a decision to let your milk dry up, see page 172.) Occasionally, the breast is so hard that the baby can have difficulty latching on to the nipple. Take a warm shower, letting water run over your breasts. Then express some milk to make the breasts softer for the baby. For more on how to express, see page 170. During this time, wear a supportive bra for your own comfort.

Blocked Ducts: As the months go by, your breasts will become so accustomed to breastfeeding and so in tune with the demands of your baby that engorgement and blocked ducts will be less likely to occur. In the early weeks, however, breasts easily fill up and sometimes are not fully emptied by the baby. This can sometimes result in a blocked milk duct. Blocked ducts can eventually lead to mastitis (see below), a painful infection. To prevent blocked ducts, get into the habit of palpating your breasts after a feed to make sure they feel loose. There should be no hard spots (full areas) left after the baby finishes

painfull, hard swelling

blocked duct

pus

breast abscess

Milk can get "stuck," leading to painful, hard swelling in the breast. If the milk is not expressed out of the area, a breast infection may result.

A handheld bicycle pump. To use, squeeze the bulb while the horn is pressed against the breast.

The syringe-style pump. To use, slide the cylinder in and out to create suction that draws out the milk.

A battery-operated pump.

his meal. If there are, you'll want to work them out on your own or try putting the baby back to the breast to finish draining the breast. Changing breastfeeding positions sometimes helps baby to drain an area that otherwise tends to remain full.

To relieve the pressure yourself, stroke the breast firmly but gently, starting at the top of the hardened area and sliding your fingers down toward the nipple. If you find breast massage difficult to accomplish or uncomfortable, you might ask your husband to do it, assuming he has a gentle touch. Ignoring those engorged areas can lead to blockage, which you want to avoid.

Mastitis: Symptoms of mastitis include fever, redness, and breast tenderness. Mastitis should not be ignored. Call your doctor. You'll need antibiotics, because mastitis is an infection. You will also benefit from continued and frequent nursing to drain the affected area. There is no danger to the infant. Mastitis is uncomfortable for you but won't bother your baby in any way.

EXPRESSING BREAST MILK

Sometimes, you will want or need to offer your baby expressed breast milk. This may be the case if, for example, you are going out and will miss a feeding. It may also be necessary if your breasts are engorged, if you have a badly cracked nipple that makes breastfeeding too painful right now, or if your baby has a problem such as cleft lip or prematurity, which can make sucking difficult for him. Depending on how often you plan to express and for what reason, you may wish to do so manually or with the help of a pump. If you just want to express a tiny bit to relieve engorged breasts, for example, manual expression would be fine. If you need to express a lot, however, then you will want to invest in a breast pump. (See illustration of two types of hand-held pumps.) An electric or battery-operated pump may be best if most or all of your baby's feedings will be from expressed breast milk, but these are much more expensive. To keep costs down, you can rent an electric pump instead of purchasing one. You should also contact your insurance company to see if the cost of a battery-operated pump is covered under your policy. It may be.

The best time to express some milk is usually right after a feeding, assuming you still have some milk left. As you try to express, you will determine which time of day is best for you (it may even be in between feedings). Some women also find it convenient to pump from one breast as the baby suckles at the other. (In the early weeks, this breast is often dripping anyway as it waits its turn.) Just remember, however, that pumping, like breastfeeding, will increase your milk supply. So if you begin to express at the same time each day on a regular basis, your breasts will be full of milk at that time and will need to be expressed or fed from then.

If you intend to use the expressed milk for a feeding, you must express into a sterile bottle. You should then refrigerate the milk. Breast milk will stay fresh for twenty-four hours in the refrigerator and for up to three months in the freezer. Label it with a date.

To express by hand, wash your hands with soap and water. Use the flat of your hand and rub in a circular motion all the way around the breast. This helps to soften the breast and stimulate milk production. Then use a C-hold to cup the breast with your thumb on top of your breast and your other fingers underneath to support your breast at the bottom. Push into your breast, toward the chest wall, then stroke out and downward toward the nipple. (See illustration.) The milk should begin to squirt out. If you plan to save the milk, be sure to have a sterile container underneath to catch it. A wide-mouthed jar might be best unless your aim is very good. Some

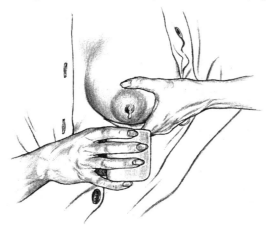

Support your breast with four fingers underneath, leaving the thumb on top. Using your thumb, press in toward your chest and down toward the nipple.

Supplemental Bottles
According to one recent study completed at Dartmouth Medical School, the use of one supplemental bottle a day will not affect your breastfeeding success, assuming you are committed to breastfeeding. In this study, babies were not confused by the different methods of feeding.

✦

Tips for Easier Expressing
To enhance the flow of milk:
1. Express early in the day when energy levels and milk production are up.
2. Look at your baby while you pump.
3. Look at a photo of your baby while you pump.
4. Imagine your baby at your breast.
5. Pump in a relaxed, comfortable environment where there will be no interruptions. (If someone else is home, ask him to handle phones, doors, and children.)
6. Place warm towels on breast before you begin.
7. Gently massage and stroke the breasts to "prime" them before you begin to pump.

people find hand expression a natural and easy method. Other mothers find that they can't get more than a few drops out. Keep trying to see if you can get the hang of it. Alternate with some hand or battery-operated pumps to see if they are easier for you. Use the method that gives you the best results.

DRYING UP YOUR BREAST MILK

If you choose not to breastfeed at all, you will need to let your milk dry up. Your body is unaware of your decision at first and will fill up with milk sometime between your second and seventh day postpartum. This can lead to uncomfortable engorgement (see page 169), which *cannot* be relieved as it would if you were breastfeeding (by feeding, hand expressing, or using hot towels). Instead, you'll need to wait out the discomfort and let nature takes its course. As your body realizes that none of the milk is being taken, production shuts down. Breasts are designed to make only as much milk as is needed. The most painful period probably won't last more than forty-eight hours, although it may take as much as a week or so for milk production to cease altogether. In the meantime, you can try ice packs to relieve some of the discomfort. Hot towels or hot showers will only encourage milk flow. Wear a well-fitting bra (at night too, if it makes you more comfortable). Continue to drink plenty of water. It is a mistake to believe that decreasing your fluid intake will decrease milk production or engorgement. Some doctors do prescribe medication to stop lactation, but these drugs are not always advisable. If you are interested, talk with your doctor about the benefits as well as the side effects.

FORMULA FEEDING

Although breast milk is considered superior, infants still thrive on formula. Every family is different and bottle feeding may be the most comfortable and appealing to you in your particular situation. Only you can make this decision. Formula feeding should be discussed with your pediatrician so you can make a wise choice among the many brand names and types of formula on the market. Most formulas are iron-fortified. Most are based on cow's milk. Some are based on other proteins such as soy. All brands sold comply with strict safety regulations, but some may be more suitable for your newborn than others. Formula milk should as closely approximate breast milk as possible. Once you and your pediatrician have chosen a particular brand, stay with that brand unless you have a problem with it and your pediatrician tells you to switch.

Formulas usually come in powder form or liquid concentrate and must be mixed with water. You should follow the instructions to the letter when preparing milk for your baby. If the formula is too concentrated, it may make your baby sick or overweight. If you dilute the formula too much, your baby may not get the nutrition he needs. Infant formula is also available in ready-to-use cans and ready-to-use disposable bottles (with attached nipples). These require no measuring or mixing. Ready-to-use disposable bottles are perfect for traveling and ideal for an occasional supplement to breastfeeding. For everyday use, however, they can become expensive.

Formula should be prepared fresh each day. You can make enough bottles each morning to last through a twenty-four-hour period. Prepared bottles should then be refrigerated until you are ready to use them.

As with breastfeeding, formula-fed babies should be fed on demand. Allow the newborn to take as much as he thinks he needs. It is unwise to coax him into emptying the bottle. Your newborn will probably drink about five or six bottles in a twenty-four-hour period.

Babies should continue to drink formula right up to their first birthday. After that, your doctor will probably switch them to whole cow's milk. Regular milk has more salt and protein than formula or breast milk and can put an added strain on the kidneys of a child under age one.

> **A Nurse's Opinion**
> *"In the early days of breastfeeding, I think people tend to turn to bottles when breastfeeding is not going well. I would rather see mothers work their breastfeeding problems out first, and then when successful breastfeeding is established, supplement. Once breastfeeding is established, mothers needn't feel guilty about offering a bottle of breast milk so that they don't have to be anchored to baby."—Linda Kobokovich, R.N.C., M.Sc.N., Clinical Nurse Specialist, The Birthing Pavilion, Dartmouth Hitchcock Medical Center*

WARMING BOTTLES

Although it is not necessary, many parents seem to like the idea of warming the formula for the baby. (Do not microwave or cook expressed breast milk, because the heat causes it to lose its immunologic properties. Instead, just run the bottle under warm water.) The conventional wisdom is: Do not place a bottle of formula in the microwave because it can get hot spots that may burn the baby. Instead, it is safer to place it in a pan of hot water. (So many parents

have ignored this advice, however, that three Ph.D.'s published a list of microwave safety tips in the September 1992 issue of *Pediatrics*, the journal of the American Academy of Pediatrics.) According to the authors, plastic bottles of refrigerated formula may be safely microwaved as follows:

1. Heat only *refrigerated* formula. Do not heat room-temperature formula that can be served as is.

2. Fill at least a 4- or an 8-ounce plastic bottle with the formula. Never use a glass bottle, which can crack or explode.

3. Stand the bottle upright, leaving it *uncovered* to allow heat to escape.

4. Heat a 4-ounce bottle no more than 30 seconds and an 8-ounce bottle no more than 45 seconds.

5. Remove the bottle from the microwave and screw on a top with a nipple. Turn the bottle over *10 times* to mix (hot spots tend to be at the top).

6. Always test the formula by placing a few drops on your tongue or on top of your hand. If it feels warm to the touch, it may be too hot to serve. It should be cool to the touch.

BOTTLE-FEEDING EQUIPMENT

If you are formula feeding, you'll want to have an adequate supply of bottles and other paraphernalia in the house:

- Four 4-ounce bottles (glass or plastic)
- Eight 8-ounce bottles (glass, plastic, or plastic holders with disposable plastic liners)
- Nipples (rubber or silicone)
- Bottle brush for cleaning
- Nipple brush for cleaning

No Bottle Propping
Never leave an infant alone with a propped-up bottle. The baby could choke.

✛

Lead-free Water
There has been some concern recently that, in certain communities, there are high levels of lead in the water. This is because pipes often have lead in them. As a precaution, always let the water run for a couple of minutes before using it. When cooking, be sure to boil cold water only. Hot water contains more lead.

- Funnel
- Pyrex measuring cup
- Long-handled mixing spoon
- Tongs
- A sterilizer or large pot for boiling bottles and accessories (if your pediatrician recommends this)

KEEPING BOTTLES CLEAN

When bottle feeding, great attention must be paid to good hygiene. For your newborn's health, everything must be clean, from the spoon you use to stir the formula to the cap you place over the nipple. Milk is a breeding ground for germs, so bottle and nipples must be kept scrupulously clean. After use, all equipment should first be thoroughly washed by hand and then placed in a dishwasher. Sterilization is no longer routinely recommended. If your pediatrician does advise sterilization of bottles, use a large pot or stove-top sterilizer tank. Fill with water and bring to a boil. Allow equipment to continue to boil for five to ten minutes. (Sterilization can be made easier if bottles are placed on a rack before they are lowered into the pot.) After the equipment has boiled for five minutes, remove the pot from the heat and allow it to cool. Remove the bottles from the pot with sterilized tongs, or if they are on a rack, lift out the rack. Try not to touch the nipples with your fingers. When placing them on bottles, handle them by the edges.

Currently, most pediatricians believe a hot-water wash in the dishwasher is enough and you don't have to be so fastidious about sterilizing everything! Check with your own pediatrician for advice.

Prevent Tooth Decay
Do not put a baby to bed with a bottle. The milk can pool and cause needless cavities. For more on this, see "Bottle Mouth (Nursing Caries)," page 126.

A Tip for Night Feedings
Put the exact amount of cooled boiled water you need into a clean thermos. Measure out the powder you need and place it in a baby bottle. When your baby wakes up and wants to be fed, just pour the lukewarm water from your thermos into the bottle, screw on the nipple, and shake. Your baby's bottle is ready quickly, with no trips to the kitchen for warming or mixing in the middle of the night.

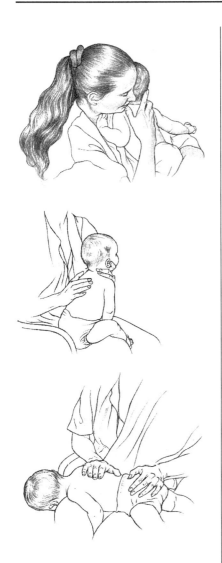

PREPARING BOTTLES

1. Read the instructions on the label on your formula.

2. Pour sterile water into a measured pitcher or Pyrex measuring cup. (Be sure this has been washed in a hot-water dishwasher.) Use the exact amount of water indicated on the formula's instruction label.

3. Using the scoop provided with your powdered formula, measure out the correct amount. Level off the scoop with a clean knife.

4. Add the powder to the water and stir it well, using a clean long-handled spoon or the knife.

5. Pour the milk formula into your day's supply of bottles.

6. Place the nipple and cap on. Shake well.

7. Store extra bottles in the refrigerator to be used later in the day.

OFFERING THE BOTTLE

Sit down with the baby on a comfortable chair. Use pillows to give your back and arms some support. Place a pillow under the infant if this makes you more comfortable. Try to have feeding times be uninterrupted moments of quiet for you and your baby. Bottle feedings take just as long and require just as much attention to what you're doing as breastfeedings. If you have warmed the milk, test the temperature by shaking a few drops out onto your wrist. Touch the bottle to your baby's cheek and he will turn toward it and latch on to the bottle's nipple. Allow the baby to take what he needs from the bottle. Throw away whatever he can't finish, because it will spoil.

BURPING

Although not necessary for every baby or at every feeding, burping is often a good way to bring up swallowed air that may be interfering with a newborn's feeding or quiet enjoyment. There are several methods of burping (see illustrations).

1. Hold the baby in an over-the-shoulder position and pat him gently, but firmly, on the back. There's no need to pound or thump.
2. Sit the baby upright in your lap, supporting him with one hand on his chest and chin and your other hand on his back.
3. Lay the baby stomach-down across your knees. Rub him gently on his back.

SPITTING UP

Babies often spit up milk when being burped. This is normal. As many as 80 percent of all babies spit up, but most will stop by around six to eight months of age. Spitting up is not serious and will not interfere with your baby's weight gain. Bottle-fed babies tend to spit up more than breastfed babies. Spitting up may occur less frequently if you burp the baby. Spitting up is different from vomiting. When your baby spits up, stomach contents easily dribble out of the mouth. Vomiting is the forceful expulsion of the stomach contents. If your baby vomits forcefully, so that it travels across the room (known as projectile vomiting), call your pediatrician to let him know about this. Any frequent or forceful vomiting should be reported to your pediatrician immediately.

WHEN TO WEAN

There is no law that says you must stop breastfeeding once solid foods are being offered. You can really continue to breastfeed as long as you and your baby are still interested in doing so. It is now believed that there are some health benefits in continuing to breast-feed past the six- to nine-month mark. One study in Finland is reported to show that middle ear infections are more prevalent in babies who've been bottle-fed than in babies who've been breastfed longer than six months. There should be no embarrassment in continuing to breastfeed even after your child is taking solids, gets teeth, or can walk or talk. Naturally, over the first year, breastfeeding times decrease, until finally you may only be breastfeeding at night

A Mother's Reflections
"I knew I probably wouldn't have any more children, so I was in no rush to stop breast-feeding."

✦

Around the World
Worldwide, the average age at which children are completely weaned from the breast is a surprising 4.2 years of age (according to Dr. Ruth A. Lawrence in her book *Breastfeeding: A Guide for the Medical Profession*)! Perhaps equally surprising: In the United States, most mothers (about 70 percent) wean the baby by three months of age and 80 percent of babies have been weaned by six months of age.

Dad? Robbie's rejecting his first solids!

or during an early-morning snuggle. You can follow your child's lead and allow him to give up the breast when he's ready or you can have the child follow your lead by slowly weaning him off the breast when you feel you've had enough.

If you wean your baby well before his first birthday, he will need to drink formula. If you wean between ten and twelve months, however, your baby may be old enough to take whole cow's milk, although whole cow's milk is usually not recommended before the first birthday. Talk with your pediatrician about the switch from breast milk to formula or breast milk to whole milk. If you are advised to offer cow's milk, remember that whole milk is preferred over skim milk for a young child. Reduced-fat milk is generally considered inappropriate to use during the first year.

You may wean straight from the breast to the cup or from the breast to a bottle. The process of weaning should be gradual, with one formula feeding replacing a breastfeeding. This is usually more easily accomplished at a noontime feed than a nighttime feed, when your baby is likely to feel more attached to the comfort of the breast. Sometimes weaning occurs so naturally and slowly that you don't even have to think about it. Depending on his age, the baby may already be taking solids, juice, and either formula or whole milk by bottle or cup. Breastfeedings naturally become fewer and farther between until they can be dropped altogether.

If, owing to an illness or other problem, you need to stop breastfeeding abruptly, speak with your pediatrician about what's best for your baby and for you. An abrupt end to breastfeeding can be very uncomfortable and your doctor may be able to help you get through this with suggestions for ice packs or, rarely, medication.

Occasionally, mothers who stop breastfeeding say they feel blue and moody. Hormonal surges, as you become a nonlactating mother, are often at the root of your mood swings, just as they were during pregnancy and the immediate postpartum period. Weaning is also an emotional time for mothers because it involves a first separation from the infant. It can help to talk to other mothers, to a sister, or to your partner. It also helps if you increase cuddling time with your baby, to take the place of the physical comfort breastfeeding gave to you both.

INTRODUCING SOLID FOODS

Just when to introduce a baby to solid foods is open to some debate. Most doctors seem to agree that solids should not be introduced before about five or six months of age. Your baby probably won't become an instant eater. A baby's first natural reaction to having a spoon of solid foods placed in his mouth is to push his tongue against it and push it out of his mouth. The first few feedings are really just taste tests for the baby. He may smack his lips a few times and make a funny face, but he has officially been introduced to solid food. At this age, of course, all foods must be pureed smooth and strained. Babies are not able to chew well until seven to nine months (and even then, they're basically toothless so chewing is not terribly effective). Your pediatrician will probably have some specific suggestions for those first meals, but here is a basic schedule to follow:

- 5–6 months: fortified baby cereals and pureed fruits (a well-mashed, overripe banana makes a perfect first fruit).
- 6–7 months: as above, plus pureed and strained meats and vegetables (try cooked and pureed carrots, sweet potato, cauliflower, turkey and chicken).
- 8 months: as above, plus cooked egg yolk.
- 9–10 months: as above, plus cooked whole egg.

Don't be too concerned about how much solid food your baby is taking. Under one year of age, a baby's main food source is still milk and provides him with much of what he needs. Many would argue that it provides him with all his needs for the first six to nine months, and that the early introduction of foods is more to get the baby used to foods than it is for nutritional purposes.

CHANGES IN BOWEL MOVEMENTS

As you begin to offer more solid food, you may notice that bowel movements become firmer and smellier. This is especially true if you are offering foods to a heretofore totally breastfed baby. These changes are normal and to be expected. Do not be alarmed, either, if some of what you feed baby seems to come out the other end much the same as it went in. Some foods that weren't chewed well or that

A Mother's Reflections
"When my child was a baby, I would prepare more than what I needed for the meal and freeze the rest for later. I would freeze the food in small, one-meal portions, however, by placing tablespoons onto a piece of aluminum foil and putting them in the freezer just long enough to freeze them. Then I would place the food into a sealed, plastic freezer bag. I built up a store so that, at dinner, I could defrost a helping of applesauce and a helping of squash, supplemented with a little rice cereal for a delicious three-course meal!"

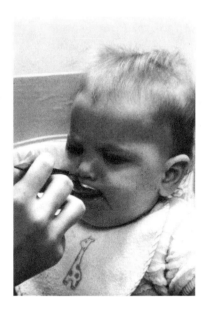

An Apple a Day
The apple is a versatile, good first food for babies and is unlikely to cause an allergic reaction. Peel and grate a raw apple and offer it to your baby on a spoon. Or you can cook, cool, and then puree the apples into an applesauce.

A baby-food grinder

were hard for the baby to digest will simply reappear in the diaper! You may want to hold off for a while and try again later if a certain food is not well digested by your baby. Be advised that color changes in the stool may be startling as well—especially if you've just fed your baby carrots or beets. Try to remember what you fed baby so you won't get an unpleasant shock at the next diaper change! Of course, if you notice an unusual change in bowel movements or if they become mucousy, frequent, and watery, you should contact your pediatrician.

HOMEMADE FOODS

Once you begin solid foods, your choice is to make it yourself or buy it ready-made. Which is better for baby? Which is better for you? The foods you can make yourself at home are excellent for your baby, but the commercially prepared foods are good too. When you make it yourself, of course, you have more control over the ingredients and the consistency of the puree. You may also feel better knowing you prepared the food yourself. Since babies under one year of age do not eat large quantities of food, you may feel you have enough time to prepare what he needs and that cooking is not too much of a chore.

You can make your own baby foods at home from fresh ingredients. A baby food grinder is a good thing to have in the house for pureeing the foods you cook. (See illustration.) Extra baby food you make can be poured into ice cube trays and frozen for later use. Do not add any sugar or salt to your baby's food. These represent adult taste preferences and do not add anything to the nutritional value of the food.

COMMERCIALLY PREPARED BABY FOODS

Commercially prepared baby foods are also an excellent choice for your baby. Today they are prepared under special guidelines that do not allow artificial additives, colorings, or preservatives. All jars are clearly labeled with the information you need listing all the ingredients. Read the labels to make sure you are using the type appropriate for your baby's age. You may find prepared foods more convenient for your lifestyle. Once you start introducing meats, you may find that the consistency is smoother in the jarred foods than what you can achieve at home. Store-bought baby foods can be especially convenient when you are away from home or on a trip with your baby. They don't have to be heated. Buying baby foods is more expensive than preparing your own foods at home, however.

ADDITIVES

Additives include any item, whether artificial or "natural" such as salt or sugar, that is added to the food during processing. Babies under age one are better off eating foods as close to their natural state as possible. It is not necessary to alter the taste or appearance of these foods with the addition of salt, sugar, or food colorings. If you are making your own baby foods at home, do not add sugar or salt. If you purchase a commercial baby food, you should read the label. Most do not contain additives.

ALLERGIES

An allergy is an abnormal reaction to any substance. Signs of a food allergy include rashes, watery eyes, diarrhea, stomachaches, and muscle cramps.

Let your pediatrician know if there is a history of allergies in your family. If allergies are common, consider breastfeeding (without any supplemental formula feeds) for the first six months. It is believed that this can help prevent allergies from developing in your child. A bottle-fed baby may be allergic to cow's milk. If your baby has such a milk intolerance, your pediatrician will probably switch him to a soy formula or perhaps suggest that you return to exclusive breastfeeding, if possible. Some babies are also sensitive to soy formula and may need a specialized formula or breast milk. Babies are not allergic to breast milk, but some may react allergically to food the mother has eaten, traces of which are passed on in the breast milk. In some specific cases, it may be beneficial for a breastfeeding mother to follow a hypoallergenic diet herself (for example, no cow's milk or egg white), although this is open to debate. Check with your pediatrician right away if your baby is exhibiting allergic reactions. Do not self-diagnose or change your diet on your own.

There is no reason to rush into solid foods, especially if you suspect that your child might be susceptible to allergies. When you begin to add solids to your baby's diet (around six months), start

Nature's Gift to Mothers
It comes in its own package. You don't need to wash it or cook it. It's the banana! The banana is a perfect first food. It's easy and it's nutritious, full of potassium and vitamins. Use a well-ripened banana and mash it with a fork or put it through a baby-food grinder. You can make the consistency as smooth as you like. Babies over the age of six months may like ripe banana slices as finger foods, too.

✦

Healthy Snacks
Once your baby is six months or older and used to solid foods, he may want something to munch between meals. Here are some good finger foods to offer:
Plain breadstick
Piece of soft cheese
Slice of Italian bread
Cheerios
Cooked potato wedge

Adequate Weight Gain
Your baby will be weighed at routine baby checkups over the year. Your doctor will monitor baby's growth against a curve showing normal ranges for babies during the first year. Typically, babies will triple their birth weight by the end of the first year. Many parents worry about whether or not their babies are eating enough. These periodic weigh-ins should reassure you that your baby is, in fact, thriving on his diet.

with foods that are the least likely to produce any allergies, such as bananas, apples, pears, and peaches. Start with rice cereal and leave wheat, oats, and barley until later. Avoid egg whites because of the chance of allergic reaction. Try one new food at a time so you can easily determine which foods cause allergic reactions. Be on the lookout for rashes and runny noses, which may indicate a bad reaction.

CHOLESTEROL

You may worry about your own cholesterol. But should you be worrying about your baby's cholesterol levels too? Probably not. Although we know that high cholesterol levels can be a risk factor for heart disease in adults, we don't know as much about cholesterol and young children. It is difficult to predict who will face problems in later life based on current diagnostic techniques. Furthermore, when severe dietary restrictions are made in a child's diet, there is justifiable concern that the diet may not be able to support a child's normal growth and development. It is especially important not to restrict the diet of a child under the age of two, who needs those fats and calories to grow. In its latest statement, the American Academy of Pediatrics states that "Dietary guidelines that restrict fat and cholesterol should *not* apply to infants from birth to age 2 years." Skim and low-fat milk is not recommended in the first two years of life. *After* two years, a parent and doctor can begin to think about a slow transition to a lower-fat diet, through the use of lean meats and lower-fat dairy products. The recommended diet for children *over* the age of two includes 30 percent of total calories from fat, less than 10 percent from saturated fats, and less than 300 mg of cholesterol per day.

WATER

A healthy, breastfed baby does not need anything besides breast milk for the first five or six months. Still, if you wish, you can offer a bottle of water. A formula-fed baby might also occasionally take some water. It is not necessary to put sugar in the water to get the baby to drink it.

CUPS

After six months of age, some babies enjoy drinking from a cup. First drinks should be offered in a training cup that has a lid and a spout. Try water or juice in the cup first, rather than formula or breast milk. Most young babies don't like to have anyone playing around with the serious business of drinking their milk from breast or bottle. Some babies resist the cup and may not accept one until after their first birthday. There's no reason to force the issue.

PLATES

Unbreakable hard plastic plates are perfect for the first year, when babies are likely to overturn their dinners or knock lunch onto the floor. Preferably the plates should have sides to help keep the food where it belongs. Small bowls also work well for baby food. Some plates stick to the high chair with a suction pad, and you may wish to try them. Some plates have room for hot water in the bottom to keep food warm. In general, however, babies do not seem to care about the temperature of the food, and this seems to be done more for parental prejudices than baby's likes and dislikes.

SPOONS

Choose a small plastic-coated baby spoon. In the beginning, you will be handling the spoon. When you first offer food on a spoon, remember that both the food and the spoon are foreign to your baby. Put only a very little bit on the spoon and tip the contents into your baby's mouth. Let your baby be the guide throughout the first year. When your child is giving you clues that indicate he has had enough (turning away, closing his mouth), do not try to slip a few more spoonfuls into him. Past the six-month mark, babies may enjoy some finger foods. They may also want to take some initiative in spoon-feeding themselves. At this point, it's a good idea to use two spoons at the meal—one for him to play with and one for you to use, to ensure that some food actually makes its way into his mouth.

BIBS

Bibs are what every fashionable baby will be wearing this year! Until your baby gets the hang of more polite table manners, feeding can be a messy proposition. There are many styles, including a tie or snap around the neck and even a pullover variety. Some even have sleeves that cover the arms. They come in fabric and in plastic (even paper for traveling!). The plastic bibs with a catch-all at the bottom are easy to wash but obviously cannot be used as a face wipe the way soft terry-cloth bibs can be. Some babies also object to the stiff feel of the hard plastic bib and prefer the fabric ones. A clean bib at every mealtime is the best idea, so you'll need to have plenty on hand.

CHAPTER 19

Medical Problems You and Your Baby ✤ May Be Facing ✤

New babies can face some minor or major medical problems ranging from jaundice to prematurity. The problems may entail some treatment, including time in the hospital nursery, or they may reflect ongoing problems that you and your child will have to deal with throughout the years to come. This section will help you to get some initial information on the problems at hand. For more in-depth treatment of the particular problem that affects your baby, ask the pediatrician or neonatologist for suggested reading, or go to a library and find the most up-to-date books and articles that concentrate on the medical problem you and your baby are facing. The more you know, the more comfortable you may feel in your new role as parent to this baby.

✤   ✤   ✤

NEWBORN INTENSIVE AND INTERMEDIATE CARE UNITS

Sometimes, owing to a medical complication, rooming in is not possible. Instead, you may receive the very upsetting news that your baby needs to spend time in either the intensive care or the intermediate care nursery. You may have expected this if you were rushed in for a premature delivery or if you had a high-risk pregnancy owing to diabetes or another medical problem. On the other hand, it may come as a total surprise when doctors find a problem in your newborn that needs medical attention. The prognosis for most babies who spend time in the NICU is quite good.

The newborn intensive care unit is not a pleasant place to begin parenting, but parenting can and does begin there. Your partner

Infant Mortality Rates
The United States infant mortality rate has dropped to a new low for us: Out of 1,000 babies, 9.2 babies under one year died in 1990. Part of the reason behind these more encouraging figures is the use of surfactant to treat undeveloped lungs in premature and low-birth-weight babies. We are still well behind other developed countries, however. In a list of infant mortality rates among twenty-three developed countries, the United States ranks twentieth, just above Italy and Greece. Japan currently has the world's lowest infant mortality rate.

may be the first one to see the intensive care nursery. Usually, he is able to accompany the newborn within minutes of the birth, even when you cannot. Once you have spent some time in the NICU, the clinical (and possibly intimidating) atmosphere will seem more familiar to you, as will the wires and machines your baby may be connected to. Newborns in the intensive care unit must be monitored continuously. They may be placed either in Isolettes or on warming trays. Open warming trays are used when constant emergency access to the baby is necessary. The closed Isolette can be used when the baby is in less danger. Your baby may be hooked up to machines which monitor his respiration and heartbeat. Frequent blood tests may be taken. X rays, ultrasound, and CAT scans may be ordered as well.

The first thing you will want is reassurance about your baby's health and prognosis. Unfortunately, this is not always easily given, especially if you had a premature or very small baby. A tiny baby's condition can change radically from day to day, even from hour to hour. You should, however, be kept abreast of every change in your baby's condition and the medical care being given to him or her. Talk with the doctor in charge of the NICU, and get to know the nurses. You are this baby's parent.

The guilt felt by parents of ill babies can be a heavy weight to bear. Most likely, you did nothing to cause your baby's medical problems—whether that problem is prematurity, meconium aspiration, or cleft palate. It is natural to assume you did something wrong and to berate yourself for whatever you believe caused the problem. Speak with the physician in charge of your child, as he or she should be able to reassure you that you were not responsible for your baby's condition. You *are* responsible for helping to make your baby's stay in the NICU as comfortable and loving as possible, however. This may mean long days and nights by your baby's side, offering whatever solace you can, from a gentle stroke to holding, to breastfeeding, if possible, or just being there.

THE LOW-BIRTH-WEIGHT BABY

Babies weighing less than 5 pounds, 8 ounces are low-birth-weight babies. Low-birth-weight babies may be either premature, or on time and growth-retarded. Prematurity is the most common cause of low birth weight. Intrauterine growth retardation (IUGR) is another cause of low-birth-weight babies. IUGR has nothing to do with mental retardation. It is a term used to signify a baby who, for a variety of reasons, was not growing well in utero. An IUGR baby is a very small baby whose birth weight is below the norm for the number of weeks spent in utero. Low birth weight can also be the result of planned early delivery because of the mother's high blood pressure, diabetes, or other pregnancy complication.

Low-birth-weight babies often need monitoring in an intensive care or intermediate care nursery before discharge. They are at risk for a number of possible health problems, from respiratory distress syndrome (RDS) to jaundice. In recent years, we have been able to offer a new treatment to babies at risk for RDS. Using a substance called surfactant (which a full-term baby naturally has), doctors can now help prevent a tiny baby's undeveloped air sacs from collapsing as he breathes. It is this treatment that has brought down death rates so dramatically in the last year or two.

Happily, the outlook for even our tiniest babies is improving all the time. Of course, the smaller the baby, the greater the chances for medical complications. Improvements in the care medical science can offer these babies is also helping to reduce the number of long-term disabilities facing these children on discharge.

THE PREMATURE BABY

A premature baby is defined as any baby born before thirty-seven weeks gestation. Premature babies vary widely in appearance, weight, ability, and maturity. They may experience many medical problems or only a few. A premature baby (born too soon) is different from a baby with IUGR (intrauterine growth retardation). Some babies are both premature and growth retarded, however.

A premature baby looks very different from the full-term baby you were expecting. The abdomen is large, the rib cage visible, the skin transparent. A premature baby does not have fat deposits, so veins often show through the thin skin. A premature baby's genitalia will not yet be well formed. A boy's testicles may not yet have descended into the scrotum, for example.

A premature baby cannot yet act like a full-term baby either. A preemie's organs are immature and this can have the greatest effect on his health. Many preemies are born before their lungs were able to manufacture surfactant, the substance that allows the lung's air sacs

Low Birth Rate
In 1989, 7 percent of all babies born in this country had a low birth weight (under 5.5 pounds). This was the highest number of low-birth-weight babies since 1978.

✛

Learning Problems?
Will a baby who spent time in the NICU have learning problems as he reaches school age? Not necessarily. One study published in *Pediatrics* (March 1992) says that the NICU graduates it tracked (excluding those with sensory or physical impairments) do as well in school as those who came out of normal newborn nurseries. Authors Michael Resnik et al. write, "Our findings . . . suggest that any effect low birth weight and severe neonatal illness may have in early life can be overcome as NICU graduates progress through public school." Factors such as poverty and parents' limited educational backgrounds do have a negative impact on a child's educational progress, however.

Stay in Touch

If you have a premature baby, stay close by. As difficult as it may be to believe with all the nurses and equipment surrounding your child, your presence is extremely important. Studies and clinical experience have shown that babies whose parents are nearby, stroking and if possible holding, will thrive. Babies who do not have this special kind of physical and emotional contact with the same person every day unfortunately are weaker and less able to surmount their medical problems.

Useful Reading

For more information on caring for and coping with prematurity, read *Parenting Your Premature Baby*, by Janine Jason, M.D., and Antonia van der Meer (New York: Delta Books, 1990)

to open and close easily. For this reason, many preemies have trouble breathing and develop RDS (respiratory distress syndrome). Right after delivery, we are now able to give many premature babies the surfactant they need. Surfactant is mixed into the oxygen that the baby breathes in, either by mask or respirator.

The cardiovascular system, brain, and nervous system are also not fully developed and can cause a number of medical problems for the baby. Happily the outlook for these babies is constantly improving, and great strides have been made in the care of premature babies.

MECONIUM ASPIRATION

Meconium is found in the amniotic fluid in 8–15 percent of all deliveries. In 2–6 percent of these cases, meconium aspiration occurs. Meconium aspiration is believed to occur when the infant takes a breath and inhales the meconium-stained fluid into his lungs. Some experts believe that this gasping may occur in utero, and others think it occurs during the first breath of birth. No one really knows why this occurs or whether, in fact, it is always an independent sign of fetal distress. In any case, aspiration of amniotic fluid (whether with meconium or without) can cause significant respiratory problems. Suctioning would be performed at birth in an attempt to pull the fluid out of the baby's nose and airways. The baby would have his lungs X-rayed, and assuming the problem is mild, he may need to spend time in an intensive care nursery in an Isolette, receiving extra oxygen for forty-eight hours or less. In the case of more severe problems, though, a ventilator may be needed and the baby may need oxygen or other treatment for longer than forty-eight hours.

JAUNDICE

Jaundice is related to an immature liver and its inability to break down bilirubin in the blood. Symptomatically, the baby's skin and sometimes the whites of his eyes take on a yellowish cast. Press lightly on your baby's nose with your finger, watching as the skin blanches white and then the color returns. If he's jaundiced, you'll notice the yellow then. Of course, the hospital staff and your pediatrician will be on the lookout for jaundice at all examinations during the first month. A blood test can be done to confirm the diagnosis of jaundice and to gauge its severity. The test will check for the level of bilirubin in your baby's blood. Bilirubin is a colored pigment that is the result of the normal breakdown of red blood cells.

Mild newborn jaundice occurring in the first seven to ten days of life is so common as to be almost normal. It should always be reported to your doctor, however, as serious cases can be dangerous to your baby. Mild jaundice can be managed with frequent feedings to help stimulate bowel movements and lower bilirubin levels. Occasionally, however, the jaundice is more severe, and your doctor may suggest more aggressive treatment, from phototherapy to a forty-eight-hour interruption in breastfeeding (with formula offered instead). If the bilirubin level is deemed to be high, your doctor will take immediate steps to treat the jaundice and reduce the level in your baby's body so that it won't cause any damage to the brain. Your baby will probably be placed under ultraviolet lights. The lights help your baby to break down the pigment and help it to be excreted from the body. Your baby will wear eye patches to protect his eyes from this light. There is some disagreement in the medical community about jaundice, how normal it is, at what levels treatment is necessary, and how aggressively it should be treated. Ask your pediatrician about how decisions are being made regarding your baby's particular case.

Apparently, phototherapy can be used at home as well. Many doctors and parents are excited about the home treatment plan, because it is less disruptive to breastfeeding and family life in general since the baby doesn't need to be in the hospital. Not all pediatricians feel comfortable with this home method, however, and may prefer to be the ones responsible for the treatment. Talk to your pediatrician about it if this interests you and if you think you could handle the responsibility.

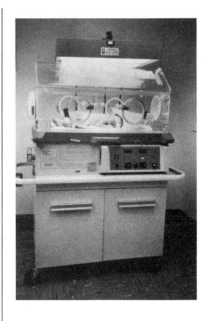

CEREBRAL PALSY

Cerebral palsy is a neuromuscular disorder. Damage to the brain may occur prenatally, at the time of delivery, or immediately after birth. Mild CP may affect a limb on only one side of the body or both arms or both legs. More severe CP can affect almost all muscle use. Muscles may be very stiff (spasticity) or floppy (hypotonia). Although many children with CP have normal intelligence, mental retardation is more common in children with CP. Other possible

CP Resource
For information, educational materials, and referrals, contact the United Cerebral Palsy Association, 66 East 34th Street, New York, NY 10016, (212) 481-6300.

associated problems: epilepsy, vision problems, scoliosis, and hearing loss. Depending on the severity of the CP, a child may be able to overcome the difficulties of this disorder, as he learns to walk, speak, and feed himself. Some of these children can grow up to lead normal lives. Others may have much greater difficulty walking, talking, and controlling bladder and bowel.

CLEFT LIP/CLEFT PALATE

A cleft lip is the separation of the two sides of the lip and possibly the upper gum as well. It appears as a split in the upper lip and gum. Cleft lip ranges from the mild (a slight notch in the lip) to the severe (separation extending up to the nose). It may occur on only one side (unilateral cleft lip) or on both sides (bilateral cleft lip). A cleft palate is an opening in the roof of the mouth. The cleft may involve only part of the palate (incomplete cleft palate) or it may run the entire length of the palate (complete cleft palate). No one really knows what causes cleft palate, but it is believed to be influenced both by genes and by environmental factors. Together, cleft lip and cleft palate make up one of the most common of all birth defects. According to the Cleft Palate Foundation, about 1 out of every 700 to 750 children is born with a cleft lip and/or cleft palate. Some infants with nonsevere cleft lips and soft palates will have little or no trouble feeding. Others, with more severe problems involving the hard palate, may have difficulty creating pressure on a nipple. If you choose to breastfeed, ask for guidance from a knowledgeable pediatrician or lactation nurse. You may be able to successfully breastfeed your baby, especially if your infant has an isolated cleft of the lip or soft palate. Infant nourishment and mother/infant satisfaction with feedings are the most important factors in any feeding decisions. For some, bottle feeding may prove a satisfactory alternative to breastfeeding. There are various nipples that can be used and there is even a dental appliance that can be worn by the baby to take the place of his palate during a feeding. Feeding an infant with cleft palate can call for some creative solutions and a lot of patience. Try various methods and stay in touch with your doctor to find the most comfortable feeding techniques for your family. Whatever method of feeding you choose, it will be a success as long as your baby is getting enough nourishment and the two of you are happy. The baby born with cleft lip and/or palate will need surgery (and additional sur-

Parent Resource
For more information and referrals, contact the American Cleft Palate Craniofacial Association, 1218 Grandview Avenue, Pittsburgh, PA 15211 (1-800-24-CLEFT).

✤

Ear Care
Children with cleft lip and/or palate are at greater risk for ear infections. Make sure they have frequent ear exams and hearing tests.

gery later as he matures), dental work, and possibly speech therapy to correct the problem. You may wish to choose a team of specialists, called a cleft palate/craniofacial team. The team may consist of a plastic surgeon, pediatrician, dentist, speech therapist, otolaryngologist, and more.

CLUBFOOT

Affecting 1 in every 400 children, clubfoot is not a painful condition but it is one that can interfere with walking later if it is not corrected. Clubfeet turn inward or outward. Mild cases can be treated with physical therapy. More difficult cases can be treated with casts, corrective shoes, or rarely, surgery. Good, early treatment provides the best results.

DOWN SYNDROME

Down syndrome is a chromosome disorder typically characterized by strikingly oval-shaped eyes, mental retardation, delayed development, small ears, a large tongue, and short stature. The degree of retardation varies. According to the National Down Syndrome Congress, about 1 in every 800–1,100 children is born with Down syndrome every year. Down syndrome is the result of an extra chromosome that occurs at the time of conception. The exact causes of the chromosome rearrangement are not known, although the likelihood of giving birth to a Down syndrome child increases with maternal age. That being said, however, 80 percent of Down syndrome babies are born to mothers *under* age thirty-five. Many children with Down syndrome go on to lead happy and fulfilling lives. Some, as adults, can live in groups or even independently. Many can be mainstreamed in school. There is a wide variation in abilities among these children. Unfortunately, some will face physical challenges as well—with 30–50 percent being born with heart defects and 8–12 percent having gastrointestinal abnormalities.

Down Syndrome Resource
For more information, write the National Down Syndrome Congress, 1800 Dempster Street, Park Ridge, Illinois 60068-1146 (1-800-232-NDSC).

SPINA BIFIDA MANIFESTA

Occurring in about 1 in every 1,000 births, spina bifida is an incomplete closure of the spinal column, which can be physically disabling. It occurs prenatally when the spinal bones fail to close. As

Spina Bifida Resource
For more information, write the Spina Bifida Association of America, 4590 MacArthur Boulevard, NW, Washington, DC 20007-4226, or call 1-800-621-3141 for information and referrals.

a result, legs may be weak or paralyzed. In the most severe form of spina bifida, known as myelomeningocele, associated problems can include hydrocephalus (excessive fluid around the brain); bowel and bladder control problems; deformities of the hips, knees, and feet; and learning disabilities. Children with spina bifida are usually cared for by a team of specialists, including pediatrician, neurosurgeon, urologists, physical therapists, orthopedic surgeons, and more. Almost all of these children can expect a normal life span.

HEART DEFECT

About 1 in every 175 babies is born each year with a heart defect in the United States. Congenital heart defects may be caused by infections (such as maternal rubella during pregnancy) or by the genes. Surgery may be required to treat the heart defect. Most treatment is quite successful.

CELIAC DISEASE

Characterized by ongoing diarrhea, low appetite, and poor growth, celiac disease can usually be controlled by proper diet. Children with celiac disease are sensitive to gluten, found in wheats and grains. A gluten-free diet must be followed for life. Other treatment may also be necessary.

CYSTIC FIBROSIS

Cystic fibrosis is a genetic disease occurring in about 1 in every 2,500 live births. For a child to get cystic fibrosis, both parents would have to be carriers of the disease. The disease is not usually discovered at birth but is typically diagnosed sometime in the first three years of life. CF involves changes in the glands (especially the sweat glands and glandular cells in the lungs and pancreas). Children with CF have excessive amounts of salt in their sweat. If CF is suspected, the amount of salt in the sweat would be tested. CF causes the production of thick mucus in the lungs. This can result in more coughs, possible pneumonia, and progressive loss of lung function. Sometimes children with CF also have trouble digesting food, grow more slowly, and do not gain weight easily, owing to a blockage in the

Cystic Fibrosis Resource
For more information, write the Cystic Fibrosis Foundation, 6931 Arlington Road, Bethesda, MD 20814, or call 1-800-344-4823.

pancreatic ducts. Life expectancy is shorter than average, but children with CF now live much longer than was possible before. Over the past 25 years, life expectancy has jumped from 7.5 years to 27.6 years and can be higher with effective treatment. For now, treatment depends on how far the disease has progressed and which organs are affected. Soon there may actually be a cure. The CF gene was discovered in 1989, and in laboratory tests, copies of the normal gene corrected defective CF cells. This new gene transfer therapy should lead to a cure soon.

SICKLE CELL ANEMIA

Both parents must be carriers in order for a child to get sickle cell anemia. It is more common in children of black African descent, although it is also found in whites of Middle Eastern or Mediterranean descent. In sickle cell anemia, the red blood cells are abnormal and are not able to function properly. Symptoms may include unexplained fever and swelling of the hands and feet, increased susceptibility to infection, fatigue, and shortness of breath. Symptoms can be treated but there is currently no cure. Sadly, the life expectancy of children with sickle cell anemia is much shorter than normal.

TAY-SACHS DISEASE

A serious and fatal disease, Tay-Sachs usually strikes babies of Central and Eastern European Jewish descent. Both parents must carry the gene in order for the child to get the disease. Babies with Tay-Sachs can appear normal at birth only to later regress, with most sufferers dying by age three or four. The disease interferes with the body's ability to break down fat deposits in the brain and nerve cells, clogging and eventually causing the nervous system to shut down.

THALASSEMIA

Most commonly found in children of Greek or Italian descent, thalassemia is a type of anemia. Cases can range from the mild to the severe. Children appear pale and listless, with increased susceptibility to infection and slowed growth. Those with mild forms of the disease are likely to live normal lives with few or no symptoms. Those with moderate to severe problems may require frequent blood transfusion and possible bone marrow transplants. In severe cases, life span is not expected to exceed the teens or twenties.

PYLORIC STENOSIS

Spitting up is common in infants and is not a sign of a problem. Frequent, forceful vomiting, however, should be brought to the attention of your pediatrician. It may be a sign of pyloric stenosis, a condition in which the muscle at the stomach exit thickens and prevents food from passing out of the stomach into the intestines. Surgery is usually recommended to correct the problem.

INGUINAL HERNIA

You or your pediatrician may notice a small lump or bulge in your baby's groin area, a typical sign of hernia. A hernia occurs when part of the intestine slips through a hole in the abdominal wall. Normally, this hole would have closed before birth. Hernias are more common in boys than girls. Your pediatrician will examine the hernia and let you know whether and when surgery might be necessary to correct it. Sometimes, emergency surgery is necessary.

UNDESCENDED TESTICLES

About 3 to 4 percent of the time, boys are born with undescended testicles. This is more common in premature babies. Undescended testicles will descend by themselves over the period of the first three months to a year. If they have still not descended after a year or more, surgery would be recommended to correct the problem. In most cases, no one knows what causes undescended testicles. Some factors that can contribute to it, however, include prematurity, hormonal problems, or physical blockage.

HYDROCELE

Some boys have extra fluid around the testes in the scrotum and the testes appear unusually large. This is known as a hydrocele and will usually correct itself. Although it may look uncomfortable, it apparently does not bother the baby. Some of those babies with hydroceles, however, may have an underlying hernia. Your pediatrician will be able to determine whether your son has a hydrocele or a hernia.

EMERGENCY ROOMS

Each year, 80 million visits are made to this country's emergency rooms. Children account for one third of these visits. Most emergency rooms are general emergency departments, giving medical attention to all age groups. Some hospitals, however, now have separate pediatric emergency departments. These are usually staffed by pediatric emergency specialists, pediatricians, and pediatric residents.

Emergency Room Visits
Injury and fever are among the most common reasons for a visit to the emergency room. Injuries appear to be more prevalent in the summer and fall. Emergency room visits for earaches are more likely to occur in the fall and more likely to be an evening or nighttime complaint, according to one study of emergency departments.

PART II
✦ Your Body ✦

✤ Introduction ✤

You're a mother now, eager to concentrate on the needs of your baby. But you are still a woman with a body that makes its own demands and needs attention. The postbaby body you look at now in the mirror has served you well and you need to treat it with the respect it deserves. That means good attention to nutrition and exercise, two topics that will be covered here. This part will also guide you through the first twenty-four hours following the baby's birth, tell you what you can expect by the six-week checkup, address your most common postpartum concerns, and explore your new body image and your sex life and contraceptive needs. The part ends with a chapter on your feelings: from baby blues to energy levels and moods.

CHAPTER 20

✦ You: The First Twenty-four Hours ✦

While you are busy getting to know your new baby during the first twenty-four hours after delivery, you are also coming to terms with your new role as parent, both physically and emotionally. Luckily, nature has designed things so that you are in pretty good shape right after birth. This makes sense since your job now is to care for a needy, dependent newborn. You may feel especially energetic right after having a baby, surprising after all the hard work but a nice benefit, and one that helps you to enjoy your new baby right away. There are some changes which are taking place in your body, and some things which may worry you during the first twenty-four hours, especially if there has been some medical intervention in your delivery (such as an episiotomy, catheter placement, epidural, cesarean, etc.). Here are some of the changes and concerns you may encounter in those early hours after giving birth:

✦ ✦ ✦

DELIVERY REPAIR

While you are still on the delivery table or in the delivery bed, your doctor or midwife will inspect your perineum for any damage caused by an episiotomy or natural tearing. The perineum is the area between the vagina and the rectum. Sometimes, this area is cut by the doctor to make room for the baby's head at birth. Other times, the area tears a little on its own as the baby exits the vagina. It is also possible that the perineum stretches to accommodate the birth of the baby and does not tear at all.

If you had an episiotomy, you will be stitched. If you had a birth without an episiotomy, you may not need any repair. If there was some tearing, however, your doctor or midwife will repair it. With the exciting part over and the baby in your arms, this can seem to take

Four Degrees of Tears

First-degree: Just the surface is nicked. A first-degree tear may or may not demand repair.

Second-degree: The lining and a little bit of the connective tissue underneath has torn. Stitches are advised.

Third-degree: This is a tear that has extended to the sphincter (the round muscle) in the rectum.

Fourth-degree: This is the most serious tear, one that has extended clear through into the rectum.

forever! You're anxious to get back to your room, spend time with your baby, and call all your relatives and friends! It's not necessarily that you need so many stitches. It's just that stitching in this area takes time and patience. The doctor or midwife is working to make sure that the perineal area is the same *after* the cut or tear as it was before. You should not feel any pain during the stitching, assuming you have been given a local anesthetic. If you already had an epidural, of course, extra anesthesia is not necessary.

All cuts and tears can be repaired. Obviously, some are more difficult to stitch and will take much longer to recover from. If you have had a serious tear (see sidebar), you will want to get as much information as you can about the recovery process. You will also want to discuss your feelings: after such trauma to the area, you may be naturally apprehensive about everything from toileting to your sex life. Even though damage to the perineum and repair are common, this is probably the first time it has happened to *your* body. You have a right to your feelings and questions. For more information, see perineal swelling (page 208) and healing of episiotomy or tear (pages 213–214).

CESAREAN SECTION REPAIR

In an emergency, the cut can be made and your baby can be out within minutes. Repair can take a lot longer. Remember: Many layers were cut to arrive at the baby, and they all need to be sewn back together. Both the skin and the uterus have been cut to get your baby out. Repair can take fifteen to forty minutes.

The type of incision your doctor made and the stitches used depend on decisions he or she made at the time of the birth. You may have absorbable stitches or stitches that need to be removed. Your doctor may have used surgical clamps instead of stitches or surgical steel staples to close the wound. The uterine incision may be vertical or horizontal. Most doctors prefer the transverse (horizontal) incision because this will allow the greatest possibility of a safe vaginal delivery next time.

Many women have an epidural (a regional anesthetic) for the cesarean delivery. In the first one to two hours afterward, your legs may still be numb. As the feeling returns, you may notice an uncomfortable tingling. It can take several hours for you to regain full control of your legs and move them. If you had general anesthesia, you may feel a little confused, drowsy, and disoriented on waking up.

Once the initial anesthetic effects wear off, you will begin to feel the pain of the incision. Nurses will check the incision, as well as take your blood pressure and temperature often during the early hours. They will also check to make sure your uterus is contracting as it should be. You will be bleeding vaginally, just as you would after a vaginal delivery. This is the uterus shedding the lining it no longer needs.

Assuming all is well with your newborn, you can ask to have your baby with you in the recovery room. This may not be possible if doctors are checking on the baby's vital signs and condition, especially if the operation was due to some type of fetal distress or other medical problem. If the baby cannot be with you, usually the father is allowed to accompany the baby to the nursery for the checkup. If you had general anesthesia, you will be shown the baby, but it is unlikely that you will be allowed to hold or have the baby with you until you are completely awake and the effects of the anesthesia have worn off.

With an epidural, you will be in better shape to hold your baby immediately after the operation. If possible, you may ask to breast-feed your new baby before the effects of the regional anesthetic have worn off. This can help you to start breastfeeding in a more relaxed manner without the additional discomfort of a sore incision, which can make you tense up as you go to feed your baby.

As soon as permissible after the operation, you should try to get up and move around with help. Even before you get up, you can do an early exercise while still in bed: flex and point your toes. Moving around will help you to recover faster and helps to prevent possible postoperative complications such as phlebitis. It also gets you breathing more deeply. A nurse will help you to walk around sometime within the first twenty-four hours. This can be an unpleasant experience, but it is better done now than later, as it only gets harder to move the longer you put it off. Walking encourages healing as it improves circulation and gets your body back in working order.

For more information on continued cesarean recovery over the first six weeks, see page 215.

URINARY CATHETER USE AND REMOVAL

If you had an epidural or a cesarean, you may have a urinary catheter in place. The urinary catheter is placed prior to surgery to

A Doctor's Thoughts

"The mother coming out of general anesthesia may be somewhat disoriented. Still, her first question is usually about the baby. As a matter of course, I always tell her as soon as she can hear us, 'Everything's fine. We're finished. You had a beautiful baby.' It's natural to be a little frightened, so I try to reassure her right away that everything's okay."—Dr. Susanne L. Bathgate, Assistant Professor of Obstetrics and Gynecology, The George Washington University

Pillow Talk

When you have to move, talk, cough, or breathe deeply, your incision can bother you most. Yet all these things are important for your speedy recovery. One tip: Place a soft pillow (or folded towel) against your incision and apply light pressure when you have to move or breathe deeply. This can lessen the discomfort.

Deep Breathing
Following a cesarean, it is important to try to breathe deeply. Unfortunately, taking deep breaths can be uncomfortable so your tendency is to avoid doing so. If you don't breathe deeply enough, your lungs won't fully inflate and you run the risk of contracting pneumonia. Try concentrating on deep breathing. Some hospitals may offer you an incentive spirometer to help you get started. You breathe into a tube and deep breaths cause the Ping-Pong balls in the apparatus to move up and down. Breathing more deeply causes even more motion of the balls.

✦

Good News
Usually, by the third day, most cesarean section patients need only a little Tylenol to help them cope with the postoperative discomforts.

empty your bladder and prevent damage to it. A catheter is often used with an epidural because the drug causes you to lose feeling from the waist down, including the urge to urinate. The catheter will probably remain in place for the first twelve to twenty-four hours after the birth. It is left in place after the surgery or epidural because the bladder may not be able to resume normal function right away. If you want to get up and walk around before it is removed, you can carry the catheter bag with you. In most cases, however, by the time you are ready to get up and walk, the catheter has been removed.

Sometimes, the catheter was not used during the delivery but may be necessary after the birth if you are having a lot of trouble emptying your bladder. See the section on urinating, page 209.

Occasionally, catheterization can result in a urinary tract infection. If this happens, you will be treated for it with antibiotics and/or other drugs.

POSTPARTUM PAINKILLERS

Following a normal, vaginal delivery, it is unlikely that you will feel much pain or need any painkillers. A cesarean is another matter. Once the anesthetic used for the operation wears off, you will feel it! You will be offered painkillers during the first twenty-four hours following a cesarean. Since everyone's pain tolerance and recovery time are different, your doctor may prescribe painkillers past the first twenty-four hours as well. Try to move around while you are still under the effects of the painkiller. Ask your doctor whether breast-feeding is advisable while you are taking the painkiller he has prescribed for you. Usually, it presents no problem.

INTRAVENOUS OXYTOCIN

Even if you made it through the entire labor and delivery without a single drug, you may need one now. Right after birth, your doctor needs to make sure that your uterine contractions are sufficient to slow the flow of blood from your uterus. A nurse or your practitioner may massage the uterus to stimulate contractions, and to check on the state of the uterus. Your baby will be put to your breast, as nursing can also stimulate contractions. But often, this is not enough, and many practitioners will give some intravenous oxytocin to new mothers in the first twelve hours after delivery. You may be given the drug by an intramuscular shot or through an IV drip. If you were already on an IV, this will just be added to the drip. The bag is usually attached to a stand on rollers next to your bed. If you need to get up to go to the bathroom, the nursery, or take a walk down the hall, you'll have to take this with you. It will likely be removed after about twelve hours or sooner. The goal is to prevent the rare occurrence of a postpartum hemorrhage, which can be life-threatening.

HUNGER

One of the first things you'll do with relish after the delivery is eat. This is one meal you've earned! You may be very hungry in the first twenty-four hours after delivery. This is a natural reaction to hours of labor and delivery, probably spent with no food or drink. Unfortunately, you may have a wait before the next scheduled meal is served if you delivered in a hospital. If you delivered at home or in a birthing center, of course, you can have your meal when you want it. If you don't think you can wait until tomorrow morning when breakfast will be served, a loved one may be able to run out to an all-night coffee shop and bring you back something to eat. Now is the time to refuel, so don't be shy about cleaning your plate.

Now that you're a mom (and possibly a breastfeeding mom, at that), you'll want to be as careful about your diet as you were when you were pregnant. Choose fresh (not processed) foods from all the major food groups. Continue to take your prenatal vitamins if your doctor so prescribes. During the early days, opt for as many fresh vegetables, fresh fruits, and high-fiber foods as you can, to help you avoid constipation. Since hospital foods are notoriously poor and may include very little fiber, you might want to ask your partner to bring in some more appropriate foods. He may bring in some fresh fruit or vegetables for you. A sprinkle of bran over some of the hospital foods can also help. (Do not do this if you are recovering from a cesarean. See below.)

EATING AFTER A CESAREAN

Your doctor will leave instructions about what and when you should be fed. Often, the first meal is a liquid one. Early meals may consist of soft mashed foods, which are easier on your postoperative digestive system. Gas pains are a common postoperative complaint.

Abdominal Massage
If you feel comfortable doing so, you can massage the uterus yourself. Rub your lower abdomen. This can help to expel clots and lessen bleeding.

Here's to You
Toast your new baby with a tall glass of water or milk! New mothers, especially if they're breastfeeding, need plenty of liquids. Be sure to wash down everything you eat with plenty of water, milk, and/or juice. The liquids will also help to keep constipation at bay.

To minimize the problem, try to move early and often. Avoid eating foods that might cause gas.

AFTERPAINS

Even though labor and delivery are over, some uterine contractions continue. They may be more or less noticeable to you. Women who have already had a child may find that they are stronger, although this is not always the case. The afterpains tend to be more noticeable while you are nursing because the baby's sucking at the breast causes the hormone oxytocin to be released, the driving force behind uterine contractions. Although they may be mildly to somewhat uncomfortable, they are a sign that your uterus is doing what it needs to do. Afterpains are noticeable only for the first few days to a week. Many mothers probably won't even notice these contractions. Don't worry, it doesn't mean your uterus isn't working just as hard.

THE DELIVERY IN RETROSPECT

Now that it's all over, you have time to look back over the delivery and think about how it all went. It's natural to replay parts over in your mind, just like an athlete might after a big sporting event. You may have been surprised by some things, disappointed by others. Maybe you didn't get the doctor you had hoped for because he wasn't on call last night. Maybe you didn't get to use the birthing room. Maybe you're wondering why you had to push for two hours, or the reasons behind a certain procedure or test. Maybe you'd like some feedback on how the delivery went. When your doctor or midwife comes back to see you on rounds, this is the time to ask questions about the delivery. For example, you may want to find out why the doctor decided he had to use forceps, or what it meant when the nurse noticed meconium staining in your waters. Whatever is still on your mind about the delivery is worth bringing up, not in a confrontational way, but as a way of putting your mind at ease. Of course, most important, you can now lie back and at least feel good about what that delivery ultimately produced: a beautiful little baby and a mother with the energy and good health to enjoy him.

A Mother's Reflections

"I felt it was pretty unfair . . . after hours and hours of contractions, it's finally all over, and then I breastfeed my baby and feel more contractions! Granted they're not so intense, but I thought to myself, 'I'm too tired for this now!' Luckily, the contractions I felt when I breastfed disappeared within a day or two."

HOSPITAL NECESSITIES

Hopefully, you packed a bag in advance and came to the hospital with it in hand. If not, send someone home now with the following list of items you'll need:

- Two nightgowns with button fronts or pleated slits for nursing or a pajama set with separate bottoms and top (also easy for nursing)
- A bathrobe
- A loose-fitting track suit or sweats for "dress-up" during visitor hours
- A pair of socks or slippers for cold hospital floors
- Two to three pairs of underpants
- Two nursing bras
- Toiletries (toothbrush, toothpaste, shampoo, perfume, deodorant)
- Hairbrush
- Blow-dryer
- Money (for gift shop items like newspapers, gum)
- Loose-fitting going-home outfit for you
- A travel clock
- Your address/telephone book

A Note
As your room fills up with presents and flowers from visitors, you may want to start sending some of it home with a family member. Or why not pass some of the flowers along to the nurses on the floor who've been especially nice and attentive? They might appreciate the gesture and it'll make your load a lot lighter when you leave.

A Brief Stay
In the 1940s, women stayed in the hospital for seven to ten days after having a baby. Today, the average stay is only twenty-four to forty-eight hours following an uncomplicated delivery! Among other factors influencing this shift, insurance companies have been encouraging hospitals to discharge healthy women early to help cut medical care costs.

- A baby care manual like this one
- A pillow from your bed at home
- Going-home outfit for baby
- A baby car seat (see page 11) for the trip home
- A baby name book (if you're still deciding)

LOCHIA (BLEEDING AFTER BIRTH)

Lochia is the medical term for the afterbirth bleeding you will experience. The bleeding begins immediately after birth, so the hospital or birthing center will give you extra-large sanitary napkins to use. Lochia is actually a combination of tissue, mucus, and blood from your uterus—the leftovers of a successful pregnancy. Bleeding can be fairly heavy at times and you may notice a sudden surge or even a clot of blood when you get up after lying down. This occurs because the blood pools while you are lying down and then is discharged when you change positions. Seeing a clot of blood pass is not unusual and should be no cause for concern. During the first twenty-four hours, this bleeding will be quite red and fairly heavy. Over the coming days and weeks, it will change in color from bright red to pink to brown. Expect the lochia to continue for four to six weeks. During this time, take things slowly and give your body a chance to go through the healing process.

PERINEAL SWELLING

Even without an episiotomy or tear, your perineum will likely be sore or swollen. The stretching and battering it takes may cause some mild to moderate afterbirth discomfort. With a tear or episiotomy, your perineum will be especially sensitive. How much discomfort you feel will depend on the severity of the cut. The nicest thing you can do is to apply an ice pack to the area in the first eight hours after birth. Ask the nurse to get you some. The sooner you start applying ice, the greater the chance of keeping the swelling down. When the first bag melts, ask for more, or find out where you can go to get your own refills. Ten minutes with the ice pack on, followed by fifteen minutes with it off, is a good schedule to follow in the first few hours after delivery. Sometimes, a topical anesthetic can also be prescribed. Talk with your caregiver if you think you need something. Your own urine can sting the perineum the first few times you go to the bathroom after delivery. Urine is an irritant. Use a squeeze bottle to pour warm water over the area after you urinate. Pat the area dry afterward, or use a blow-dryer to dry the area. (Do not aim directly at the vagina.)

GETTING OUT OF BED

Hospital beds are sometimes high off the floor, making it hard for new mothers (especially those with stitches) to climb in and out of bed. Luckily, hospital beds are adjustable. Ask the nurse to show you how to lower the bed to make it easier for you to get in and out. If it's still too high, see if you can requisition a stool to keep near the side of the bed. If your doctor or midwife needs to raise the bed for an examination, he or she can do so at that time.

URINATING

It's important to try to urinate as soon after giving birth as you can. Any toileting can be a little scary in the first few hours after delivery, but going to the bathroom is perfectly safe. Urinating soon after birth (within six hours) will help ensure the return to normal bladder function and decrease the chance of a urinary tract infection. Because you may have just spent hours without food or drink, it's a good idea to have some liquid refreshment as soon after birth as possible. If you're dehydrated, you won't have any fluid to excrete. Running the faucet in the bathroom can help you focus on the urge to urinate. Alleviate the possible sting of urine by using a squeeze bottle of water, as mentioned earlier. If you have to use a bedpan, urinating can be psychologically difficult. One trick: If possible, sit up on it as you would on a toilet, close your eyes, and try to imagine you are in the bathroom, not in bed.

If you had an epidural or other drug at birth, you may find urinating more difficult. (See urinary catheter use and removal, pages 203–204.) The drug may interfere with the normal signals that tell you your bladder is full and send you to the toilet. If drinking liquids and running water don't do the trick after eight hours, you may have to be catheterized. A catheter is a thin tube which is inserted into the urethra and empties the bladder of urine.

Keeping Clean and Dry
With all the bleeding in the first week, it can be hard to feel clean and fresh. Keep clean with frequent showers, and the use of a peri bottle (plastic bottle with nozzle used for cleaning after toileting). If you've had an episiotomy or tear repaired, when in the shower, bend over to allow the warm water to run over your stitches. Dry gently, but well, when you get out. Hospitals use Chux pads (disposable pads with blue plastic backing) to protect the sheets as you lie in bed. Ask if you can take a few home with you for the same reason.

A Soothing Wipe
Wiping the vaginal area with a premoistened towelette like Tucks (which contains witch hazel) can help reduce the minor itching, burning, and irritation you may experience as a result of your stitches.

A Mother's Reflections
"The thought of possible urinary catheterization was enough to make me go to the toilet right away. There was no way I wanted any more things done to me!"

THE FIRST BOWEL MOVEMENT

Perhaps more frightening than getting up to urinate is the first bowel movement. The idea of pushing again after all you've been through can be daunting, to say the least. Combine this with mainly unfounded fears that your stitches will rip and the pressure put on you by nurses who constantly ask if you've gone yet, and you can see why the first bowel movement becomes such a momentous occasion. Don't worry about your stitches. They will not rip from using the toilet. (If you had a fourth-degree tear that extended through the rectum, you may have some special problems. Talk with the nurses and your doctor for ideas on how to make the first bowel movement easier.)

In general, stay relaxed, eat plenty of fibrous foods, and drink lots of liquid. Do not, in fear, hold in your stool or it will become harder to pass. Some hospitals offer stool softeners (in the form of a pill) to make the first bowel movement easier. Once you've accomplished this, you're in the clear, and subsequent movements will not appear so daunting.

CHAPTER 21

Continued Postpartum Recovery:
✦ The First Six Weeks ✦

Your baby needs a lot of attention right now. But so do you. Neglecting yourself will not benefit your baby or the rest of your family. Once the cord was cut, you took on a new and very demanding role: that of parent, with all the worries and responsibilities connected to it. Physically, your body not only must work to provide for your newborn but also to return itself to a prepregnant state, a process known as involution. Your body's job right now involves healing itself while catering to the physical needs of the baby. It may sound like a tough assignment, but happily, this is what your body was made to do. This chapter will cover your postpartum recovery, from the healing of an episiotomy to bathing and more.

✛   ✛   ✛

UTERINE INVOLUTION

Your uterus will slowly shrink over the first six weeks until it returns to its prepregnancy size. Your body will shed water weight and extra pounds. Lochia (vaginal discharge that looks like blood) will continue for 4–6 weeks. Although your body does all these things on its own, you can help the recovery process by resting when you can, eating well, and beginning a few safe, moderate exercises (see page 231).

The Nonpregnant Uterus
Over these six weeks, your uterus will shrink from its pregnant high of 11 × 9½ × 8½ inches to its prepregnant size of only about 3 × 2 × 1 inches.

HEALING OF EPISIOTOMY OR TEAR

Once you leave the hospital, make sure you continue to take care of yourself. Keep the site of the episiotomy or tear clean—with the help of a squeeze bottle of water, which can be used after toileting, and plenty of warm showers. Always pat dry afterward.

Stair Master

Until your stitches have been absorbed or removed, take it easy on the stairs. If possible, try to pack up and spend the day on one floor rather than going up and down all day. Use a bassinet for the baby to sleep in downstairs and have a supply of diapers and clothing changes with you too.

If you've had stitches, exposing the area to the air also helps. Lie on a large Chux pad and let air get to the area. You might even direct the light of an ordinary lamp toward the perineal area to help warm and dry the area. A sitz bath can also promote healing (see below). Kegel exercises should be begun again soon after delivery to increase circulation to the perineal area (see below). You may find them pretty difficult to do in the first week after birth, but by the end of the first month, you may be able to work up to twenty a day.

SITZ BATHS

When you were in the hospital, you may have been introduced to the sitz bath, a plastic basin that you fill with warm water and put on top of the toilet. With a bag of water hung above it, the sitz bath swirls warm water over the perineum, increasing circulation and helping the area to heal. Usually, the hospital will let you take the sitz bath home with you when you leave. Use it every day once you are at home.

PELVIC FLOOR EXERCISES

The pelvic floor is a strong sling of muscles that you count on to support your uterus, fallopian tubes, ovaries, bladder, and rectum. Pelvic floor exercises, known as Kegels, can be done after the birth to help these muscles regain their strength and improve their tone. This can, in turn, help you to avoid problems of urine leaking out and, some say, help to improve your sex life. To do, simply contract, or squeeze, the muscles of the vagina tight and try to hold it a few seconds, then release. To find the right muscles and to get the hang of the exercise, try to stop the flow of urine and start it again while you are on the toilet.

Even if you were doing these exercises during the pregnancy, you may find it hard to do them in the early weeks after delivery. Keep trying. Muscle tone will return. Speak with your caregiver to find out how many you should be doing a day. Depending on the condition of your muscles, you may be advised to do 20–100 or more a day. This sounds like an enormous amount, but they can be done while you are watching TV, reading, talking on the phone. You do not need to take time out of your day to do Kegels, but you do need to remember to work on them.

RECOVERY FROM CESAREAN

The cesarean, because it is surgery, involves a longer recovery period than a normal vaginal delivery. (For information on the first twenty-four hours following a cesarean, see pages 202–203.) You may be asked to stay in the hospital for 3–10 days following the birth. How quickly you recuperate and how uncomfortable you find the first few postoperative days depend on the circumstances surrounding your particular delivery. No two women will have the same recuperative powers or the same tolerance for physical discomfort.

With stitches or clamps in place and a wound healing, the little things can become difficult. Just getting up and moving around, or sitting down to breastfeed, can be painful. To breastfeed, try lying on your side with the baby next to you. This method allows you to feed without any pressure on the site of the incision. When you have finished feeding from that side, hold the baby to your chest and roll to the other side. Or, if rolling seems too hard, allow baby access to the other breast by leaning farther over baby until it reaches him. If you can sit up comfortably with some pillows behind your back, the football hold also works well because it keeps pressure off the incision. (See pages 164–165.)

Once at home, you'll need to avoid climbing stairs, lifting heavy things, or doing housework. Rest as often as you can. Ask for help and take it when it is offered.

BATHING

During the first six weeks following the birth, you may be advised to shower rather than bathe. The uterus needs a full six weeks to fully close and return to its prepregnancy size and shape. Until the cervix fully closes, it's possible that bathing could lead to an infection. Other practitioners dismiss this as highly unlikely and allow baths. A sitz bath, however, is encouraged by both camps. (See page 214.)

POSTPARTUM CHECKUP

You will be asked to return to see your physician or midwife six weeks after the birth of your baby. If you had a cesarean, you will probably be asked to come in at three weeks, also, so that your incision can be looked at. The postpartum checkup is scheduled to

---

Questions You May Want to Ask at the Postpartum Checkup

1. Has the episiotomy or tear site healed the way it was supposed to? (If you have used a mirror to look at the site, and have any specific questions about the healing, ask now.)

2. If you had a bad tear, you might also ask: Do you have any tips on how to make the first postpartum sexual experience any easier?

3. When can I expect to lose the rest of my weight gain?

4. How can I get relief from my hemorrhoids/varicose veins/other problems?

5. What would be the best form of birth control for me to use now?

6. If you have been feeling depressed, you might ask, "Why have I been feeling so miserable and what can I do about it?"

7. Jot down any other questions on your mind so you don't forget to bring up the topic with your doctor.

ensure that you have both healed physically from the birth and are coping emotionally with your new baby. You will be given an internal exam to determine if the cervix is closed. Your abdomen will be palpated to determine if the uterus has returned to its prepregnancy size. If you had an episiotomy or if you tore and had stitches, the external genitalia will also be checked to make sure they have healed. If you had a cesarean, the site of your incision will be examined. Your weight will be recorded and your blood pressure will be taken. You will probably be given the green light for resuming sexual relationships, and birth control will be discussed. See the section on postpartum sex (pages 237–238) and contraception (page 238) for more information.

MENSTRUATION

Throughout most of the time you are breastfeeding, you will probably not get your period. At some point during the first year, it will probably return even if you are still breastfeeding. Occasionally, women do not get a period again until they stop breastfeeding. The return of menstruation should have no effect on your milk or your baby's penchant for it. If you are not breastfeeding, you may get your period at any time, although usually not before a few months have passed.

Breastfeeding is not considered an acceptable form of birth control in the United States. Even though you might not be menstruating, there is still a chance that you can get pregnant. If you are trying to avoid pregnancy at this time, see pages 238–248 for information on forms of contraception.

CHAPTER 22

Your Most Common
✦ Postpartum Concerns ✦

Being a new mother is a fantastic experience, but your transformation to parent doesn't always come without a price. You won't feel like the winner of the lottery every day. Some days you will find you barely have enough energy to get to the grocery store, or you may find yourself suffering from a bad back or sore nipples or other spoilers of parenting enjoyment. Your body is going through some changes right now that make these ups and downs understandable. This chapter covers some of the physical changes and common problems in the early months that may be of concern to you, from backaches and fatigue to leaky breasts.

✦ ✦ ✦

BACKACHE

You thought you had it tough during your pregnancy, but now that you're carrying that little bundle of joy around on the outside, backache can still be a problem. Breastfeeding without proper back support can add to your troubles. Always sit in a chair with a back when you breastfeed. Lean back against the chair and insert a pillow for extra support at the base of your back. If possible, put your feet up on a stool while you feed. Use an extra pillow under the baby or under your arm to get the baby to the breast comfortably. Relax your shoulders. Don't hunch up or slouch during the feedings. Continue to bend and lift items using your legs, not your back, just as you were instructed to do during pregnancy. Remain aware of your posture: shoulders down and relaxed, arms at your sides, pelvis tucked under. Poor posture will stress your back muscles. Take warm baths and ask your partner for back rubs. After all, motherhood is hard work and you deserve a few perks.

Eliminate back and shoulder stress by breastfeeding with a pillow behind you and feet up on a low stool. For added comfort, bring the baby closer to you by placing a pillow under him as well.

HAIR LOSS

Hair loss following pregnancy and childbirth is very common. Happily, it is only a temporary problem. Hair, which was in a state of rapid growth during pregnancy, begins to fall out about two to four months after delivery. Estrogen and other pregnancy-related hormones are declining and your body is returning to its prepregnant state, causing hair to enter a resting state. This can cause hair to fall out in substantial amounts. Do not be concerned. The overall appearance of your hair usually will not change, as new hair had been growing in to replace the old. Just expect a lot of drain cleaning after shampoos! A small number of women, however, may actually feel that the appearance of their hair has changed—with sparse hair around the hairline and crown area. A little mousse or a change of hairstyle (sweeping up from the sides and piling on top, for example) can help to conceal the sparser areas.

A Mother's Reflections
"I went to have my hair done and the hairdresser actually asked me if I was on some kind of drug because so much of my hair fell out during the shampoo."

URINARY INCONTINENCE

Many women experience some urine leakage during pregnancy when the baby is pressing on the bladder. Why does this problem persist for some even after the baby is out? Having one or more babies can weaken the muscle tone unless you work to regain it.

Kegel exercises strengthen the muscles in the vaginal wall and help support the urethra and bladder, usually eliminating the problem of urinary incontinence. See the section on Kegel exercises on page 214 to find out how to do them.

FREQUENT URINATION

During the early weeks following the birth, the body has a lot of extra fluids to get rid of. Many women find that they are in and out of the bathroom, just as they were during the pregnancy. This will not last long. As soon as the body has, through perspiration and urination, lost its extra water weight, all should be back to normal. Frequent urination can irritate the sensitive perineal tissues right now, however. Be sure to drink plenty of water to dilute the strength of your urine. A squeeze bottle that sends a spray of warm water over the area after toileting also helps.

FATIGUE

Although it may not be so bad as anything you experienced during the first trimester of pregnancy, motherhood can be pretty tiring. You're not getting much sleep, your body is still recovering physically, and you're using up any extra energy you have worrying about how many minutes have lapsed since the last feeding. Luckily, newborns sleep a lot more than you realize. Whenever your baby naps, you must as well. Even if you are not a natural napper, at least lie down. It can be tempting to use the time to do chores, such as writing thank-you letters or folding baby clothes, but these are things that can be done (albeit not so quickly or efficiently) when baby is awake. It may also make sense to defer as much responsibility for non-baby work as possible—leaving all the laundry for your partner, or postponing thank-you notes for a few weeks.

COMMON COLD

Unfortunately, the common cold even dares to strike new mothers. Whether you're breastfeeding or bottle feeding, you may be more worried about whether your baby will get sick than you are about yourself. Can you continue to hold and feed your baby when you have a cold? Yes. Be sure, however, to wash your hands with soap and water before handling the baby and turn away to cough or

Quotable Quote
"Life is one long process of getting tired."—Samuel Butler, nineteenth-century British novelist and essayist

Medical Questions
Your doctor is the best source of information regarding which drugs are contraindicated during lactation.

sneeze. If you are breastfeeding, you can also feel better knowing that your milk protects your newborn against germs. You should continue to take precautions, however, by keeping your baby away from people with colds.

If you have a serious infection or need to be hospitalized, speak with your doctors about the advisability of continued breastfeeding. Also, if your doctor suggests any medication, make sure he knows if you are breastfeeding. He may want to change or cancel the drug he has in mind. Or in the case of a necessary drug, you may have to stop breastfeeding.

PIGMENTATION

Some of the dark patches you may have gotten during pregnancy should begin to fade now. The linea nigra, the dark line that ran down your abdomen, should also lighten and fade in the weeks following the delivery. Some mothers complain of continued difficulty with their skin during breastfeeding. Take special care in the sun to use a sunblock. The sun can make brown patches even darker.

SKIN BREAKOUTS

Between the changes in your hormones and the demands of caring for a newborn, you may suddenly be facing a breakout. Stress is a major cause of adult acne. To treat mild cases (a few pimples or blackheads), wash your face daily with a mild cleanser. Try to reduce the stress in your life (always easier said than done) by getting more help with the baby, joining a new mothers' exercise program, taking naps when the baby does during the day, and so on. If your acne is severe, see a dermatologist for advice.

HEMORRHOIDS

Hemorrhoids can strike during or right after pregnancy. They often appear in the last trimester of pregnancy, although sometimes they appear for the first time in the immediate postpartum period.

They are varicose veins of the anus. They can ache, cause pain, itch or burn, or even bleed, none of which leads to good feelings in the early days of motherhood. To minimize the discomfort, stick to a healthful diet (see pages 226–229) to help lessen the chances of constipation. Straining on the toilet can make hemorrhoids worse. Warm sitz baths can provide some relief as can ice packs for some women. Rest on your side and stay off your feet as much as possible. Usually, nothing more has to be done and hemorrhoids will go away on their own. If your problem persists, however, or worsens, speak with your doctor.

LEAKY BREASTS

Unless you're out in public, there's really no reason to worry about leaky breasts. After a few weeks, milk production will better match your baby's eating habits and breasts will stop overflowing. For now, let nipples air-dry whenever possible. Covering nipples up can trap wetness in, making it more likely for slightly cracked nipples to get infected. When going out, many women use breast pads tucked into their bras to absorb wetness. Just be sure to change these frequently so that bacteria doesn't get a chance to breed. It's also a good idea to try to time your outings so that breasts don't become overfull while you're out. Try to go out right after a feeding, when breasts are empty and less likely to leak.

ENGORGED BREASTS

It is not uncommon for breasts to become painfully engorged in the early weeks when your milk production is still fluctuating to keep up with baby's demands. Your milk supply comes in by the third day postpartum—often at the same time that you're released from the hospital or your partner has decided to go back to work. This can be terrible timing for the mother who has to cope with hard, swollen, painful breasts on top of the sudden realization that she is alone with her baby for the first time. If you are breastfeeding, relief comes as the baby drinks and empties the breasts but engorgement returns as soon as breasts start filling up again with milk. It can take a few days to a couple of weeks for the breasts to adapt to your baby's appetite and produce just the right amount of milk. In the meantime, apply

Spraying
Don't be surprised if milk actually sprays out of your breasts sometimes. This is most likely to happen to the waiting, full breast as you have begun to let your baby feed on the other one. If you've been trying to collect a little expressed milk for use later, this may be a good time to catch the overflow. Use a sterile baby bottle.

On the Lighter Side
"This morning I woke up with breasts that could force Chesty Morgan into retirement. They were huge, hard and hot. . . . A pile of [mail] arrived and, generally feeling I'd escaped the weeping and wailing and congratulating myself on coming through this potentially upsetting time pretty unscathed, I opened the first envelope. It was from two people I haven't seen for a couple of years and to whom I've never been particularly close. The card carried a simple message: 'Congratulations.' I wept buckets. I haven't been so moved since Bambi. I sobbed continuously for two hours. At the same time milk started to pour from each breast, and this appears to be prompted by the phone ringing. Every time it rings they are filled with an extraordinary sensation that borders on both orgasm and pain, and then milk issues forth quite copiously."—Julie Walters, British comedienne, *Baby Talk* (London: Ebury Press, 1990)

warm compresses to your breasts before feeding time to help the milk begin to flow. Wake the baby up if you have to get him to feed. Breastfeed in a variety of positions (see pages 164–165) and switch sides to make sure your baby drains all parts of both breasts. Wear a supportive nursing bra in between feedings. For more on breast engorgement, see page 169.

If you have decided not to nurse your baby, you'll have to live through a few days of discomfort as your body starts to shut off the milk supply. Cold compresses and a supportive bra may offer some relief. See page 172 for more on letting your milk dry up.

BIGGER BUST

If you are breastfeeding, your breasts will remain large throughout the nursing period. You will need to reevaluate your bra size and purchase nursing or other bras that fit well and offer the right amount of support for your fuller figure. The first few weeks breasts tend to be unusually full and oversized. Once breastfeeding is established and all is going smoothly, breasts should no longer be quite so large or tender. During lovemaking, you may leak some milk. This is nothing to worry about. If it bothers you, however, you might want to refrain from breast play until breasts are less sensitive.

When you stop breastfeeding, you may see a noticeable decrease in bust size. After pregnancy and nursing, breasts may be somewhat more pendulous, though this is not necessarily true in all women.

NURSING BRAS

As a breastfeeding mother, you may wish to invest in at least two nursing bras. These bras offer good support, comfort, and a "drop cup." They unhook in front (one side at a time) to allow baby access to a breast at feeding time while giving the other breast needed support. You're likely to find the best selection in a large department store, although they are also offered through mail order catalogs and in maternity shops. You can also get by with your regular bras, if you wish. Just pull one cup up or down to feed the baby. Because breasts are larger than normal, however, your old size may be uncomfortable now. Invest in a larger size when necessary.

STRETCH MARKS

Some babies like to leave their signatures on your belly, in the form of stretch marks. The stretch mark occurs when skin is stretched beyond its normal capacity to do so, not an uncommon occurrence during pregnancy. A telltale sign of motherhood, these silvery lines may fade, but they will remain with you. You may notice them most on your abdomen, but you can also get them on your thighs, breasts, and buttocks. Creams and lotions are appealing but apparently do little or nothing to relieve the appearance of stretch marks.

HOT FLASHES

Some women experience hot flashes in the first few days after the delivery. Your face may actually become red and feel hot. They are caused by the hormonal changes in your body as you shift gears from the pregnant state to the nonpregnant state. Fortunately, they pass quickly.

SWEATING

In the first few weeks after the birth, you may notice that you are sweating more than usual. This is not just the hard work of being a mom! The excessive perspiration occurs because of the extra water weight your body is trying to lose. One of the ways your body is now getting rid of it is through perspiration. Continue to drink plenty of fluids to make sure you don't get dehydrated, however.

FLABBY BELLY

It can be bewildering to look down and see a belly that still looks pregnant weeks after you've already had the baby! Even after most of your extra water weight has dropped away, the puffed-out belly remains. This is because your uterus is still enlarged. It will take six weeks for your uterus to return to its prepregnancy size (a process known as involution). Stretched-out muscles and ligaments also take some time to regain their snap. Breastfeeding will help your uterus

On the Lighter Side
Here is some advice from humor writer Dave Barry: "How to Get Your Body Back into Shape After Childbirth the Way All the Taut-Bodied Entertainment Personalities Such As Jane Fonda Do: Don't kid yourself. Those women have never had babies. Their children were all borne by professional stunt women." (from Dave Barry, *Babies & Other Hazards of Sex*, Emmaus, PA: Rodale Press, Inc., 1984)

to contract faster and a mild exercise plan can get you back on the road to a flat tummy. Be sure to consult your physician before you embark on any exercise program. (See page 231 for ideas on early exercises that are safe and effective.)

POSTPARTUM FASHIONS

There's nothing worse than the thought of putting on a maternity outfit once pregnancy is behind you. Instead, try elastic-waist skirts and sweatpants, loose-fitting dresses, even your partner's clothes! If all else fails, and you're too heavy for anything you own, go out and buy yourself a new pair of shoes or a new ring. With the pregnancy behind you, at least your feet and fingers should be thinner!

CHAPTER 23

✦ Healthful Food for New Mothers ✦

For many moms, the first year becomes a struggle to regain the body you once knew and loved (tolerated?) and, at the same time, to maintain your energy level during the demanding first year with a new baby. Eating well with a new baby in the house can sometimes be a challenge. New mothers tend to push their own needs aside in order to cope with the demands of an infant. Keep in mind, however, that by taking care of yourself you put yourself in a better position to take care of your baby. Whether you are breast-feeding or bottle feeding, good nutrition is important. Your good health is vital to your new role as mother. This chapter gives you information on weight loss and nutrition.

✦   ✦   ✦

WEIGHT LOSS

Many postpartum women are interested in weight loss first and good nutrition second. The two do not have to be mutually exclusive. Some of your weight will naturally drop off as your body returns to its prepregnancy state. By your six-week checkup, you will probably be about twenty pounds lighter than you were when you were pregnant. You will gradually begin to see a flatter tummy and pounds will continue to drop away. Once the birth is six months behind you, you may even be back to your prepregnancy weight.

Although you lose a lot of weight in the first few weeks, you will still look pregnant, a fact that is disconcerting to some. The enlarged uterus is still shrinking back to its prepregnancy size during the first six weeks and so the abdomen retains its pregnant appearance during the first month and a half after the birth. There is really nothing that you can or should do about weight loss during the

Who Loses?
In a study of mothers' weight losses over the first six months postpartum, published in *Obstetrics & Gynecology* (March 1992), researchers at La Crosse Lutheran Hospital in Wisconsin discovered that first-time mothers tend to lose more weight than other mothers. Women who return to work lose more quickly than those who don't and those who returned earlier lost the most.

An Expert's Opinion
"Some studies show that breastfeeding mothers lose more weight than nonbreastfeeding mothers. Other studies show the opposite, particularly if the nonlactating women were dieting. Postpartum weight loss is extremely variable. Over the long term, there is probably not a big difference in weight loss between the groups."—Dr. Nancy Butte, Associate Professor, Department of Pediatrics, Children's Nutrition Research Center, Baylor College of Medicine

first few months following the birth. Maintaining a healthful, balanced diet and following a sensible exercise plan are the best course of action. Dieting this early on would be a mistake.

Once you have passed the six-week mark, you may be anxious to drop pounds. If you are breastfeeding, however, it is unwise to restrict calories. When calories are severely restricted, milk supply may diminish. Neither, however, should you view this as a time to allow yourself unlimited calories, especially not from nutritionally empty foods such as candy, chips, and soda. You need good nutrition to help provide for your baby. Even if you are not breastfeeding, beware of crash or fad diets. There are only two real ways to lose weight: by eating less (but sensibly) and by exercising more (and wisely). Take a look at your own weight goals. Are they reasonable? Are you working to return to your prepregnancy weight or are you hoping to come out slightly below (or above) this mark. (Some superskinny moms hope they may be able to retain some of that pregnancy weight!) Recent evidence points to the belief that not all bodies are created equal—some people have a lower metabolism or higher fatty tissue level, thus making it more likely that they will remain slightly overweight in spite of dieting attempts. Perhaps you need to accept your body weight as is. This does not mean, however, that you should be unhealthy. You may want to concentrate on toning, strengthening muscles, and building endurance through exercise rather than on losing weight. See page 231 for more on exercise.

NURSING MOM'S DIET

You'll need to pay as much attention to your eating habits now as you did when you were pregnant. Remember, as a nursing mother, you are sustaining a new life with your own.

As a breastfeeding mother, you'll want to be sure you're getting enough nutrition to keep up with the demands of a growing baby. This is as much for your sake as it is for your baby's. Nursing a baby can use up as many as 500–700 extra kilocalories a day. It is a physically demanding job and one that requires more energy intake than usual. Some of the needed energy comes directly from your own fat stores. The rest comes from food intake, meaning you may want to add about 500 k calories to your diet. For women with inadequate gestational weight gain or whose weight falls below the standard for height and age, 650 k calories is the recommended addition. As when you were pregnant, remember that not all calories are created equal. A candy bar can add extra calories to your diet, but does not add any extra vitamins or nutrients.

Although you may be interested in slimming down, do not attempt a severely restricted or fad diet. Your health and that of your baby depend on your eating a well-balanced and nutritious diet. Dramatic weight loss can mean lower milk production. Make sure you're eating a balanced diet of low-fat protein-containing foods, whole grains, fresh fruits, vegetables, milk, and water. This type of balanced diet will help you to avoid constipation as well, a problem that plagues some new mothers.

DIETARY RESTRICTIONS FOR THE NURSING MOTHER

You do not need to rule out certain foods on the grounds that babies don't like them—unless you notice a definite connection between something you eat and irritable crying or gassy problems in your baby. Obviously, women in Mexico and India consume spicy foods with no problem. Maybe you can too. Just watch for a reaction in your baby. If you believe there is a reaction, it's probably best not to repeat that food. Mothers of infants with colic may try eliminating milk from their diets after consulting the pediatrician. Occasionally, the mother's consumption of milk products is at the root of baby's colic. If the baby does not respond positively after a trial elimination, the mother should resume consumption of dairy products.

NEEDED NUTRIENTS

The major nutrients (energy sources derived from foods) are proteins, carbohydrates, and fats. You need to get the proper amount of each nutrient.

Proteins are found in all animal products: from fish and meats to eggs and milk. These are known as complete proteins. Vegetables and whole grains contain protein but are considered incomplete because they do not contain all the essential amino acids. A common way to "complete" a vegetable or whole grain protein is to combine it with an animal product (mixing lentil beans with yogurt, for example). Dried beans and rice can also be combined for a

An Expert's Opinion
"If colic is suspected, see your pediatrician and come to an agreement with him/her first that this is a colicky baby. Then try eliminating milk products from your diet. In some cases, this may be effective."—Dr. Nancy Butte, Associate Professor, Department of Pediatrics, Children's Nutrition Research Center, Baylor College of Medicine

Shop Smart
When on an outing with your baby, why not take a stroll past a vegetable or fruit stand? Away from the temptations of processed foods available in the supermarket, you may be more likely to choose a healthful array of colorful fruits and vegetables for your meal. Be colorful: look for orange, green, yellow, and white-colored veggies. The more colorful you get, the more likely that you have a rainbow of vitamins and nutrients in your shopping bag!

Healthful Snacks
Fresh fruits (apples, grapes, bananas, pears, oranges)
Peanuts (fresh from the shell)
Bran or other whole grain muffin
Whole wheat crackers
Low-fat cheese and yogurt
Unbuttered popcorn
Fresh vegetables (celery, carrots, cucumber, broccoli, etc.)
Dried apricots
Raisins

A Note of Caution
Vitamins can be dangerous in large doses, so take only the recommended amount.

No Sharing
It's tempting to eat a little bit of everything your baby eats. Watch out! You may be setting yourself up for a bad (and fattening) habit—especially once your baby is old enough to be eating cookies. What your baby doesn't finish should be thrown away, not polished off by you. Keep baby food separate from low-fat, low-cholesterol Mommy food.

complete protein with no animal products used. Most of us already consume more protein than we need. Many of the sources we turn to for protein also happen to be high in fat and calories. When choosing your proteins, opt for skinned chicken and fish over red meats, skim milk instead of whole, and so on. This way, you'll get the protein you need without the added fat!

Carbohydrates give you your best source of fuel for energy production. (Fats and protein give energy, too.) Complex carbohydrates, found in grains, vegetables, and fruits, are your best selection. Too many sugary sweets (simple carbohydrates) can be a problem, predisposing you to obesity, dental caries, and blood sugar problems. Candies and pastries should be reserved as "treats" and can be consumed in moderation, as long as they don't interfere with your consumption of needed nutrients.

Fats are not always an evil to be avoided. They represent a necessary part of your diet and are a source of energy. Fats help the body to absorb and use vitamins A, E, D, and K. Unfortunately, most Americans tend to have high-fat diets, a trend that has been linked to cancer and heart disease. It is important to keep saturated fats and cholesterol-rich foods to a minimum in your diet. Whole milk, butter, cheeses, and red meats are common sources of saturated fats. Foods like liver, kidney, and egg yolks all contain cholesterol. (Only foods from animal sources contain cholesterol.)

VITAMINS

Although there is disagreement on the necessity of vitamins for a woman with a normal, well-balanced diet, your doctor may advise you to continue taking your prenatal vitamins if you are breastfeeding. The vitamins may provide you with a little extra security, especially if you know you don't always eat right. Of course, the proper solution here is really to correct your diet. Pills cannot substitute for healthful eating.

BEST BITES

Looking for easy ways to eat right? You can eat well even though you don't have the time to be a gourmet cook. Prepare a lean meal of baked or broiled chicken or fish. Try using ground turkey in place of ground beef for hamburgers or tacos. Both of these are high-protein, low-fat dinners. Serve them up with a baked potato (with a microwave, this good-for-you food can be ready in minutes with no fuss) and add a vegetable (frozen, for convenience, or fresh if you have just a few minutes extra for trimming and rinsing). Instantly, you have a nutritious and tasty meal.

Give yourself an extra boost of vitamins and nutrients by adding to old standards: stir-fry some red and yellow peppers in with your boneless chicken. Sprinkle nuts or dried beans on your salad. Have celery sticks and cucumber slices with your tuna sandwich. Slice a banana over your breakfast cereal. Keep Minute Rice in the house for a quick addition to almost any meal. Add peas to the rice. Serve French-cut green beans with slivered almonds. Be creative. Be colorful. Be fast. Then, sit down and enjoy as leisurely a dinner as your baby will allow!

WATER

You will need plenty of water in your diet to make sure you are well hydrated. You may already have noticed that you are thirstier than usual. If this is true in your case, pay attention to this reaction. As a habit, when you sit down to nurse, have a glass of water or milk next to you. Water is necessary to good health. If you are beginning an exercise plan, have water on hand during and after exercise. Water helps to carry nutrients throughout your body and helps to remove waste. Don't let your urine get too concentrated. Eight glasses a day is not too much to be drinking now that you're a mom—if that's how much you crave! It is not necessary to force too many fluids for adequate milk output.

CAFFEINE

Caffeine, which you may have been careful about during pregnancy, should still be consumed in moderation. It is recommended that you do not drink a lot of caffeine (more than 2–3 cups of coffee or other caffeine-containing beverages a day). Amounts that pass through the breast milk can cause some babies to become irritable or restless. Individual infants respond differently. If you believe the caffeine you drink has a strong effect on your baby, you may wish to cut it out altogether. Chocolate contains caffeine, too, so consume that carefully as well.

Read All About It
Buy a good cookbook, one that emphasizes quick and easy meals. Various parenting magazines usually also include recipes with a frazzled mom in mind. Try them for inspiration and to motivate yourself to prepare nutritious meals.

The Mother of Invention
Many supermarkets now offer convenient, user-friendly fresh vegetables that provide you all the nutrients without any of the work: a chopped mixed green salad sold by the bag, peeled carrot sticks, broccoli florets, peeled and halved squash, trimmed green beans, and so on. If they look good, take advantage of these timesavers. It may mean the difference between eating well or skimping on good nutrition.

Get Help
If you smoke, speak with your caregiver for help kicking the habit. He or she may be able to recommend a formal program to you. Hopefully, it will become a lifetime resolution.

NO SMOKING

You were advised to give up cigarettes during pregnancy for the good of your baby, and hopefully you did. But if you were thinking it would be safe to light up again after the baby was born, think again. Besides clearly being a health hazard to you, it is believed that smoking after the birth can present a danger to your baby through secondhand smoke. Problems believed to be connected to maternal and paternal smoking include respiratory infections, asthma, and even modestly impaired cognitive development. There is now also some evidence linking maternal smoking both during and after pregnancy to increased rates of behavior problems in children. Although more studies would be needed to make this connection definitive, it is wiser for now to limit or quit smoking. If you are a nursing mother, smoking can affect both the quality and the amount of the milk you produce.

ALCOHOL

Breastfeeding mothers need to be aware that alcohol passes into breast milk and may have an effect on the baby. For this reason, it is recommended that breastfeeding mothers not drink. If you do have a drink for a special occasion, it is recommended that you do not breastfeed until at least two hours after the drink. Whether you are breastfeeding or not, large amounts of alcohol can have a negative effect on your own health. Large quantities of alcohol can suppress your appetite and make absorption of nutrients difficult, thereby diminishing your chances of good health. Without the benefits of good nutrition, breastfeeding or even simply mothering your baby can become difficult. Obviously, too, moderate to large amounts of alcohol can impair your senses, leaving you unfit for the serious care a newborn demands.

CHAPTER 24

✢ Exercises for the New Mother ✢

Whether you were relatively active or relatively inactive during your pregnancy, you may now want to regain control of your postbaby body. Moderate exercise can be an important part of being a new mother. Rather than wearing you out, it can help to make you feel more energetic and up to the task of baby care. Caring for a young child and possibly working outside the home as well, you may wonder if you can find the time to add one more thing to your day. Think about this: regular exercise will pay back dividends on your time investment, helping you to a healthier body and often an improved self-image, too. This chapter will show you the way to get involved in a rational exercise program, with your lifestyle and needs in mind.

✢   ✢   ✢

FIRST EXERCISES

Assuming you had a normal, uncomplicated delivery and have consulted your physician, after the first twenty-four hours have passed, you can begin doing some very mild exercises. Although it may seem early, this is a good time to get back into an active mode. Getting up and getting muscles moving may help you to get back to your former self sooner. Try these slow, easy exercises while still in the hospital or while recovering at home:

The Pelvic Tilt: Lying on your back, with your knees bent and your feet flat on the bed, press the small of your back into the bed and squeeze your buttocks to tilt your pelvis up. (See illustration.) Relax. Repeat three times.

Chin to Chest: Lie down on your bed with your knees bent, your feet flat on the bed, and your arms at your sides. (See illustration.) Lift

The pelvic tilt

Chin to chest

Bottoms up

The crunch

Back track

Lean machine

your chin to your chest four times. As you do so, make sure you are pushing your back to the bed and contracting your abdominal muscles.

Bottoms Up: Lie down with your knees bent, feet flat and your arms at your side. Squeeze your buttocks and lift your bottom up off the bed an inch or so, then roll back down. (See illustration.) Repeat four times, at your own speed.

Flex and Point: Flex and point your toes as you lie in bed.

The Stroller: Take a slow, easy walk down the hallway before returning to bed.

EXERCISES IN THE FIRST SIX WEEKS

During the postpartum period, while you are adjusting to your new role as mother and your body is returning to its prepregnancy state, you can do some mild exercising. Remember, however, your hormones are still fluctuating and your body has not yet entirely recovered from pregnancy and birth. Your joints are still loose, so you'll need to avoid any bouncy or jerky exercise movements. You're still dealing with some extra blood volume as well as extra weight. Because of the added stress on your heart, you'll want to avoid aerobic activity in the first six weeks postpartum. Instead, concentrate on moving with an eye to increased activity later.

A perfect first exercise during this postpartum period is to walk. An easy three-minute walk, either pushing the baby stroller or alone, is a good start. You can gently add more minutes and eventually some briskness to the pace over the coming weeks.

You might also want to concentrate on some back exercises to regain flexibility and strength. Your back has been through a lot—first the extra weight of pregnancy, then the strain of delivery, now the demands of feeding and carrying an eight-pound baby! Try these exercises:

The Crunch: Lie flat on the floor with knees up and bent. Cross your arms over your chest. Press your lower back into the floor. Begin to raise your upper body until your shoulder blades are about three inches off the floor. (See illustration.) Roll back down to the floor. Do one set of ten crunches. If you feel that this is too much for you to do all at once, break it down and do two sets of five or six.

Back Track: Sit on the floor with one leg extended straight out in front of you and the other bent so that the sole of your foot is against the thigh of your extended leg. Pull yourself up, straightening your spine so you are sitting tall. Then, leading with your belly button, lean forward over your extended leg. (See illustration.) Reach both hands toward your foot and hold for ten easy counts. Do not bounce. Do not overstretch. Stretch only as far as is comfortable. Remember, during the postpartum period, your joints are still lax. Relax. Repeat three times. Switch legs. Repeat three times. (You should feel this stretch in your hamstrings and your lower back.)

Lean Machine: Sit on the floor with both legs straight out in front of you. Place your hands on your thighs. With a straight back, lean toward your toes. The movement will be very subtle. Maintain this lean for ten seconds, without bouncing. Repeat three times.

EXERCISE DURING THE FIRST YEAR

Once you have seen your doctor for the six-week postpartum checkup, you should be able to get the green light for continued exercise and a return to all the sports you love. Although you may be counting on exercise as a way to lose weight, you should think first of exercise as a way to achieve fitness and health. Don't quit even if the pounds seem to stay glued to you in the first six months of the year. Exercise has many benefits besides helping you look better: it increases your aerobic capacity, builds muscular strength and endurance, and encourages flexibility. When choosing an exercise program or sport, make sure it includes all the basics of a good fitness program:

1. A good, cardiovascular warm-up period
2. A muscular warm-up, or stretching period
3. A cardiovascular conditioning session in your target heart rate range (see sidebar)
4. A cool-down period
5. A toning and strengthening segment
6. A flexibility development period

You'll want to choose an exercise program that you're going to enjoy and keep up. Anything you're likely to do is good—whether

Heart Rate Range
To determine your target heart rate, subtract your age from 220. If you are thirty, for example, your age-predicted maximum heart rate (APMHR) range would be 190. Use this figure to determine at what heart rate range you should be exercising. For example, if you are thirty and your doctor has suggested that you exercise at 70 to 75 percent of your APMHR, you would have a target heart rate range of 133 to 142 beats per minute during exercise. Determine your heart rate by taking your pulse at the wrist or neck. Take your resting pulse, your pulse about five minutes into exercise, and again in the middle of the program. If your pulse is too high, slow down until you are in the right heart rate range.

you choose to exercise at home, with a video, or in a class or club. Walking, often overlooked as a sport, is cheap, easy, always available, and a very effective means of exercise. Take a brisk walk at least three times a week. If you're really trying to lose body fat, walk five times a week. Walk for twenty minutes in your target heart range (see sidebar, page 233) for optimal cardiovascular fitness. Continue walking past that twenty-minute mark, and you'll start to lose body fat. Plan to walk for at least thirty minutes if your goal is to lose body fat. Be sure to work up to this pace gradually. If you're not sure you want to brave the elements every day of the year, you might also wish to invest in exercise equipment such as a stationary bicycle, treadmill, or rowing or skiing machine. Choose a well-lit, airy, pleasant room. If you push your exercise equipment off into a damp corner of your basement, you won't be too likely to use it. To help you maintain interest in your exercise program, play music, watch TV, or read as you use it.

Write an exercise prescription for yourself. Set goals for yourself, in your effort to get back to a certain level of fitness. Assuming you did some exercise during the first six weeks, you can now begin working out at least three times a week, exercising at 75 percent of your heart rate (see sidebar, page 233) for twenty to twenty-five minutes. Gradually increase the time you spend exercising until your workout lasts thirty-five minutes to an hour, at 65 to 85 percent of your heart rate range, assuming your doctor agrees.

HOW TO CHOOSE AN EXERCISE CLASS

When looking for an exercise class, ask your doctor, as well as your friends, for suggestions and recommendations. The local YWCA often offers a wide selection of exercise and sports programs, including some classes specifically geared to the postpartum mother. Many fitness clubs also offer prenatal and postnatal exercise classes. The benefit of taking a postpartum class, of course, is the camaraderie that often develops among the new mothers. You all have something in common and you have the same basic exercise needs. If you sign up for a regular class, just remember that these women have not been through childbirth recently. You may need to take things more gradually and proceed at your own pace. Don't worry about keeping up with the rest of the class.

Here are some things to look for in a health club or fitness class:

WEIGHT LIFTING (#1)

Also known as walking to the playground.

SIPRESS

1. Proximity to your home. If you have to go out of your way to get there, you may not go at all.
2. Convenient hours. If they're not flexible, you may never fit an exercise class in between all the feedings, baby play groups, and/or hours back at your job.
3. Clean facilities. Obviously, you'll want to exercise in a pleasant place where you feel comfortable.
4. A nursery. Some clubs offer baby care while you exercise. This can be a real boon to new mothers, who may otherwise find it difficult to leave a young baby long enough to get to the club, exercise, and get back home. It's also a big help to mothers who don't have routine child care in place at home.
5. A safety-conscious program. The class should include a warm-up and cool-down period to keep you exercising safely. The class should be small enough so that the teacher can see you and correct your body position, if necessary. The staff should be willing and available to help you use any of the exercise machines safely and effectively.

BODY IMAGE

As some of the weight comes off and you return to the feeling that your body is your own again, you'll begin to take stock. How have you changed since you last took a good look in the mirror? Your new body may seem a relief (you thought you'd look a lot worse), it may look the same (some women bounce back with little or no changes), or you may be in a panic (everything's saggy and stretched out). If you're nursing, your body is still reacting to the physical demands of being a parent, with larger bust and maybe some extra padding elsewhere too.

Don't be overly critical of your body. You need to learn to love it the way it is. It's useless to compare yourself to an unmarried friend with no children or a superslim model in a magazine. This doesn't mean that you should give up and accept extra pounds that you don't need, only that you need to set reasonable goals and then be happy with the ones you manage to achieve.

All in Good Time
It will take you at least ten weeks of exercising for you to notice a change in the way you feel and look. After twelve weeks, you should notice a measurable difference in your general fitness, strength, endurance, and flexibility.

An Expert's Thoughts
"I would like to think that exercising helps women to get back on their feet sooner and to begin to feel like themselves again. Your baby has needs but you have your own needs as a woman, too. Exercise gives you a sense of control, a way of saying 'I'm back to me.' "—Dana Brown, Director, Women's Exercise Research Center, The George Washington University

CHAPTER 25

✢ Postpartum Sex and Contraception ✢

Postbaby sex can be as good or better than prebaby sex, as long as you and your partner give yourselves time and have patience with each other. Even though you are parents now, you are both still sexual beings who need and enjoy time alone together. You have both been through a life-changing event (birth) and you did it together. Concentrate on the ties that bind you closer together rather than on the little tugs that pull you apart. This chapter will guide you through some of the early rough spots, good feelings, and contraceptive needs in the first year.

✢   ✢   ✢

FEELING SEXY AGAIN

Immediately after the birth, sex is probably the last thing on your mind. A short five or six weeks down the road, however, and you may be raring to go. Don't be surprised, however, if sexy feelings are a little slow to return. You have a lot of physical demands on you right now (getting up in the middle of the night, carrying an 8-pound baby around, nursing) and you are also on the receiving end of a lot of physical pleasures (snuggling, cuddling, suckling a warm little bundle of baby). It may be that by the end of the day you just can't handle any more touching. On the other hand, maybe you are ready for a little grown-up stroking. Try to give your (often clueless) partner some clues as to your feelings. When you're in the mood, let him know; don't wait for him to guess. As moments alone may be fleeting, catch as catch can. If there's time (baby's napping) and you're both home (it's Saturday) and you're feeling sexy, who cares if it's three in the afternoon? Nighttime isn't the only time for sex.

Positive Changes
Although there are a lot of jokes about what a new baby can do to your sex life, there are bright spots as well. Many couples may note a newfound respect for each other once they become parents. There is a sense of shared accomplishment and pride. There can be a new closeness that will, happily, spill over into your love life, perhaps making it better than ever before.

POSTPARTUM SEX

It may have been a while, but your sex life is still there waiting for you. Once your energy, spirit, and appetite return, you will find that being a parent does not take the place of being a loving partner.

It is unlikely that you will want to resume an active sex life in the first month. Some doctors will advise that you wait until the six-week postpartum checkup. At this point, the cervix should be fully closed and there should be no chance of infection. The optimum time to resume your sex life is when you and your partner feel ready to do so.

On that first magical night (and it *will* feel like a first), go slowly and tenderly. As with other firsts, however, you have a certain sense of newness, excitement, and intimacy going for you! You may, of course, be a little tense, given the trauma this area only recently experienced. If you have recovered from an episiotomy, you may wonder if you are "the same." Meanwhile, your partner may be a little nervous, too, given the miracle he witnessed your body perform only weeks ago and the concern that everything will feel different to him too. Take your time and don't rush things. Talk about the doubts, fears, or desires on your mind.

SEX AND THE SINGLE EPISIOTOMY

Unfortunately, the stitching required with a bad tear or episiotomy can sometimes leave you feeling "different." You may feel that the vagina is a different size, is tight, dry, or unfeeling along the scar tissue line. To ease some of these problems, use K-Y jelly as a lubricant. Guide his penis into you with your hand, so sex moves at your pace and in your comfort range. Try the woman-on-top position, which offers you more control over the depth of penetration. Assuming all systems are go, you'll proceed as usual. If you have a real problem, however, do not suffer in silence. Return to your doctor to discuss your concerns or report any physical discomfort you may have experienced.

CONTRACEPTIVE NEEDS

In order to prevent pregnancy from occurring again, you will have to choose a birth control method before resuming your sex life.

There is no safe time following the birth. Breastfeeding reduces your chances of conception but is not a guaranteed method (for more on this, see "LAM [Lactation Amenorrhea Method]," page 246). At the six-week checkup (earlier if necessary), talk with your doctor or midwife about the choices available to you and your partner. You may or may not wish to return to the method you were using prior to becoming pregnant. When considering a method, you will want to take into account your desire to have more children (and how soon), your own general health, your willingness to follow whatever usage rules your method demands, your lifestyle (monogamous or likely to have multiple partners), and so on.

DIAPHRAGM

A diaphragm is a latex dome that, when placed over the cervix, prevents sperm from entering the uterus. For maximum effectiveness, the diaphragm should be used with a spermicidal jelly or cream. The diaphragm is a barrier method, meaning that it prevents the sperm from reaching the egg. It can be an appealing method for the nursing mother, since it does not involve the ingestion of any hormones. It can be a fairly effective method when used properly. There is a failure rate of eighteen pregnancies per one hundred women per year. If you're well motivated and you use it each time you have sex, it is more effective. If you sometimes leave it in the drawer, obviously it becomes a much less effective method over time.

If you had a diaphragm before, you cannot simply return to it. You have to be resized and given a new one after a pregnancy and birth (unless it was a cesarean birth). This is because the vaginal walls have been stretched by childbirth. You must be fitted for a diaphragm at your six-week postpartum checkup, according to the size and shape of your vagina. There are basically three types of diaphragms: one that bends in any direction (flexible coil spring), another that bends only one way (flat spring), and a third that bends in all directions and folds into an arc shape for insertion (arcing spring diaphragm). Both the flexible coil and flat spring diaphragms are good for women with strong vaginal muscle tone. For the woman who has given birth, the arcing spring diaphragm may be best, as it is able to

We've Come a Long Way
Contraceptives were illegal in the United States in the early 1900s! Margaret Sanger, nurse and activist, is credited with being the first to openly defy this law and bring contraceptive information to the American woman. Her sister was arrested and jailed for dispensing diaphragms that had been illegally imported from Germany. Margaret herself served thirty days for opening the country's first birth control clinic.

Diaphragm History
According to *The New Birth Control Book* by Howard Shapiro, M.D. (New York: Prentice Hall Press, 1992), primitive diaphragms appear in Egyptian writings and drawings as far back as 1850 B.C.! Much later, the famous lover Casanova invented his own barrier method: using the rind of half a lemon placed against the cervix.

Not a Moment Too Soon
Nonnursing mothers may be ovulating as early as the sixth week postpartum, so you will want to have your contraceptive method in place early. Don't have sex without using some method of birth control.

work well even if you have poor vaginal muscle tone. Diaphragms come in sizes and you will be given the largest one available for your size. Do not use a fit-free diaphragm (a one-size-fits-all model that does not require a doctor's prescription), because these have been associated with a much higher rate of pregnancy, especially in women who have given birth before.

Diaphragms are safe to use, though there has been some evidence that users may be somewhat more susceptible to urinary tract infections and yeast infections. There is also the slight possibility that a woman or her partner may be allergic to the latex from which a diaphragm is made. Rarely, diaphragm use has been associated with toxic shock syndrome, a serious and potentially fatal infection. Such a rare occurrence is even less likely to occur if the diaphragm is removed six to eight hours after intercourse. Women who leave it in place twenty-four hours or longer would be at slightly higher risk.

To use, a teaspoon of spermicidal jelly or cream is placed inside the dome, the diaphragm is inserted, and the user checks its placement with a finger to make sure the cervix is covered. The diaphragm must remain in place at least six hours after sex and should not be inserted more than six hours before sex. If you have sex again before the initial six hours are up, you will need to leave the diaphragm in place and insert more spermicidal jelly into the vagina, then leave it in place six hours after that last act of intercourse. Upon removal, the diaphragm should be washed with soap and water and, if desired, sprinkled with cornstarch and returned to its case. You should periodically check your diaphragm for tears by holding it up to the light or filling it with water to see if there are leaks. If you notice any cracks, tears, or puckering, it must be replaced immediately.

THE PILL

Birth control pills combine synthetic estrogen and progestogen, two hormones that work to inhibit the growth of an ovarian follicle, and create a cervical mucus that is hostile to sperm. The pill also helps to make the uterine lining unreceptive so that, if an egg were fertilized, implantation would be unsuccessful. The pill must be taken every day for twenty-one days, followed by seven days off the pill (or seven days on a placebo), when you will have some bleeding. The pill is a very effective method, with only 3 pregnancies per 100 women per year (based on 1990 statistics).

There has been increasing good news about the pill in recent years. Its use has been linked with lower rates of ovarian and endometrial cancer, for example. Unfortunately, like any drug, it can have side effects, ranging from minor problems such as nausea, fluid retention, mask of pregnancy, weight gain, and dizziness to more serious complications such as migraine headaches and urinary tract infections. Some complications caused by the pill can actually result in death (most commonly by heart attack or stroke). This serious side effect has almost been eliminated, provided the pill is not given to heavy smokers. The highest risk group appears to be smokers over age thirty-five. Mild complications such as nausea, fluid retention, and weight gain may be corrected by changing brands. There are currently more than twenty-five different pills on the market to choose from. Nonsmokers under age thirty-five appear to be in the lowest risk group for pill use. Pills that contain low doses of estrogen appear safer than high-dose pills. Before recommending the pill, your doctor should review all this with you and do a careful check of your history and health to determine if you are a risky candidate for the pill. (There are many factors that can make the pill a poor choice for some women.) If, for example, you smoke, or have a history of certain medical problems such as diabetes or high blood pressure, consider other methods of contraception.

Although the pill may appeal to some postpartum women, it is not usually recommended for nursing mothers. Some experts believe that the estrogen in the pill can reduce the quantity of milk you're able to produce. Others disagree, including the American Academy of Pediatrics, which believes that low-dose oral contraceptives will not affect milk supply in a woman who has already nursed successfully for the first six weeks postpartum. The minipill, a birth control pill that contains progestogen only, apparently does not change the quantity of milk you produce, but some research shows it can change the quality slightly: lower protein content, less milk fat, lactose, calcium, magnesium, and so on. Furthermore, we do not know what, if any, the effects of progestogen are when ingested over a period of time by the nursing baby. Many in the medical community are awaiting more studies. Ask your doctor.

Pill Popularity
Birth control pills were once the most popular form of contraception in the United States, with a high of 10 million women using the pill in 1974. Worries about its safety caused the numbers to tumble to 6 million users today. Recent reports have stressed the pill's relative safety, especially for healthy nonsmokers, although many women continue to eye the method with some suspicion. Recent reports citing the benefits of oral contraceptives may soon change their minds: the pill is now being associated with a lower rate of endometrial cancer, cancer of the ovary, pelvic inflammatory disease, osteoporosis, and ectopic pregnancies.

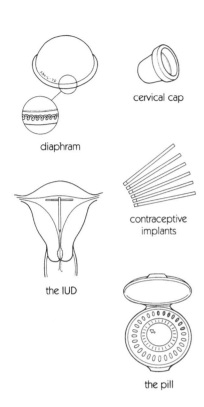

cervical cap

diaphram

contraceptive implants

the IUD

the pill

IUDs

The intrauterine device (IUD) is inserted into the uterus and left there. Made of polyethylene plastic, the device also has a nylon tail that protrudes out of the cervix into the vagina. The tail is there so the woman and/or her doctor can check and make sure the IUD is still in place. It can also be used for removal of the IUD. Until recently, there were various types and shapes on the market. Now, owing to heavy litigation and difficulty getting liability insurance, there are only two: a T-shaped IUD that contains synthetic progesterone and must be changed annually, and a T-shaped plastic IUD containing copper, which is good for eight years.

No one knows for sure how the IUD works, but it is believed that it either interferes with the implantation of a fertilized egg or that it works as an inflammatory agent (the body creates macrophages to rid itself of the foreign body; these macrophages destroy sperm and fertilized eggs). The IUD is very effective, with a failure rate of 6 pregnancies per 100 women per year. IUDs do have side effects, ranging from severe cramping and heavy menstrual bleeding to serious fallopian tube infection and pelvic inflammatory disease (PID). They have been associated with some deaths. Insertion can be painful and the IUD does not always stay where it was put. It may, in fact, be expelled by the body. The IUD should not be used by women with abnormalitics of thc utcrus, nor should it be used by women with tumors or fibroids.

An IUD should not be inserted until your six-week checkup or later. If you are considering using an IUD, discuss it with your doctor, being sure to explore all the potential complications of IUD use. You will likely be asked to sign an informed consent. Owing to its association with fallopian tube infections, it is best for women who have completed their families. The IUD is not recommended for women who have not yet had any children or who wish to go on to have children later, as fallopian tube infections can cause infertility. (The risk of PIDs is higher in IUD users who have multiple sexual partners.) Make sure your doctor knows all the facts about your health history. If you are nursing, be sure to say so. Some research has suggested that perforation of the uterus during insertion is more likely to occur in nursing mothers. Other research does not support this, so ask your doctor. The IUD should not be used by a woman with a history of ectopic pregnancies. If, after insertion, you have any questions or notice any adverse reactions, call your physician immediately.

CONTRACEPTIVE SPONGE

An over-the-counter contraceptive method, the contraceptive sponge is small and round and contains a spermicide. One size fits all women. It is inserted by the woman into the vagina and placed over the cervix (there is a small indentation on one side for this purpose). Acts of sex can be repeated without any additional applications of cream. The sponge can be left in place up to twenty-four hours. It should be removed six to eight hours after the last act of intercourse. If it is left in place longer than twenty-four hours, the risk of toxic shock syndrome, a serious and potentially fatal infection, is increased (though still rare). The sponge is thrown away after removal.

The sponge, while it has its benefits, is not so effective against preventing pregnancy as the diaphragm. Its effectiveness rate appears to drop even lower in women who have given birth before. This may be due to the fact that the sponge is too small to fit well over the woman's larger cervix or to the fact that a woman who has given birth often has poorer vaginal muscle tone, which may allow the sponge to shift during sex. Pregnancy rates are as high as 28 per 100 women per year among women who have had one or more babies. To increase effectiveness some couples combine this barrier method with another: the condom.

CERVICAL CAP

The cervical cap is similar to the diaphragm but it is smaller, and made to fit just over the cervix. It works by preventing the sperm from entering the cervix. The cap can be left in place for days. Complaints about the cap have ranged from a bad odor after it has been in for two days to lacerations of the cervix, as it sits and rubs against the tissues. Pap smears may become abnormal as well. Unfortunately, the cap has also been known to become dislodged during intercourse. In studies so far, it is not so effective a method of preventing pregnancy as the pill, a condom and foam, or the IUD.

Famous Quote
Margaret Sanger, a leader in the advancement and availability of birth control for women, once said, "No woman can call herself free who does not own and control her body. No woman can call herself free until she can choose consciously whether she will or will not be a mother."

The condom and foam is a good method because it is both mechanical (the condom prevents the sperm from entering the vagina) and chemical (the spermicide can kill any sperm that may get in). Failure rates when using the condom alone have been reported at 12 pregnancies per 100 women per year.

A Look to the Future
Eventually, there may be a two-year contraceptive implant product. Down the road, there may be one that works for only one year and then is absorbed by the body so it does not even have to be removed.

Insertion and removal of the cap may be difficult for some women. Pregnancy rates for the cervical cap are 18 per 100 women per year.

CONDOM AND FOAM

The condom, a thin sheath unrolled over an erect penis, prevents the sperm from entering the woman. Used diligently in conjunction with spermicidal foam, it can be a highly effective method of birth control. Condoms typically come in only one size and are available over the counter, as are the spermicidal foams. There are many brands and types, all promising something new and different: a tighter fit, a thinner sheath, an exciting color, ribbing, and so on. Make your choice based on what appeals to you and what has worked well for you and your partner in the past. Or ask your doctor or midwife for a brand recommendation. Besides protecting against pregnancy, the condom has received a great deal of positive publicity recently because of its ability to offer protection against sexually transmitted diseases like AIDS.

CONTRACEPTIVE IMPLANTS

Contraceptive implants provide long-term, reversible contraceptive protection for five years. It is a highly effective method with a failure rate of less than one pregnancy per one hundred women per year. Six thin, flexible capsules (about the size of matchsticks) are placed under the skin of your arm through a small incision during a fifteen-minute in-office procedure. Local anesthesia is used. The capsules each contain a synthetic hormone known as norgestrel. The implants contain no estrogen. They are not recommended for women who want to get pregnant within the next year or two, but they can be removed (and fertility immediately restored) if sometime during the next five years you change your mind and want to get pregnant. It is believed safe for nursing mothers, but long-term follow-up of infants nursed by mothers has not yet accumulated.

Side effects may include menstrual cycle irregularities, headaches, nausea, and dizziness. Most common are the menstrual irregularities (spotting, prolonged bleeding, or no bleeding at all for several months). Many women find that, after a year, bleeding patterns become more regular. Women with breast cancer, thrombophlebitis, unexplained vaginal bleeding, acute liver disease, among others, should not use contraceptive implants. As with the pill, smokers should not use implants. Your doctor will know if it's a method you can consider after taking your health history. Like the pill, this method is not for everyone. Talk to your doctor if you are considering it.

INJECTABLE DEPO-PROVERA

One intramuscular injection is given every twelve weeks to women who wish to avoid pregnancy. The injection is given by a health professional in the back of the thigh or the back of the shoulder. Depo-Provera contains a synthetic version of the female hormone progesterone. The method works by blocking ovulation, and is highly effective. It should not be used by nursing women or by women who wish to get pregnant again fairly soon. Once the injections have been stopped, it can take as long as a year for fertility to return.

WITHDRAWAL

An extremely unreliable method of birth control, this involves a partner who is able and ready to pull out of the vagina prior to ejaculation. The problem, of course, is that some of the initial ejaculate may end up in the vagina as the man withdraws at the last minute. Besides being unreliable, it can be emotionally and sexually unsatisfying as well. The woman may be rushing (sometimes unsuccessfully) to achieve orgasm before the man pulls out.

RHYTHM

The rhythm method makes use of the knowledge of a woman's monthly cycle and involves having unprotected sex on "safe" days only. During ovulation, abstinence would be the contraceptive method (although some couples use condoms on unsafe days). Rhythm is the only birth control method approved by the Catholic Church. Ovulation typically occurs on or about day 14 of a woman's cycle. Since cycles can change from month to month and may range, for example, from 25-day cycles to 28-day cycles, this method alone of figuring conception times is too simplistic. For this reason,

An Expert's Thoughts
"It's fine to talk about statistics and effective rates of various contraceptive methods. The problem is that for that woman, that one in however many per year— for her, the ectopic pregnancy or the unplanned pregnancy can be a disaster."—Dr. Hakim Elahi, Medical Director, Planned Parenthood, Margaret Sanger Center

Rhythm Effectiveness
Overall, the rhythm method
is not so effective as other
birth control methods and
probably should not be used
by a couple hoping to avoid
any future births. However,
properly trained and motivated couples can achieve
highly effective rates.

rhythm users combine the calendar method with a daily temperature taking, to give them a more accurate idea of when ovulation is
taking place. There is often (but not always) a slight dip in temperature during ovulation. The woman also must check her cervix to
determine if it is softer than usual or if the cervical mucus is thinner
than usual. This would indicate that she is ovulating.

If you are interested in using rhythm, talk with your doctor. Bring a
chart of your menstrual cycles over a number of months and get help
determining your "safe" and "unsafe" days. You may have to abstain
from sex for as many as ten days each month to be sure that you have
missed the ovulation period. Ask for training in temperature taking
and cervical examination.

LAM (LACTATION AMENORRHEA METHOD)

Women who exclusively breastfeed their babies over a long period
of time often have complete cessation of menstruation, as long as
frequent nursing continues. Nursing a baby in this case does provide
some protection against pregnancy. Using this biological fact as a
method of contraceptive is common in some other countries but not
favored by the medical community in the United States. It is believed
that the average American woman does not breastfeed often enough
to make this method work. The method is effective only if nursing is
frequent, consistent, and uninterrupted by any supplemental bottles. For this reason, all nursing mothers are advised to use another
contraceptive method.

MORNING-AFTER PILLS

Morning-after pills allow women who did not use any contraception during sex to rectify the situation later by taking pills that
interfere with the survival of the fertilized egg. The pills must be
taken within seventy-two hours of the unprotected sex. Morning-
after pills should be used only in emergencies—such as in the case of
rape, incest, or a condom that breaks. Two tablets are taken in the
morning and two more in the afternoon. They cannot be used if the

woman has had unprotected sex earlier in the month (since her last menstrual period), because there would be a chance that she may already be pregnant.

RU 486

Like morning-after pills, RU 486 is considered a contragestation method rather than a contraceptive method. In other words, it can be used after conception has occurred, but prior to implantation of the fertilized egg. Only one 600-milligram pill is taken. Like morning-after pills, it must be taken within seventy-two hours of unprotected sex to be effective. RU 486 can also be used for early abortion, up to forty-seven days after the last period. Usually the dose is larger and has to be followed by an injection of prostaglandin and, later, a sonogram to make sure the uterus is empty. Interestingly, the drug has also been used in the treatment of breast cancer, Cushing's disease, glaucoma, and intrauterine death with no labor. RU 486 is not yet available in the United States, but the company that makes it is currently looking for a distributor.

STERILIZATION

For the woman, sterilization would mean a tubal ligation. It can be done at the time of the delivery or later. When done right after birth in the hospital, it involves a slightly more serious operation. The abdominal wall is cut and the tubes are burned with an electric current. Three months after birth, it can be done through the belly button. A clip or band is placed on the fallopian tubes. Since sterilization is almost always permanent and irreversible, the woman must sign a consent form anywhere from seventy-two hours to a month prior to the operation (laws vary from state to state). There must also be written proof that she has been counseled by a doctor and told of this procedure's permanence. A man can be sterilized with a vasectomy. The vasectomy is a very effective, fairly simple operation, which can be done under local anesthesia in a doctor's office. It is a permanent and often irreversible method of birth control. The vas deferens is tied and part of it removed. The man is instructed to use

An Option
For couples who are absolutely sure that they do not wish to have any more children, sterilization may be an option.

a condom for the next fifteen ejaculations. He then brings in a sample of his semen, which can be tested to make sure that no sperm are present. For women undergoing tubal ligation, there is a failure rate of fewer than 1 pregnancy per 100 women per year.

CHAPTER 26

✛ Your Feelings ✛

As you approach your new role as mother and combine it with all the other roles you play in life (wife, daughter, sister, friend, employee), you may find your feelings in a constant state of flux. One day you're happy, the next you're miserable. One day life seems pretty perfect and another may leave you with a list of endless resolutions for improving it. This chapter covers your moods, postpartum depression, ways to deal with stress, and more.

✛   ✛   ✛

BABY BLUES

Your hormones remain in a state of flux in the early days. During the early weeks with a new baby, your emotional state may remain rather unpredictable. You may feel at once like a lottery winner and a down-and-out loser. Some women barely notice these blues while others are hit hard by blues that make them weepy and angry.

Often, you are sent home from the hospital on day 3, the very day your milk comes in and hormones rage. You may find yourself in tears in your first hours back at home. This isn't a sign of your incompetence as a mother. This is simply a sign of active hormonal changes. Just as you learned to live with a few ups and down during your pregnancy, you need to accept your changing feelings now. There are a lot of pressures and demands on you right now. Luckily, babies have as many ways of charming and flirting with their parents as they do of driving them to distraction. For this reason, just as you're starting to regard your baby suspiciously as an egocentric tyrant, he suddenly becomes a lovable, cuddly newborn again and you realize you are hopelessly in love with him. The best prescription for the times you're feeling low is to accept that the down times will exist in any relationship. Rapid hormonal changes, lack of sleep, new-mother anxiety, and physical discomfort as your body heals are all to blame. You should feel much more settled after a few weeks have passed.

It's a good idea to discuss some of these feelings with your partner and close friends or relatives. It can also help to discuss them with your pediatrician at one of your baby's first exams or with your obstetrician or midwife at your six-week checkup. If you believe you are spiraling down into deeper depression, you'll need help to pull yourself out of it. Read the following section on postpartum depression, and contact a doctor you trust for advice on where to go for help.

POSTPARTUM DEPRESSION

The combination of hormonal changes, lack of sleep, anxiety over parenting, and excitement of having a newborn can sometimes add up to mild to severe depression. (See the section on baby blues above if your blues are mild.) If you had a complicated and difficult pregnancy, you may be more susceptible to postpartum depression than usual. (See sidebar.)

Symptoms of serious postpartum depression include inability to sleep or eat, excessive irritability with those around you, a desire to retreat from the outside world, and the feeling that you don't want to see anyone. Hopefully, your doctor or midwife is asking about your feelings: how well you're sleeping, how you are coping with motherhood, and so on. If not, you may have to bring the issue up yourself. Serious depression should not be ignored. If you have suffered from depression before you had a child, you probably already know how important it is to get some help and to have someone to talk to.

WORRYING

A newborn can be incredibly demanding, and the first month can be as scary and exhausting as it is exhilarating. But by the end of the first month, you'll at least be able to look back and see that in spite of anxieties and inexperience, your new little family is getting along quite nicely. By then, you will probably have made a few mistakes and realized that everyone survived them. You'll also have noticed that your baby is nowhere near so fragile or helpless as you might have thought at first. Don't expect to stop worrying, however. Once you have a child, worrying is something you'll probably continue to do until he's fully grown—and beyond!

If you had a complicated pregnancy (even if it was followed by a healthy newborn), you may be more likely to worry about your baby's health. (See the sidebar on page 250.) Don't be shy about discussing these fears with your pediatrician and giving your doctor the chance to reassure you. The more you know about your child's health, the more comfortable you may feel and the more likely you will be able to put the past to rest.

YOUR ENERGY LEVEL

Having a new baby in the house and recovering from delivery can be overwhelming at times. You're tired, overexcited, simultaneously full of energy and drained. Lack of sleep and the seemingly constant demands of a new baby can sap your energy. To keep energy levels as high as possible, make sure you're eating well (see Chapter 23), napping when you can, and doing some moderate exercise. When possible, get a change of scene. Take your baby out for a walk. Pack your baby up and go visit a friend. Or leave your baby with your partner and go out alone to recharge your batteries. Turn to your immediate family for help. If your friends and family are supportive and encouraging and understanding, your burden can be eased.

Quotable Quote
"Worry is interest paid on trouble before it falls due."—William Ralph Inge, theologian and author

A Mother's Reflections
"I'd been home with the baby for maybe three days when I decided I wanted to go out to a store and buy something for the baby. I remember feeling if I didn't get out of the house and get some air that minute, I'd go crazy. I guess I had cabin fever."

PART III
✤ Your New Family ✤

✤ Introduction ✤

No matter whether you are married or a single parent, with the birth or adoption of a baby you become a family. A family is a unit that lives together, learns together, and cooperates with one another. It is a group of individuals finding a way to relate to and support one another.

A new baby is an addition that changes the dynamics of many of your relationships—with your mother, your brother, your partner, your friends, your other children. This part of the book devotes itself to understanding those changes.

There's a chapter on the importance of the father's role in bringing up baby, another on siblings' reactions, plus a chapter discussing the role and relationship of grandparents. Child-care arrangements often become part of the larger picture of your family life as well. There is a chapter on choosing and finding appropriate care for your baby. In this day and age, family issues do not stop inside the home. Often, part of what you do for your family is to provide financial support. For this reason, there is a chapter on returning to work and balancing your two identities of parent and employee.

CHAPTER 27

✦ Your Partner Is Now a Dad ✦

No one should for a minute think that the father is not a vital and important part of the baby team in the first year. There will certainly be times when you'll have more than your fair share of the baby workload, but there will also be times when your partner will step in and take over just when you need him most. Thankfully, sex roles have changed enough in the past twenty years that, while your own father probably rarely changed a diaper, your baby's father may not only change them but wash them too. With more and more men attending prenatal classes and witnessing births, the stage is set for greater continued involvement—not just because it is becoming socially "expected" but because it is enjoyable and rewarding to be an active father.

✦   ✦   ✦

PATERNITY LEAVE

According to a 1990 *Time* magazine poll, 48 percent of polled men aged eighteen to twenty-four were interested in staying home with their children. Unfortunately, most men don't get the chance to follow that dream—either because finances won't allow them or because they feel socially pressured to remain on the job. The sad fact is that society tends to view dads who stay home as being uncommitted to their careers. This perception of paternity leave obviously causes men to hesitate and worry about how their careers might be affected by time off. Furthermore, many men remain tied to the feeling that their main job as parent is to provide for a child by making money. To make matters even more complicated, children are often born when the father is in his thirties—a crucial time in any career and years during which men may feel compelled to put in the most time at work.

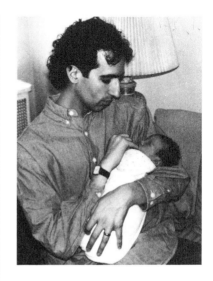

House Husbands
In March 1992, the U.S. Department of Labor reported that 578,000 fathers were at home while their wives worked. That may sound like a lot until you realize that there are 24,460,000 fathers in two-parent families.

Some companies offer a limited-time paid paternity leave. Employers of 50 or more employees must allow parents (male or female) to take up to 12 weeks of unpaid leave for the birth or adoption of a child and guarantee the same or equivalent job on their return. The family's finances obviously must be taken into consideration. Assuming the father is by far the higher earner, it may be financially inappropriate for him to be the one to take time off from work right now. With enough in savings, however, a short unpaid paternity leave may be financially feasible.

FATHER-TIME

Feeding times are not all that a newborn needs in his life right now. He spends many hours in a quiet, alert state—a perfect time for getting to know Dad. A father who spends time holding his baby and allowing the baby to focus on his face will come to feel very close to this child. Seeing his tiny baby's face brighten when he looks at him lets the father know that he is an important person in his baby's life already. The more time a father spends with his baby, the better he gets to know baby's moods and the easier it becomes for Dad to calm the baby, coax a smile, read a nonverbal cue, or soothe him to sleep. Dressing and undressing babies and changing diapers also take practice. The more frequently fathers do these tasks, the more familiar they become and eventually dads develop their own little tricks to make baby care easier.

Of course, father-time is not all diapering duties. So much of what a parent does (and which is so important to child development) is simply playing. Although mother and father may find different ways of playing with baby, both styles are important. During the early months, of course, roughhousing can be physically harmful to a baby, and a father should certainly be as aware as a mother of this fact. Instead he should spend time holding and talking to the newborn, showing him toys and watching his reactions. Toward the end of the first year, some rough-and-tumble play is not only appropriate but a lot of fun for baby and Dad. Moms can be roughhousers too, of course, but dads typically see this as their role—giving piggyback rides and bouncing baby around. Clearly, in a family where Mom is the principal caregiver, she has a lot less time in her day for such play. Dad fills the gap, then, blissfully free of the hours of picking up toys and grocery shopping and cooking that Mom may already have logged today. During Mom-time, she might play with the baby as he sits in the grocery cart, sing along with baby as they drive back home, offer baby pots and pans to play with while she cooks. Dads who are not involved in the primary caregiver role obviously can devote full physical attention to the baby because they are not trying to do something else at the same time. Babies love this attention and playtime with Dad and clearly benefit from it.

Father-time spent with the newborn has another benefit as well: it allows the mother to have some free time to nap, bathe, read a newspaper, or make a phone call uninterrupted. As a father becomes more and more involved with his child, he may notice that he has a better relationship not only with the child but also with the mother. So many women these days hold two jobs—mothering and working outside the home—that father-time is all the more necessary and appreciated. About 54 percent of married women with children under the age of one are working outside the home, according to 1990 U.S. Bureau of Labor statistics. Women who work outside the home tend to end up putting in more hours altogether, when baby-care hours are added to paid employment hours. When fathers pitch in, this lightens the load (see "Fair Shares," p. 262), and will inevitably expand a woman's love for and pride in her partner.

STILL A MATE

Fathers have another role in the first month, which is caring for mothers. Most women don't have extended family around anymore, so they are even more dependent on their loved ones for help during the early weeks and months. Since fathers do not have the physical demands placed on them that new mothers do, nor the postpartum recovery to drain them, they can be of great help around the house, preparing meals and doing all the day-to-day tasks that might otherwise be left to moms.

Often, a dad provides his wife with her only feedback on how she is doing at being a mother. The father may also be her one source of outside news and adult companionship in the first month or two. Men need to be sensitive to this.

Obviously, still acting the part of mate means continuing sexual relations. Although this is usually no difficult assignment, some men

Have Times Changed?
First, a look back at a 1972 study of dads and their daughters: Fathers tended to be less involved with their daughters than mothers were. When fathers were involved, they tended to be more action oriented, physically helping the child to do something. Mothers, on the other hand, were found to be more supportive and encouraging. According to a new 1990s study, it seems that things haven't changed much: When sociologist Diane Lye at the University of Washington observed 700 families, she found that fathers who had only daughters played with them less frequently, talked to them less often, attended fewer family outings, and even ate fewer meals at home than did fathers who had only sons.

A Doctor's Thoughts

"Mothers have to have a lot of self-confidence and self-esteem to do this job. There aren't any outside rewards, there aren't any school grades with this. It's important for dads to say, 'You're so good at this job! It's so great the way you knew she'd had enough playtime when she began to turn away,' and so on."—Mary Howell, Assistant Clinical Professor of Pediatrics, Harvard Medical School

A Father's Reflections

"One night when I was holding a fussy Ben, [my wife] said, 'Let me have him. Maybe I can make him stop.' The suggestion annoyed me. Even worse, once he smelled her, heard her voice and sensed her touch, he quieted immediately. I was actually angry for a few seconds until a sign lit up in my head: 'Jerk!' The point was that Ben felt better."—from "A Father's Eye View of Birth" by Steve Kemper, published in American Baby, *June 1991*

do find that they have some trouble switching gears from parenting to partnering. If this is true in your case, talk about it together and give yourselves a little time. Romance will typically rekindle once the initial trauma of birth and early newborn care has passed. See the section on postpartum sex, page 238.

JEALOUSY

The early relationship between mother and child can be particularly intense in the first year. Unfortunately, some men may actually become jealous of that intimate relationship with the new significant other in your life. They may be jealous of the time you spend with baby and the time taken away from couple activities. Or they may be jealous of your "way" with the infant, who, if you are the primary caregiver, may sometimes act more desirous of Mom's attention than Dad's. Meanwhile, the mother who gives all day (both physically and emotionally) to her infant may not have much energy left over for Dad by day's end. This can add up to occasional, and natural, feelings of jealousy. Of course, not all dads experience feelings of jealousy. Dads who are highly involved in child care along with their wives may be less likely to view the relationship between mother and child as "exclusive" and would therefore be less likely to be jealous of this relationship. Also, a dad who does his fair share of child and home care allows his partner the time she needs to occasionally separate herself from this pervasive role of mother and slip back into her other roles of person, employee, friend, wife, daughter, whatever.

Both parents, of course, will benefit from time spent together. Try to get a babysitter lined up for occasional nights or afternoons out. Just because your child may be in day care for much of the week doesn't mean you should feel guilty about also allowing yourself the occasional outing for socializing. If you do feel strongly about not being away from baby a minute longer than you have to be, however, then be creative. If you are working, arrange to meet for lunch during the work week—when you'd normally be out of the house anyway. Or if you're at your mom's house and the baby has just gone down for an hour nap, your partner and you can take advantage of the free time and the built-in babysitting by taking a walk or going out for coffee and cake.

SUPPORT OF BREASTFEEDING

A lot of attention is paid to a dad's ability to get involved by bottle feeding. But what if his baby is not bottle-fed? Must he be left out of the breastfeeding experience? Breastfeeding is not necessarily a time from which Dad must be excluded. This can be a nice time to snuggle together as a family on the couch or in bed. It can be the perfect time for a quiet, pleasant conversation. (This is not the time to start ranting about tax returns. Stressful conversations or arguments do *not* enhance milk flow!) Dads can support breastfeeding by allowing their wives the time to breastfeed. As mentioned above, breastfeeding is a quiet time for mother and baby. It helps if Dad plays with an older toddler during this time or does a chore his partner is unable to get to right now, like unload the dishwasher. He should not assume that just because you are sitting in a chair staring out into space that you are doing nothing. Hopefully, he will come to respect this time as extremely important both to you and the baby.

Unfortunately, a recent study published in *Pediatrics* does indicate that many men do not understand the benefits of breastfeeding and may be unsupportive of it. Breastfeeding women with unsupportive husbands, in turn, may end up choosing to formula-feed or even wean the baby from the breast earlier than they might otherwise have done. This study indicates how important a father's support can be in helping his wife to breastfeed successfully. It is particularly helpful to have a supportive dad if other members of your family, such as your own mother, are initially unsupportive of your choice.

A FATHER'S FINANCIAL WORRIES

Although obviously a concern of both parents, dads sometimes feel the financial burden of children weighing heavily on their shoulders. This may be tied to the stereotypical view of a man's role as the one who brings home the bacon (whether or not the mother also works). When children arrive in the world, he may take this role even more seriously and therefore become more worried about his job and the amount of money the family has. Unfortunately, the end result sometimes is that dads start spending *more* time at work after the baby is born rather than *less*.

Fathers' Attitudes About Breastfeeding

In a Texas study published in *Pediatrics* (August 1992), men whose partners planned to breastfeed exclusively were more likely to understand the benefits of breastfeeding than those whose partners did not plan to breastfeed. The breastfeeding group was more likely to believe breastfeeding was better for the baby, helped with infant-mother bonding, and protected their baby from disease. The formula-feeding father group was more likely to think that breastfeeding was bad for the breasts, made breasts ugly, and interfered with sex. "These fathers would presumably have a nonsupportive or even negative outlook toward breastfeeding and could be expected to discourage their partners from attempting to initiate lactation," write Doctors Freed, Fraley, and Schanler. They conclude, "We recommend that fathers be included and actively solicited for participation in all breastfeeding education courses currently taught in hospitals."

FAIR SHARES

As much as we like to think that male-female relationships are on equal footing these days, the unbalance often becomes painfully clear when the first child is born. Typically, the mother gets the often delightful, but sometimes draining and thankless, job of caring for the child and the home. Even women who work as many hours outside the home as their husbands often find that, when they return home, they have many more hours ahead of them doing the domestic tasks that are presumed to be the domain of the woman: dinner, laundry, bathing, bedding of children. Arlie Hochschild, a professor at the University of California, who wrote a book called *The Second Shift,* discovered that working moms put in an average fifteen hours a week more than their working husbands when she added in their domestic chores.

To try to equalize the parenting forces in your house, think about trying the following things:

1. If both of you are willing to do so, you might make a schedule of parenting and home care activities and divide them up. For example, you'll do the bills Thursday night while he does the laundry. Or you'll do the dinner dishes while he gives the bath. You can set up an actual written calendar of events or just make a loose verbal agreement to split certain tasks.

2. Remind yourself and your spouse that whether your outside job brings in 10 percent of what he makes or surpasses what he makes is not the issue. You both are putting in a lot of time, attention, and energy to your paid jobs. Both of you deserve respect for this, regardless of the monetary awards, and therefore, both of you (not just the lesser earner) should be involved in the child care and household care at night.

3. Ask yourself if you have been inadvertently interfering with your partner's attempts at child care. Do you criticize the way

Cost Conscious

The average cost of raising a child for eighteen years in the United States today is about $105,000. Most of this money goes simply to feeding and housing the child. About $7,000 is spent on clothing; the same on medical care. This figure is based on 1989 estimates for a child in a Midwestern urban area.

he gives her a bath? Rush into the room to remind him which shirt matches those overalls? Disapprove of the fact that he fed her a snack of Cheerios so close to lunch? Nagging, hovering, and complaining obviously aren't going to do much to foster a father's feelings of self-esteem or his desire to do this job. Back off. It may be quite true that you know a lot more about bringing up baby than your husband does (assuming you are the one who does the lion's share of the child care), but your partner will never learn if you interfere. He's going to have his own way of dealing with your son or daughter and it's going to be different. In the long run, this will be healthful for your child. After all, a child doesn't need two identical mothers; he benefits from having two different parents. No matter how inexperienced Dad may seem to you, the baby will certainly come to no harm by being dressed in a mismatched outfit or going out for a walk in moderate temperatures without a hat on. Allow Dad his distinctively male way of relating to the child. He may play in a messier or rougher way. He may throw what you consider caution to the wind by leaving the pack of baby wipes at home. Assuming the new dad is honestly trying to nurture and care for this baby, you can feel entirely comfortable leaving the two of them to their own devices and allowing the relationship to take its own course. The more time he spends with his baby, the more ways he will develop for responding to her needs (soon you may even learn something new from him . . . so don't be so smug).

4. Reinforce the truth that babies are not superfragile. Dads should not be made to feel that they are clumsy or too large to handle such a tiny being. A baby is not made of glass and will not break. It is extremely unlikely that a dad would accidentally drop a baby or hurt him just by holding him, even though he may be fearful of this. (Of course, exuberant bouncing and roughhousing are not acceptable in the early months, since they can harm an infant's developing brain.)

5. Redesign your view of the father's role. If you and your partner view fatherhood in strictly old-fashioned terms, it is unlikely that either of you will feel comfortable with shared parenting roles. Dads today are not only the breadwinners, the disciplinarians, and the baseball tossers. Dads should be allowed the space and permission to be the cuddlers and the

A Look Back, A Look Forward
Openly discuss the roles your own fathers played in your lives and how you hope your child's view of a father will be different (or the same). How much time did your father spend at work and at home? What, if any, was their involvement with you as children? Then, decide together to take constructive steps to help your husband become the father that your kids will eventually look back on with respect, pride, and love.

kissers and the feeders and the book readers as well. By loosening the definition of what a dad is, you allow for an easier and potentially more loving relationship between father and child.

6. Remind the new father that he is not spoiling a baby by going to him when he cries. Sometimes, a man's lack of action may be due to his perception of how to parent rather than his refusal to parent. If your husband can sit and listen to crying that would make you jump up, talk to him about why he didn't go to the baby. Some dads may mistakenly believe that responding to every little cry is just spoiling the baby (not a manly image by any means!). In fact, responding to an infant's cries actually helps nourish and sustain a child's growing sense of trust and security.

WHEN DAD IS NOT AROUND: SINGLE MOTHERS

Raising a baby without the help of the father can be trying—from the first month through the college years. It's important to develop and use a network of supportive friends and relatives. You may also wish to make arrangements for your child to spend time with his father, if this is an option in your situation. A lawyer or social worker may be best suited to helping you work out the details of such an arrangement.

On the positive side, you and your child or children will probably develop an extremely close relationship. If it was your choice not to live with the baby's father, you obviously did what you thought was in the best interests of all involved. Choosing to be a single parent does not make you any less a family.

On the negative side, you're missing an extra pair of hands and an extra perspective on childrearing. This is where friends and relatives can help. For support, you might also want to contact a group like Parents Without Partners, 401 N. Michigan Avenue, Chicago, Ill. 60611-4267 (1-800-637-7974), or 1-312-644-6610 in Chicago.

Single Statistics
There has been a steady increase in the number of single-parent homes. Today, about 25 percent of all American children are being raised by single parents. Of these single parents, about 90 percent are women.

CHAPTER 28

✦ Full House ✦

A new baby may be turning a two-some into a threesome or a three- or foursome into more-some! Bringing a new baby home when there is already a child in the house is a wholly different experience from last time, when you returned home to an empty house. There's noise and toys and demands for your attention, housework and preschool schedules and little feelings to contend with. On the positive side, there's a certain excitement and pride in adding to your family and making your once-baby an older sibling. On the other hand, there's less of you to go around and you have to be a little more creative and patient now! A number of issues may come up during the first year, from regressive behavior in older children to sibling rivalry. This chapter also takes a quick look at birth order (just for fun), plus issues surrounding the only child and advice on how to live happily with a pet and baby (just in case it's your collie that's becoming the older sibling).

✦   ✦   ✦

SIBLINGS AT THE BIRTH

Your child may have been at the delivery itself or, at least, near enough to have seen your new baby within minutes of the birth. Hopefully, all went as you expected it would. Having children at a birth is a very personal decision. In retrospect, it may or may not have been ideal for your family. Assuming it was a positive experience for all, you can be happy that your older child was able to be so intimately involved with the birth of her new baby brother or sister. Hopefully, this will spill over into a caring, responsible sibling attachment. If, however, your child became bored by the birth and walked out, do not be too disappointed. You were right to let her come and go as she pleased, even if this meant she missed the big event in the end. It would have been a mistake to insist that she stay. If your child did stay throughout and for one reason or another, seemed to be upset with any of the sounds or sights, give her a chance to discuss these concerns with you now. There's no need to drone on with lengthy discussions of the birth in retrospect. Just be there to answer any questions she may have. You may be able to set her mind at ease about something that has been bothering her: for example, maybe she felt like she was in the way when the doctor asked her to move. Just as you have questions about the birth in retrospect or replay parts of it in your mind, your child may also. If you are sensitive to this, you should be able to allay any concerns quickly by answering her questions.

HOMECOMING OF MOTHER AND NEWBORN

An older sibling is likely to be a lot more excited about seeing you come home than he is about meeting a new baby. You are the older child's universe right now. The baby is just a shooting star passing through it. With this in mind, it helps to leave the baby in the car seat for a moment so you have both arms ready to meet and greet the older child who rushes out to greet you. You could also ask Dad or Grandma to hold the baby while you and your firstborn get reacquainted. Another favorite homecoming tip is to come bearing gifts—from the baby—for your other children. Let them know that they are being honored as a big brother or sister. There can be just as much excitement surrounding their promotion to this new role as there is about the baby's arrival.

Once they've enjoyed some time with just Mom, they'll be curious about seeing the new baby. Assuming your older child is healthy, allow the child to hold the newborn with supervision. By having him sit down on the couch, perhaps with a pillow in his lap and the baby resting on the pillow, you can make the first holding session safe and comfortable. Take the baby away before your toddler gets truly bored with this experience. (Your toddler may be quite disappointed that this baby doesn't *do* anything!)

Once the baby is tucked quietly into a bassinet and your suitcase has been put away, sit down with your older child for some quiet time. It may be nice to go through some old photo albums, showing him what he looked like when he was a baby. This can head off feelings of jealousy as you point out to your older child how you did the same things for him when he was a newborn. It also makes children feel very important to see how they have grown and become a "big boy or girl" over the years.

If there's time and your kids are at the age to enjoy it, why not have a real celebration? Older siblings can bake a birthday cake and plan a party for the family. All children love the excitement and promise of a birthday party.

SIBLING INTERACTION

Small babies are often of immediate interest to older siblings but ways to play with them are not immediately apparent. You may find an older sibling trying to force a sleeping baby's eyes open ("Just checking, Mom," they'll say) or throwing unsuitable toys into the crib. In the very beginning, you'll have to think of acceptable ways that they can "help": getting a diaper for you, turning on a music box, telling you a story while you breastfeed. Remember to thank them for their help and to reinforce this positive behavior. By two months, you and the new baby will have a little more patience and time for playing with older siblings. Show the older sibling what the baby likes: how to shake a rattle at the baby or hold up a plastic mirror for the baby to make faces in. Older siblings also delight in the way a new baby will squeeze their fingers or stare delightedly at their faces. The positive reinforcement that a new baby gets from older siblings helps him become an active, social little person. The older sibling will almost certainly delight in a baby's every smile and gurgle, and will respond in kind, "playing" in this way for many minutes while you look on.

REGRESSIVE BEHAVIOR IN OLDER SIBLING

In spite of your best-laid plans and near-perfect Mommy skills, some children will not respond happily to the arrival of a new baby. They may seem fine until you notice that there is a return to more babyish behavior: wetting the bed at night, wanting to get back in a crib, soiling underwear, wanting a bottle, pacifier, or blankie back. This is a natural reaction to the arrival of a new baby. The older sibling sees how babyhood appeals to everyone: the big fuss made

On the Lighter Side
Here's a quick look at your family, as defined in *The Dictionary According to Mommy*, by Joyce Armor (Meadowbrook, 1989): "Father: The guy who says, 'C'mere, honey, I think his diaper needs changing.' Brother/sister: A combination punching bag and best friend. Relatives: People who you wish lived nearby so they could baby-sit on long weekends."

Role Playing

If you like, let her role-play and pretend to be a baby for a while. Then, if she tries to talk, remind her, "Babies can't talk." If she gets up to get something for herself, remind her, "Babies can't walk." She'll soon find being a baby a pretty dull game.

over the baby, the way she is instantly held and hugged if he whimpers, and so on. It can seem appealing to return to that stage. Plus, your older child reasons, the accoutrements of babyhood may win her some of the attention she sees baby getting. Often, however, it is met negatively by parents, who are shocked to see their responsible "big boy" suddenly sticking a pacifier in his mouth or refusing to use the toilet. At this point, it's best not to make a big fuss over the regressive behavior by saying it's bad or expressing any real displeasure. Instead, try giving your child a little extra attention (he can cuddle next to you while you're breastfeeding; sit in your lap while baby's in her bassinet, and so on).

To minimize regressive behavior, make sure your child knows that being big has real advantages. It can help to remind her of the things she can do that a baby can't (talk, put a cassette tape in the player, play with a friend). Encourage an older child to behave in older child ways. Make sure that your child knows you prefer her to stay dry, drink from a cup, or whatever by giving matter-of-fact statements. For example, say, "The potty is right here. It's for you to use." Praise her when she does the "grown up" thing and uses it.

SIBLING RIVALRY

Although classic sibling rivalry probably won't start until later when your children are on more even footing, you may see some signs of resentment or jealousy earlier on. A new sibling is a change that the older child must adjust to. Some will adjust to it well. Others will have more trouble coping with the stress of the new family dynamics. A new sibling won't necessarily be a problem for your child. In fact, it can help to make your firstborn more independent and empathetic. The positive aspects of having a sibling should not be overlooked in a parent's watchful sensitivity to sibling rivalry issues.

Many children are perfectly happy with their new siblings and remain secure in their relationship with Mom and Dad. It may not be until much farther down the road (when baby is old enough to get into her things, rip up baseball cards, or ruin a game) that some natural, and expected, animosity may surface. Some children, however, start out suspicious of this newcomer and feel slightly insecure about their own place within the changed family. Your older child may want his new sibling sent back where he came from or, at the very least, ignored completely. Although you can try to encourage a caring relationship between siblings, you are not to blame if sibling rivalry becomes an issue. So much depends on the sexes and ages involved and the temperament of the particular children.

Sibling rivalry may be noticeable in the way your child treats his new little brother or sister or even in the way he treats you. If he's able to treat the baby gently, he may turn around and treat you like a doormat. Here are some of the best ways to prevent sibling rivalry from rearing its ugly head in the first place:

1. Minimize changes in your firstborn's life. Try to keep her usual schedule and routines on an even keel.
2. Arrange for time together away from the new baby. If it's possible, get Dad to watch the baby while you and your older child play a game or take a walk.
3. Allow a healthy older sibling to touch and hold the baby (under your supervision, of course).
4. Let her know that it's okay to feel annoyed with the baby. Agree that babies can sometimes be loud and messy!
5. Ask for her help with the baby so she feels like part of the team rather than the odd person out. Let your older sibling make decisions about what the baby should wear that day, for example.
6. Make a fuss over your older child as often as you can. Show her baby pictures to remind her that she was once a baby herself.
7. Don't knock your child off your lap and run every time baby cries. Try to move a little more slowly, excusing yourself from the book or game first before going to get baby, then returning with the baby to try to finish what you were doing.

> **An Expert's Thoughts**
> *"Parents should be aware of what they are doing when they talk about the new baby. Rather than talk about how wonderful it is to have a new baby, talk about how wonderful it is to be a big brother or sister. Define a very positive role for them."*
> —*Dr. Keith Crnic, Professor of Psychology, Pennsylvania State University*

BIRTH ORDER

Much has been published about birth order and personality development. Are firstborns really different from the middle child or the

Children Are Individuals
No matter how many studies are done to show what first-borns, middle, and last-born children act like, they are all generalizations.

Although it can be fun to read about what the middle child is *supposed* to be like, don't take it too seriously and don't expect that your child will fit the bill. It would be a mistake, for example, to expect lower achievement in a middle child just because of something you read.

baby? It would seem that there is some truth to this theory, but at the same time, a parent must remember that ages of the children, spacing between children, sex, and family size also influence the effect of a child's birth order on his development. Remember, too, that these are just theories and may have no bearing on the way your own child develops.

It may be easiest to see the effect of birth order on the firstborn. Firstborn children are said to be achievement-oriented and are statistically more likely to attend college. They may also be more likely to emulate their parents' religious and social beliefs. The main reason for the firstborn's driven personality: Parents tend to be harder on the firstborn, with higher expectations and more demands for performance. They typically talk to the firstborn more and interfere more with the activities of the firstborn than later-born children. The firstborn is the only one to experience a time when he did not have to share his parents' love and attention. This may make for an especially intense relationship between the firstborn and the parents, which continues throughout life. The eldest child has additional demands on him. He or she is often expected to take responsibility for younger siblings and to use self-control in playing with the younger ones. With the greater pressures of being the firstborn come some anxieties as well. There is some sketchy evidence that firstborns don't cope so well with anxiety-producing situations. They may show less self-confidence and have a greater fear of failure than later-born children.

It is harder to characterize middle and later-born children. The middle child is often said to be caught in between—not the one in power and not the baby. Some believe that, as a result, they are more extroverted than their siblings and more humorous. At the same time, though, there is some evidence that they are less achievement-oriented than their older sibling.

The last child is considered to be the one who is indulged and nurtured by the parents as the "baby." The last child supposedly receives some of the positive attention that the firstborn received without the negative constraints and demands. As a result, the last-born is typically characterized as secure, self-confident, and achievement-oriented.

THE ONLY CHILD

In the past, the only child was considered to be spoiled and bratty simply by virtue of not having any siblings around. More recently, however, research has indicated that this is not the case. In fact, only children have some distinct advantages. Like a firstborn, they have parents with high demands and high expectations, but unlike a firstborn, they never have to deal with being displaced by younger siblings. The only child is thought by some to end up less anxious and more self-confident than most firstborns, with the same natural proclivity toward high achievement. Of course, on the negative side, an only child doesn't have the benefit of practicing social skills with siblings and there are no built-in playmates.

TWINS

Assuming you had ultrasound, you were likely prepared for the arrival of twins. Still their actual arrival can throw you, as you try to manage both newborns at the same time. If there are other siblings already in the house, this fact certainly adds to your work! Twins are often born early. If this was true in your case, see the section on premature birth on page 187. You will, of course, find your own ways to cope with the demands of two babies. If possible, get them both on the same schedule. It's possible to breastfeed both at the same time if you sit with them crossed in your lap or with both in a football hold and a hand under each head. On outings, use a twin stroller or put one in a front carrier and the other in a stroller. For bath time, alternate nights—bathing one one night and the other the next. As the months go by, you will develop creative solutions to your most pressing baby-care problems. Talking with other mothers of twins can help. See the sidebar for information on how to get in touch with other parents in your shoes.

THE FAMILY PET AND YOUR NEW BABY

You may, naturally, have some concerns about how your pet will react to having a baby in the house. You want to be sure that your child will be safe from any possible aggressive reactions on the animal's part. Never leave the baby alone with a pet.

When you first arrive home from the hospital, greet your dog or

First in Space
Twenty out of the first twenty-three astronauts were either firstborns or only children.

Twins Resource
For information on how to get in touch with other mothers of twins, contact National Association of Mothers of Twins Club, P.O. Box 23188, Albuquerque, NM 87192 (505-275-0955).

cat without the baby in your arms. Then, carefully introduce your baby to the dog by allowing the dog to sniff the baby under your careful supervision. If your baby has his own room, make it off limits to the dog or cat. If the baby is going to sleep in your room (where the dog or cat used to sleep), you'll have to block this room off. Using a gate may be helpful, allowing the pet to see into the room and still feel a part of things.

Try to give the pet attention when you can, by giving treats, petting her, or walking her. If your dog makes the slightest snarl or bares her teeth, admonish her immediately. Tie her up and keep her away from the baby if you have to. If your indoor cat is scratching, talk to your vet about having her declawed. If, for some reason, you find that your pet and the new baby simply are not a match made in heaven, you may have to give the pet away.

Mothers' Reflections

"Before we left the hospital, my husband brought a blanket with the scent of the baby on it home and let the dog smell it. When we got home with the baby, we continued to give the dog lots of attention and didn't change his habits. He continued to sleep in the bedroom with us. You could tell from the beginning it would be fine. He didn't seem jealous at all."

✦

"I had heard people say that a cat might try to get in the bassinet with a baby. I don't know whether or not it's true but it scared me, so I kept the cat out of the baby's room. I was especially careful to close the door to the baby's room when I wasn't in there."

CHAPTER 29

✤ Grandparents Are Grand ✤

Grandparents may be rarely seen, occasional visitors, weekend warriors, or even next-door neighbors. How much time your parents spend with your child depends on the physical distance between you, your lifestyle, and theirs.

✤   ✤   ✤

GRANDPARENTS AS PARENTS

Some grandparents these days care for the child in the parents' stead. If you are a grandparent reading this book, you are not alone. There are over 3 million American children living with their grandparents. If you'd like to find a place to turn for support and advice, call the A.A.R.P. Grandparent Information Center at (202) 434-2296.

LONG-DISTANCE GRANDPARENTS

If your parents or your husband's parents live far away, it is unlikely that they will get to see much of the wonder and excitement of the first year. This doesn't mean that they can't share it with you, however. See the sidebar on page 274 for tips on keeping long-distance grandparents close. If you can afford it, it can be worthwhile to make the trip with baby to visit the grandparents

(unless they can come to see you instead). Traveling with a small child (especially if you are breastfeeding) is often fairly easy. See page 118 on taking a trip with an infant. If one set of grandparents is far away and one close by, this can engender some feelings of jealousy. Be sensitive to this and try to keep the long-distance grandparents involved.

NEXT-DOOR GRANDPARENTS

When grandparents live very close, you may feel blessed and, at the same time, claustrophobic. Next-door grandparents can often be counted on for emergency babysitting or instant advice. Unfortunately, they can sometimes also be counted on for unwanted advice. Much depends on the relationship you already have with your parents. It also depends on how much you turn to them for help. If you ask for their opinion on every little thing, they may soon come to offer opinions without even being asked. If you want them to view you as a parent in your own right, take charge and make your own decisions. This isn't to say that you can't discuss problems and concerns with them. You can. In fact, one of the nicest things about having grandparents around is the way they can put parenting problems in perspective for you. After all, they have been through this before—with you.

DIVORCED GRANDPARENTS

Families are not always tidy little units. Your parents may be divorced or even remarried. Family ties may be extensive and complicated. As your children grow, they will take this in stride. They automatically assume that, if it works in their family, then it's perfectly normal. Having stepcousins and step-grandparents won't confuse them if everything is explained clearly from an early age. On the positive side, your child simply has more people to love her! From your perspective, of course, you do have more people to think about. Assuming you feel good about your relationship with all the people involved, try to make sure that no one feels left out of the new baby's life. Sometimes, however, you are naturally closer to one parent or stepparent than the others. In this case, just try to do what's best for you and for your child.

INTERFERING

New mothers and fathers usually get their fair share of unasked for advice about childrearing. Sometimes this comes straight from your own mom and dad. It is certainly natural for them to want "what's best" for your new family. The problem is: Who's to say what's best? As a new parent, you're already struggling with your own parenting style. Too many opinions from your own parents can make you feel insecure in your new role. Remember: You are the parent. You will soon be an expert about what calms your baby down, what your baby likes, what your baby doesn't like. Also keep in mind that time (and trends in parenting) have changed. What your parents advocate may no longer be the same thing that pediatricians and child development specialists are currently advocating. You can listen to everyone's opinion, but in the end, you are the parent and the decision rests with you. If your parents give advice, try to be gracious. They mean well. Let them know that you'll ask your pediatrician about it. Then go ahead and do it your way. Feel confident in your own choices. Your parents will soon come to see you as the parent in charge and may wait to be asked for advice next time. And remember—they may have very good advice.

SPECIAL NAMES

How are both sets of parents responding to the thought of being grandparents? Are they ready to be called by name? Even though they have had nine months to prepare, hearing themselves referred to as Grandma or Grandpa the first time can be a shock. Eventually, your child will start talking. When she does, she may make up her own name for her grandparents. In advance of this moment, though, you might want to ask everyone what they *want* to be called. Maybe one side of the family is more comfortable with the Italian Nana instead of Grandma or the German Opa for Grandpa. Maybe your

Famous Quote
Perhaps you should pass this famous quote along to your parents: "I have found that the best way to give advice to your children is to find out what they want and then advise them to do it."—Harry S Truman (as quoted in *Peter's Quotations* by Dr. Laurence J. Peter)

Quotable Quote
"Becoming a grandmother is the ultimate happiness. Just when you've settled for being an ordinary person, you find out you're a super person, because a grandchild comes along who holds that opinion."—Phyllis Diller (from the foreword of *Grandma Knows Best But No One Ever Listens!* by Mary McBride, published by Meadowbrook, 1987)

A Mother's Reflections
"The minute my baby was born, I was in love. It was so strong. I was crazy about him. And then I immediately thought, 'This must be how much my own mother loved me.' Of course, I always knew she loved me, I just never realized how much!"

parents prefer to be called by their first names. Once everyone has settled on a name they feel comfortable with, use it when talking with your baby. Eventually, he may make his own changes to the names based on what he can pronounce most easily!

NEW ROLES

All of a sudden, you're no longer just a daughter or son. You're a parent too! This can be the start of a new and more equal relationship with your parents. Life is starting to come full circle and you are now in the same position they were in when they had you. You're more grown up now in their eyes. You have your own child to cope with now and you can now share with them some of the secret joys and pains of what it is to be a parent.

CHAPTER 30

✦ Child-care Arrangements ✦

Other caregivers can be an important and sometimes necessary part of your family's life. Parents often need some help with, or time off from, their parenting duties. Parents who work outside the home (and that's more than half of you!) need responsible, consistent child care during their work hours. Although times have changed and there are many more dual-job families, uniformly good, easy-to-find child care is still years away. Law and policy are still catching up to the realities and needs of the families of the 1990s.

✦   ✦   ✦

RELATIVES WHO BABYSIT

You may choose to have a relative or a friend care for your child. While this presents special comforts, it can also present special problems. Try to be clear with one another from the outset. Will this be an occasional helping hand or a more permanent one? Will you pay this relative, and if so, how much? Will the child care take place in your home or the relative's home? Are you comfortable with this? Make sure everyone is happy with the arrangements. You must also be clear about your baby-care beliefs. Just because this person is related to you doesn't mean you and she see eye to eye on subjective subjects like spoiling, disciplining, or feeding. Sit down and work out schedules and answer questions, just as you would with a babysitter not related to you.

Grandma at Your Service
Twenty-one percent of employed moms with children under the age of one go off to work leaving their children with a relative, according to a 1990 National Child-care Survey, reported in a January 1993 *Pediatrics* supplement.

IN-YOUR-HOME BABYSITTERS

When choosing a babysitter, begin by determining your needs. Are you looking for someone to help while you're at home? Do you need only the occasional nighttime sitter for a night out with your spouse? Do you want a full-time child-care situation so you can return to

It's been a GREAT party, Jeff— but you know how it is... At midnight, we turn back into parents.

Wanted: Mary Poppins
In-home care is an option taken by only 3 percent of working mothers of children under age one (from the National Child-care Survey, 1990).

work? Do you need someone who can cook? Do you expect your sitter to also do laundry or care for the house? No matter what type of help you need, you'll want to look for a responsible, caring, and trustworthy person. Be sure to check references and interview several candidates before hiring. During the interview you may want to ask:

1. Do you have any other child-care experience?
2. How long were you in your last job?
3. What were your duties in that job?
4. Why have you decided to look for a new job?
5. What do you enjoy most about caring for children?
6. How long do you plan to stay in the job if I hire you?
7. What kind of hours are you looking for? Could you stay late if I needed you or if there was an emergency?

You may also want to ask some questions specific to the jobs you have in mind. For example, you might ask if the person likes to cook and what she enjoys making. Can the person drive? Does she know how to swim? If you have older children, you should ask how she plans to handle two or more children at once. If your children often have friends over, you might ask how this person would feel about playdates. As you meet and talk with the person you are interviewing, you will be looking for signs that they are honest, active, kind, patient, flexible, clean, dependable, enjoy children, and have realistic expectations of newborn behavior.

Your own gut reaction, financial situation, and family needs will decide the rest. Always ask for references and call and speak with them to find out as much as you can about how your caregiver performed in her last job. The first few times the sitter comes, you would be wise to stay at home with her, showing her the house, leading her through the basic baby-care routines you know so well. Stop by unannounced from time to time.

There has been increased awareness recently of the need to comply with laws regarding the payment of minimum wage and employment taxes. Your local Child-care Resource and Referral Agency will be able to give you more information about this.

DAY-CARE CENTERS

Women and men who work outside the home need to find good day care for their children. With so many facilities out there (not all of them regulated), the choices can be confusing and the quality of care available can vary dramatically from place to place. A day-care center differs from family child care. Center care takes place in a nonresidential setting and provides care for a group of children for all or part of the day. Family care (see page 280) takes place in a caregiver's home, and typically involves the care of a small group of children. To find out about day-care options in your neighborhood, talk with your pediatrician, your neighbors, your friends, and other working mothers. You can also use a local Child-care Resource and Referral organization. Look in the Yellow Pages or call 1-800-424-2246 for a local number. (There may be a nominal fee for their advice and assistance.)

Once you have narrowed down one or two conveniently located centers, call up and arrange for a visit. Look for a program that has been licensed by the state and accredited by NAEYC (National Association for the Education of Young Children). Accreditation shows that the center has gone over and above the state licensing standards. See the sidebar for questions to ask yourself during your visit. Once your child begins day care, you will need to keep constantly up to date on the goings-on there, making repeated checks to satisfy yourself that this day-care situation continues to benefit your child. Remember, as your child grows or the dynamics of the center change with new teachers or new kids, you may feel happier or less

Evaluating the Quality of a Day-care Center

Ask yourself:

1. Do the children seem happy?
2. How are staff members hired? What type of education and experience do they have?
3. Is the center clean and neat?
4. Are children kept in small groups? Is the ratio of child-care staff to child adequate? (Use your own judgment, of course, but for young children look for a ratio of at least one staffer to every three infants.)
5. Is the staff trained? Seasoned? What is the turnover rate of caregivers here? (You'll want to know that the staff will stick around, both for your child's sake and as a sign of a happy staff.)
6. Is there a safe outdoor play space? How is it monitored?
7. Are there enough toys, materials, and supplies?
8. Are there posted or written rules about health and safety?

Top Ten Child-care States
In the February 1993 issue, *Working Mother* magazine listed their pick for the ten best states for child care:
California
Colorado
Connecticut
Hawaii
Maryland
Massachusetts
Minnesota
Vermont
Washington
Wisconsin
Rankings were based on quality of the care, availability, safety, and commitment to quality child care.

happy with it. Children's needs change with time and centers may have to be reevaluated by you every once in a while. What may have been a perfect place for your six-month-old baby may seem less than ideal for your one-year-old.

Although, in general, your child's health should not be at increased risk by being in a day-care center, he is exposed to more children (and their germs) than he would be alone at home. Be sure your pediatrician knows that your child is in day care or family child care and what the ages of the other children are. The center should keep good health information on all the children and have proof of their vaccinations. There has, specifically, been an increase noticed in the incidence of diarrhea among day-care attendees. The day-care center you choose should be scrupulous about handwashing after diaper changing as well as washing the children's hands. Disposable diapers are apparently more hygienic than cloth in a day-care setting.

FAMILY CHILD CARE

Child care provided for a small group of children by a person in her own home is known as family child-care. This person may be looking after her own children at the same time. Fees are often lower than at a day-care center. Some family child-care centers are licensed. Others are not. Licensing rules and regulations vary from state to state. If you are interested in pursuing this child-care option, be sure to check the family child caregiver's references. Talk with the parents of children currently in her care or those whose children were recently in her care. Find out how many children she cares for during the day and at what times the children come and go. No more than four or five children to one caregiver is usually considered a desirable number.

MOM-AND-TOT GROUPS

Some mothers with children of similar ages like to get together in groups, allowing the children time to play and moms the time to chat and socialize. You may be able to start a group among moms you already know (perhaps friends in the neighborhood or women you met in prenatal classes). Or you might consider posting a sign in the local library, supermarket, or pediatrician's office. Usually, mothers take turns hosting the playgroup in their homes. On a smaller scale, some mothers team up and take turns offering child care. Two mothers, for example, might get together and decide to give each other a little time off. One watches both children while the other goes out. Next time, they switch. This method of babysitting may work well for you if you don't need ongoing part-time or full-time child care.

An Expert's Thoughts
"Always go back and visit a center more than once. Go back unannounced as well. Listen to the sounds of the center: Is it happy? dull? chaotic? Look around: Does the staff seem cheerful? Do they talk to the children at eye level? Count the number of staff and the number of children. Ask about the qualifications of the caregivers. A quality caregiver and a quality setting will appreciate parents' questions."—Denise Nelson, Community Coordinator, Childcare Aware Project, National Association Childcare Resource and Referral Agencies

For more information, you can call the National Association of Childcare Resource and Referral Agencies at 1-800-424-2246 or the National Association for Family Day Care at 1-800-359-3817.

✦

Company Child-care Help
In a study of 1,000 firms by the Society for Human Resource Management, about one third said they offer some form of child-care help, compared with only 10 percent who did so in 1988.

CHAPTER 31

✦ Returning to Work ✦

Being a mother is not always the only job a woman has. If you worked through your pregnancy, you're probably considering returning to work now that your baby is here and healthy. Sometimes, plans you made before you had your baby no longer make sense for you. Other times, everything goes pretty much according to plan and you return to work just when you thought you would. This chapter includes some of the things you may be wondering about: from maternity leave to information on how to continue breastfeeding.

✦   ✦   ✦

MATERNITY LEAVE

Hopefully, you found out your company policy on maternity and paternity leave while you were still pregnant. You may have chosen to take some of your allowed time off before the baby was born. Or you may have worked right up to the end, preferring to use all your paid maternity leave for being with your new baby. Husbands may also want to take advantage of allowed paternity leave once the baby has arrived. Companies with 50 or more employees must allow you to take up to 12 weeks without pay after the birth or adoption of a child. If your baby is sick or hospitalized, you may be able to work out a longer paid or unpaid time off.

Although the best time to work out a return schedule is before you leave, there may still be time for you to renegotiate hours or a different return time with your boss. After all, your expectations of motherhood may be different from the reality and you may need more or less time off than you originally planned for. You may be able to work out a convenient and mutually satisfying schedule with your company or boss. Assuming you are a valued employee, you may

A Mother's Reflections
"I find it insulting when people suggest that returning to work means I don't find being a mother satisfying or that I've decided full-time mothering is not for me. This is ridiculous! Even when I'm somewhere else from nine to five, I still consider myself a full-time mother. Yes, I find being a mother immensely satisfying but I also happen to work during the day."

be able to bend standard office policy to suit your needs at this time. You may be able to arrange for an extended leave or for a part-time schedule in the early months of your return.

Although some women feel energetic enough to return after six weeks off, many prefer not to return full-time before four to six months. Not everyone is in a position to indulge this preference, however. Whether or not and when you return to work should be a purely private decision and dependent on your wishes, financial needs, company's policies, and boss's views.

THE TRANSITION FROM HOME TO WORK

Before you return to work, you'll want to make the transition easier by:

✦　　✦　　✦

1. Hiring a babysitter or locating and getting to know a day-care center at least two weeks prior to your return. (For more on hiring a babysitter, see page 277. For more on day-care centers, see pages 278–279.)
2. Having the babysitter come for a few days while you're still home or allowing the baby to spend a few hours in the day-care center. This can get you used to the routines of child care that will be a part of your life now.
3. Checking in with co-workers by phone. Keep abreast of both legitimate business and office gossip while you're away so you're not out of touch when you return. You can also have someone from the office send you materials to read over or you can update yourself by reading a professional journal.
4. Taking stock of what you'll be wearing to work. If you're like most women, your prepregnancy clothes won't always fit your postbaby body. If you can't find something in your closet that fits well, you may have to invest in a new outfit or two.
5. Answering everyone's questions about the new baby prior to your return to work. In the days before your return to work, you may even want to stop in with your baby so everyone can have a peek. This satisfies everyone's curiosity and allows you time to discuss baby topics on your own time before you must return to the serious task of work. Interest in your baby and

A Mother's Reflections
"I was really worried about going back to work. Within a few hours of being back, however, I was really into it. I remembered how much I loved work and I knew I'd made the right decision."

✦

No Apologies
Some women have to return to work for financial reasons. Others simply like to work. Enjoying your job is nothing you should have to apologize for.

baby pictures are natural but, in some workplaces, are better kept to a minimum. When you return, your boss or supervisor will expect to see a woman who's still in business.

WORKING MOMS AND BREASTFEEDING

Some working moms find bottle feeding the best and most convenient way to do things. Others may want to breastfeed but wonder if they can. You can continue to breastfeed after you return to work, but you'll need to be committed and organized. It can be quite a nice feeling to return home from work and be able to snuggle up with your baby to share the intimacy of breastfeeding, offering something that only you can give to your baby. You can breastfeed again before bed. Early mornings before you head out to work can provide another quiet time for a breastfeeding session. For some women, it's also possible to head home for a lunchtime feeding or to have the baby brought to them at lunchtime. In between, your caregiver can offer feedings as you have indicated. This may include bottles or cups of formula, expressed breast milk, or in some babies older than twelve months, cow's milk. (Ask your doctor about cow's milk before giving it to a baby under age one.)

Before you return to work, you'll need to do some preparation so breastfeeding can continue smoothly. Start by getting your baby used to taking milk from a bottle. This can be done as early as six weeks of age or as late as three weeks prior to your return to work. If your baby is over six months old when you return to work but has not had or refuses a bottle, he may be able to get enough supplemental milk from a cup. Assuming your baby will take a bottle, try to give the baby one bottle feeding each day, around the same time of day, during a time when you will be out at work. You may choose to express and leave your own milk for your baby or you may ask the caregiver to prepare formula for the baby while you are out. Start following your work routine in the two to three weeks preceding your return. If you plan to express milk, this is the time to start so you are proficient at it by the time you return to work. See pages 170–171 for information on expressing milk. Expressing now will help you to build a reserve in the freezer before your return to work. Date it.

If your employer is willing, a shortened day may help you to continue breastfeeding successfully. For example, an 8–3 schedule

A Doctor's Thoughts
"I think more mothers would breastfeed if they could have day-care available within the workplace. This would make it physically possible for them to breastfeed and be with their babies. I would also like to see breastfeeding counselors made more available to mothers through insurance programs and health care programs."
—Dr. Ronald E. Kleinman, Associate Chief of Children's Services, Massachusetts General Hospital, and Associate Professor of Pediatrics, Harvard Medical School

An Expert's Thoughts
"The mother who is, at least for part of her day, occupied with something of interest in the outside world brings home a lot of gifts to her children: fresh insights and knowledge, and a clear interest in the world—all of which her kids can share in."—Dr. Mary Howell, Assistant Clinical Professor of Pediatrics, Harvard Medical School

✦

Equal Time

Married moms who work outside the home spend as many hours bathing, dressing, and later, doing homework with their kids, as stay-at-home moms. So says research by Dr. W. Keith Bryant, of Cornell University, and Dr. Cathleen Zick, of the University of Utah.

✦

Quotable Quote

"God could not be everywhere, so therefore he made mothers."—The Talmud

five days a week may work better for some breastfeeding moms than a 9–5 schedule four days a week, only because you miss fewer feedings.

If you plan to keep your baby solely on breast milk, you will need to express milk while you're at work. Not many places of business are set up for this. You may unfortunately end up with no more privacy or comfort than what can be found in a ladies' room stall. Once you have a place staked out, you'll probably need to express milk two or three times a day. Lunch hour affords at least one interlude during which you won't be missed. You may be able to work out the other breaks to coincide with coffee breaks or natural lulls in your working day. Obviously, you'll need a refrigerator in which to store this milk and a small cooler in which to take it home to your own freezer. Or use a sterile thermos to keep the breast milk cool until you get home.

WORKING MOTHER GUILT BUSTERS

Just because you grew up watching the *Donna Reed Show* doesn't mean you have to live a TV fantasy now that you're grown up. Mothers come in all shapes and sizes and from all walks of life. Your child will naturally assume that whatever you do in your role as mother is perfectly appropriate. If that means you work, your child will find it perfectly normal. If that means you stay at home, your child will find this perfectly normal as well. Children do not judge the worth of their moms based on whether they stay at home or go to work. Mothers, whether they work or stay at home, can be good role models for their children as long as they follow their chosen path without feelings of guilt or chips on their shoulders. Hopefully, our freedom to choose full-time, part-time, or at-home work will lead the way to even greater freedom of choice for our sons and daughters. Remember: guilt is counterproductive. It doesn't help you to be a better mother to your baby; it only gets in the way by making you tired, worried, and depressed.

❖ Conclusion ❖

The first year is a very special rite of passage for both parents and baby. This book was created to help you make your way through this tunnel of love with as much joy, good spirits, and good health as possible. I hope this book addressed your concerns, lightened your load, cheered you on, and helped you to cope with all the demands and exhilaration of baby's first year.

With so much more ahead of you, you can now at least look back on what I hope has been a great beginning to life with your child. Enjoy your new family!

✦ Index ✦

Boldface numbers indicate the main source of information.

Abdominal massage, 205
Accidents (*see* Safety tips)
Acne, 220
Afterpains, 206
Aggressive suctioning, 22, 23
Airline travel, 118–119
Alcohol, 102, 230
Allergies, 181–182
Amniotic fluid, 22, 23, 188
Anal fissures, 60
Anemia, 22, 131
Anesthesia, 202–203
Apgar score, 24
Appetite, 92, 147

Baby blues, 249–250
Baby bouncers, 123
Baby carriers, **9**, 65, 79, 118–119
Baby diary, 58
Baby gear, 5–13
Baby massage, **58**, 78
Baby nurses, 18
Baby-proofing, 158–159
Babysitters, 66, 125, 133, 148, 260, **277–278**, 284
Backache, 217
Back-saving suggestions, 144
Back track exercise, 232, 233
Bananas, 181
Bare feet, 140, 145, 152
Bassinets, 6
Baths, 11
  in first month, 61–63
  safety tips, 62, 63, 112, 113

Beanbag pillows, 9
Bedding accessories, 7
Beds, 157
Bedtime routines, 136
Belly button, 22
Bibs, 183–184
Bicycling, 133
Bilirubin, 189
Birthday party, first, 158
Birth length, 26
Birthmarks, 45–46
Birth order, 269–270
Birth weight, **25**, 186–187
Biting, 154–155
Blocked ducts, 169
Body image, 235
Body language, **141**, 146
Body temperature, 28–29
Bonding, 26–27
Books, 95, **115–116**
Bottle feeding, 18
  benefits of, 38–39
  bowel movements and, 60
  cleaning bottles, 175
  cleft lip/cleft palate and, 190
  colic and, 78
  equipment, 174–175
  in hospital, 28
  iron-fortified formula, 172–173
  night feeding tips, 175
  preparing bottles, 176
  supplemental to breastfeeding, 171, 173
  warming bottles, 173–174
  weaning, 177–178
  weight gain and, 71

Bottle mouth (nursing caries), **126**, 153, 175
Bottoms up exercise, 232
Botulism, 59
Bowel movements
    changes in, 135, **179–180**
    in first month, 60
    newborns, **32**, 167
    postpartum, 210
Bowlegs, **47**, 151
Brazelton neonatal behavior assessment scale,
        24–25
Breast cancer, 38
Breastfeeding
    allergies and, 181
    benefits of, 37–38
    bowel movements and, 60
    cleft lip/cleft palate and, 190
    colic and, 77, 78
    common colds and, 220
    constant nursing, 166
    contraception and, 241, **246**
    contractions, 203, 205
    demand vs. scheduled feeding, 167
    drying up milk, **172**, 222
    engorged breasts, **169**, 172, **221–222**
    enough milk, 166–167
    expressing milk, **170–172**, 285
    father's attitudes about, 261
    in hospital, 27–28
    leaky breasts, 221
    maternal nutrition, 226–228
    menstruation and, 216
    most common questions, 161–164
    night waking and, 73
    nursing bras, 222
    nursing caries and, 126
    positions, **164–165**, 168, 169, 215,
        222
    problems, 168–170
    supplemental bottles, 171, 173
    travel and, 118, 119
    weaning, 177–178
    weight gain and, 70, 71
    working mothers and, 285–286
Breast size, 222
Breathing, **23**, 54–55
Breech babies, 32
Bumper pads, 7
Burping, 53, 77, **176–177**

Cabinet locks, 112, 129, 159
Cafe-au-lait spots, 46
Caffeine, 229
Calories, 226, 227
Caput succadaneum, 42
Carbohydrates, 228
Caregivers, 15–19
Carrying babies, 64–65
Carry-on bag, 118
Car safety seats, 8, **11–12**, 65, 118
Car travel, 118
Catheterization, **203–204**, 209, 210
Cats, 272
Cavernous hemangioma, 45
Celiac disease, 192
Cerebral palsy, 189–190
Certified nurse-midwives, 17–18
Cervical cap, 242, **243–244**
Cesarean section, 22, **202–204**, 215
Changing tables, 10–11
CH (congenital hypothyroidism) test, 31
Checkups
    first month, 49–50
    second month, 67–70
    fourth month, 83, **91–92**
    sixth month, 105–106
    ninth month, 131–132
    twelfth month, 151
    postpartum, **215–216**, 239
Chest circumference, 26
Chewing, 102, 127
Chicken pox vaccine, 69
Child abuse, 75, 78
Child-care arrangements, 277–281
Chin to chest exercise, 231–232
Chlamydia, 30
Chocolate, 229
Choking, 95
Cholesterol, **182**, 228
Chuckling, 85
Chux pads, 209, 214
Circumcision, 30, **36–37**
Cleaning teeth, 109–110
Cleaning up, 140–141
Cleft lip/cleft palate, 190–191
Clinging, **123–124**, 136, 147
Clitoris, 46
Cloth diapers, 32, **40**, 79
Clothes, 5–6, **63–64**

Clubfeet, 47, **191**
Coffee, 229
Colic, 9, 54, **76–78**, 84, 227
Color preference, 85
Colostrum, 28, 162, 166
Commercially prepared baby foods, 180–181
Common colds, 219–220
Complex carbohydrates, 228
Condom, 243, **244**
Constipation, 60, 205, 221
Contraception, 17, 216, **238–248**
Contraceptive implants, 242, **244–245**
Contraceptive sponge, 243
Convulsions, 69
Cooing, 75
Cornstarch, 33, 47, 63
Cradle cap, 47
Cradle hold, 164, 165, 169
Crawling, 71, 107, 112, 115, **121–122**
Creeping, 107, 112, **121–122**
Crib gym, 80, 96
Cribs, **6–8**, 157
Cruising, **139**, 152
Crunch exercise, 232
Crying
  in first month, 52–54
  in third month, 84, 85
  in fifth month, 100
  colic, 9, 54, **76–78**, 84
  fathers and, 264
Cup, introduction of, 132, **182–183**
Cutting nails, 43–44
Cystic fibrosis, 192–193

Dancing, 55, 78, 103
Day care, 106, **278–280**, 284
Daytime sleeping (*see* Sleeping)
Dehydration, 97, 223
Delivery, **22–23**, 32, 41–42
Delivery repair, 201–202
Demand vs. scheduled feeding, 167
Dentist, first visit to, 153
Depo-Provera, 245
Depression, postpartum, 250
Diapering
  disposable vs. cloth, 40
  newborns, **32–33**, 40
Diaper rash, 33, 40, **78–79**

Diaphragm, **239–240**, 242, 243
Diarrhea, 97, 101, 109, 280
Diphtheria, 68
Dirt, 126–127
Disposable diapers, **40**, 79
Divorced grandparents, 274–275
Dogs, 271–272
Doulas, 18–19
Down syndrome, 191
DPT (diphtheria, tetanus, pertussis)
  immunization, **68–70**, 91–92
Dressing, in first month, 63–64
Drooling, 101, **109**

Ear infections, 101, 168, 190
Early waking, in sixth month, 110
Ears of newborns, 43
Ear tugging, 142
Ectopic pregnancy, 241, 243
Eighth month
  bottle mouth (nursing caries), 126
  clinging, 123–124
  creeping, scooting or crawling, 121–122
  dirt and germs, 127–128
  feeding, 127
  interest in genitalia, 128
  muscle control, 121–123
  napping, 126
  safety tips, 128–129
  separation anxiety, 125
  standing, 123
  stranger anxiety, 124–125
  toys, 129
Electrical outlets, 95, 103, 123
Eleventh month
  feeding, 147–148
  language development, 146–147
  mental skills, 147
  muscle control, 145
  safety tips, 148–149
  standing, 145
  toys, 149
Emergency room visits, 195
Emergency situations, 148
Endometrial cancer, 241
Energy level, 251
Engorged breasts, **169**, 172, **221–222**
Epidural anesthetic, 202, 203

Epiglottis, 69
Epilepsy, 69
Episiotomy, 201, 208, **213–214**, 238
Erythema toxicum (red blotches), 44–45
Estrogen, 218, 240, 241
Exercise, postpartum, 224, 226, **231–235**
Expressing breast milk, **170–172**, 285
Extroverted babies, 51
Eye color, 43
Eye discharge, 43
Eyedrops, 30
Eyes (see Vision)

Facial appearance of newborns, 41
Fallopian tube infections, 242
Family bed, **87**, 111
Family child care, 279, **280**
Family practice physicians, 17
Fathers, 257–264
Fatigue, 219
Fats, 228
Fears, 143
Feeding (*see also* Bottle feeding, Breastfeeding)
    in fourth month, 92, **94–95**
    in fifth month, 102
    in eighth month, 127
    in ninth month, 134–135
    in eleventh month, 147–148
    additives, 181
    allergies, 181–182
    commercially prepared baby foods, 180–181
    demand vs. scheduled, 167
    fussy eaters, 147–148
    homemade foods, 180
    introduction of cup, 132, **182–183**
    introduction of solid foods, 92, **102**, **179**, 181–182
    newborns, **27–28**, **37–39**
    plates, spoons and bibs, 183–184
    self-feeding, 134
    sugary foods, 134, **135**
    vitamin supplements, 167–168
Feet, 140
Female genitalia, 46–47
Female gynecologists, 17
Fifth month
    feeding, 102
    language development, 99–100

learning, 100
muscle control, 98–99
pediatric care by phone, 97–98
playtime, 103–104
safety tips, 103
sleeping, 100–101
teething, 101–102
toys, 104
weight gain, 99
Finger foods, **127**, 134, 181
First birthday party, 158
Firstborn children, 270, 271
First month (*see also* Newborns)
    baths, 61–63
    behavior, 51–52
    bowel movements, 60
    carrying baby, 64–65
    checkup, 49–50
    crying, 52–54
    dressing, 63–64
    massage, 58
    noises, 54–55
    outings, 64
    pacifiers, 57
    personality of baby, 50–51
    playtime, **52**, 53
    routines, 59
    sleeping, 55–57
    spoiling, 58–59
    swaddling, 55, 57
    thrush, 60–61
    time alone, 65–66
    toiletries, 63
    toys, 66
    umbilical cord care, 60
First twenty-four hours (*see* Newborns; Postpartum period)
Flabby belly, 223
Flex and point exercise, 232
Floor gym, 96
Fluoride, 102, **110**
Fluorosis, 110
Fontanel, 42
Food additives, 181
Food grinder, 180
Football hold, 77, **164**, **165**, 169, 215
Footprinting, 27, **28**
Forceps, 42
Foreskin, 37, 46

Formula feeding (*see* Bottle feeding)
Fourth month
    checkup, 83, **91–92**
    feeding, 92, **94–95**
    laughing and babbling, 93
    learning, 93–94
    muscle control, 92–93
    playtime, 95–96
    safety tips, 94, **95**
    thumb sucking and pacifier use, 94
    toys, 95, **96**
    vision, 93
Front carriers, **9**, 65, 118
Fussy eaters, 147–148

Gag reflex, 29
Gas pain
    in first month, 53
    maternal, 205–206
Gender differences, 155–156
Genitalia
    interest in, 128
    newborn, 46–47
Germs, 126–127
Gluten, 192
Gonorrhea, 30
Grandparents, 273–277
Grasp reflex, **29**, 71–72
Guilt, 186, 286
Gurgling, 85
Gynecologists, 17

Haemophilus influenzae B, 69
Hair care, 135–136
Hair loss, 218
Hair of newborns, 42–43
Hair pulling, 142
Hand grip, 29
Head banging, 141–142
Head circumference, 26
Head injury, 97–98
Head shape of newborns, 41–42
Heart defect, 192
Heart rate range, **233**, 234
Hemorrhoids, 220–221
Hepatitis B (HepB) vaccine, **31**, 50, 68, 70, 131, 151

Hernia, 194, 195
HIB vaccine, **69–70**, 92
Hide-and-seek, 125
High birth weight, 25
Holding skills, 92–93, 98
Homecoming from hospital, 266–267
Homemade foods, 180
Honey, 59
Hospital ID bracelet, 27, **28**
Hospital necessities, 207–208
Hospital privileges, 16
Hot flashes, 223
Hydrocele, 194–195
Hydrocephalus, 192

Immersion baths, 61–62
Immunizations, 31, 50, **68–71**, 75, 91–92, 105, 131, 151
Independence, 121, 123, 124, 143
Infant mortality rates, 186
Infant seats, 8–9
Inguinal hernia, 194
Intelligence, 24
Intensive care, 26, 27, **185–186**
Intercoms, 12
Intrauterine device (IUD), 242–243
Intrauterine growth retardation (IUGR), 186–187
Intravenous oxytocin, 204–205
Introverted babies, 51
Inverted nipples, 168
In-your-home babysitters, 277–278
Ipecac syrup, 129, 159
IPV (inactivated polio vaccine), 69, 70
Iron-fortified formula, 172–173
Iron supplements, 132, **167**
Itsy-bitsy spider, 113

Jaundice, 187, **188–189**
Jealousy, 260, 267
Jewelry, 123

Kegel exercises, **214**, 219
Knock-knees, 151

Labia majora and minora, 46
LAM (Lactation Amenorrhea Method), 239, **246**
Language development
    body language and, 141
    in fourth month, 93
    in sixth month, 106
    in ninth month, 132–133
    in eleventh month, 146–147
Lanugo, 43
Last-born children, 270
Laughter, 93
Laundry, 6
Layette, **5–6**, 63
Lead exposure, 105, 131, 151
Lead-free water, 174
Leaky breasts, 221
Lean machine exercise, 232, 233
Learning
    in second month, 72
    in third month, 85–86
    in fourth month, 93–94
    in fifth month, 100
Left-handedness, 117
Linea nigra, 220
Lochia (bleeding after birth), **208**, 213
Long-distance grandparents, 273–274
Low birth weight, 25, **186–187**

Macrophages, 242
Macrosomia, 25
Male genitalia, 46
Massage, **58**, 78, 205
Mastitis, 169, **170**
Maternal diabetes, 25
Maternal rubella, 192
Maternity leave, 283–284
Math, 101
Meconium, 22, 23, **32**, 162, **188**
Medical problems, 185–195
Memory, 147
Meningitis, 69, 70
Menstruation, 216
Mental retardation, 187, 189, 191
Messy babies, 140–141
Middle children, 270
Milia, 44
Milk intolerance, 181
Mirror images, 110

MMR (measles, mumps, rubella) vaccine, 69, 70
Mobiles, **8**, 13, 80
Mom-and-tot groups, 280–281
Mongolian spots, 46
Morning-after pills, 246–247
Moro (startle) reflex, **29**, 30, 71
Mouth trauma, 147
Muscle control
    in second month, 71–72
    in third month, 85
    in fourth month, 92–93
    in fifth month, 98–99
    in sixth month, 107–108
    in eighth month, 121–123
    in ninth month, 132, 134
    in tenth month, 139
    in eleventh month, 145
    in twelfth month, 152
Music, 55, 78, **116**
Myelomeningocele, 192

Nail clipping, 43–44
Nails of newborns, 43–44
Names, 39
Napping, 126
Neck nestle, 64, **65**
Nevus flammeus, 45–46
Nevus simplex, 45
Newborns
    Apgar score, 24
    birthmarks, 45–46
    bonding, 26–27
    bowel movements, **32**, 167
    bowlegs, 47
    Brazelton behavior assessment scale, 24–25
    breathing, 23
    chest circumference, 26
    circumcision, 30, **36–37**
    cradle cap, 47
    diapering, **32–33**, 40
    ears, 43
    erythema toxicum (red blotches), 44–45
    eyedrops, 40
    facial appearance, 41
    feeding, **27–28**, **37–39**
    footprinting and ID bracelet, 28
    genitalia, 46–47

Newborns (*continued*)
hair, 42–43
head circumference, 26
head shape, 41–42
hepatitis B vaccine, 31
length, 26
meconium passage, 32
milia, 44
nails, 43–44
naming, 39
PKU and CH tests, 31
prickly heat, 47
reflexes, 29–30
rooming in, 35–36
skin color, 44
soft spot (fontanel), 42
suctioning, 22–23
temperature control, 28–29
umbilical cord, 22
vernix, 44
vision, **31–32**, 43
visitors, 36
vitamin K injection, 30
weight, 25
Next-door grandparents, 274
Night-lights, 12–13
Nighttime sleeping (*see* Sleeping)
Night waking
in second month, 73–74
in third month, 86–87
in fifth month, 100–101
in sixth month, 111–112
Ninth month
bedtime, 136
checkups, 131–132
feeding, 134–135
hair care, 135–136
language development, 132–133
muscle control, 132, 134
outings, 133
playtime, 136–138
safety tips, 137
standing, 132
toys, 137
Nipples
inverted, 168
sore and cracked, 166, **168–169**
"No," 157–158

Noises
in first month, 54–56
in second month, 75
in third month, 85
in fourth month, 93
Norgestrel, 244
Nurse-midwives, 17–18
Nursing bras, 222
Nursing caries, **126**, 153, 175
Nursing (*see* Breastfeeding)
Nutrition, postpartum, 226–229

Object permanency, 142, 147
Obstetricians, 17
Only children, 271
Oral contraceptives, 240–242
Oral polio vaccine, **69**, 92
Osteoporosis, 38, 241
Outings
in first month, 64
in second month, 79
in ninth month, 133
travel, **118–119**, 274
Ovarian cancer, 241
Over-the-counter medications, 98
Ovulation, 245–246
Oxytocin, 204–206

Pacifiers, 55, **57**, 76, 87, **94**, 95, 128
Painkillers, postpartum, 204
Pain thresholds, 71
Pat-a-cake, 113
Paternity leave, **257–258**, 283
Pediatric care by phone
in third month, 83–84
in fifth month, 97–98
Pediatric dentists, 153
Pediatricians, 15–16
Peek-a-boo, 113
Pelvic floor exercises, **214**, 219
Pelvic inflammatory disease (PID), 241, 242
Pelvic tilt exercise, 231
Penis, 37, 46
Peri bottle, 209
Perineal swelling, 208–209
Perineum, 201–202
Personality of newborns, 50–51
Pertussis, 68–69

Pets, 271–272
Phototherapy, 189
Physical exam, 50
Pigmentation, 220
Pill, the, 240–242
Pillows, 8, 9, 59
Pincer grasp, 115, **134**
PKU (phenylketonuria) test, 31
Placenta, 22
Plants, poisonous, **129**, 159
Plates, 183
Play groups, 104, **280–281**
Playtime
    in first month, **52**, 53
    in second month, 79–80
    in third month, 86, **88**, 89
    in fourth month, 95–96
    in fifth month, 103–104
    in sixth month, 112–113
    in ninth month, 136–138
    in twelfth month, 153–154
    fathers and, **258–259**, 263
    siblings and, 267
Pneumococcal vaccine, 69
Pneumonia, 204
Pointing, 141
Poisonings, 158–159
Poisonous plants, **129**, 159
Polio, 69
Portable cribs, 7–8
Port wine stain (nevus flammeus), 45–46
Posterior birth, 42
Postpartum fashions, 224
Postpartum hemorrhage, 205
Postpartum period, 17
    afterpains, 206
    cesarean section, **202–204**, 215
    checkup, **215–216**, 239
    common concerns, 217–224
    contraception, 216, **238–248**
    delivery in retrospect, 206–207
    delivery repair, 201–202
    eating, 205–206
    exercise, 224, 226, **231–235**
    feelings and emotions, 249–251
    first bowel movement, 210
    first six weeks, 213–216
    hospital necessities, 207–208
    intravenous oxytocin, 204–205

lochia (bleeding after birth), **208**, 213
    nutrition, 226–229
    painkillers, 204
    perineal swelling, 208–209
    sexual relations, 216, 222, **237–238**, **259–260**
    urinary catheter use and removal, **203–204**, 209, 210
    urination, **209**, 219
PPD (pure protein derivative), 151
Precrawling movements, 98
Prematurity, 25, **185–188**, 194, 271
Prenatal tooth development, 102
Prickly heat, 47
Progesterone, 240–242, 245
Proteins, 227–228
Pyloric stenosis, 194

Rapid breathing, 23
Records, 58
Red blotches, 44–45
Reflexes, **29–30**, 68
Regressive behavior in siblings, 267–268
Repetition, 106
Respiratory distress syndrome (RDS), 187, 188
Rhythm method of birth control, 245–246
Right-handedness, 117
Righting reflex, 29
Rocking chairs, 11
Role playing, 268
Rolling over, 92, **98–99**
Rooming in, 35–36
Rooting reflex, 29
Routines
    in first month, 59
    in second month, 72–73
RU 486, 247

Safety tips
    for third month, 88
    for fourth month, 94, **95**
    for fifth month, 103
    for sixth month, 112
    for eighth month, 128–129
    for ninth month, 137
    for tenth month, 143
    for eleventh month, 148–149
    for twelfth month, 158–159

Safety tips (*continued*)
  baths, 62, 63, 112, 113
  bicycling, 133
  finger foods, 127
  walkers, 123
  warming bottles, 174
Scooting, 121–122
Scrotum, 46, 194
Seat belts, 12
Seborrheic dermatitis, 47
Secondhand cribs, 7
Secondhand smoke, 230
Second month
  checkup, 67–70
  colic, 76–78
  cooing, 75
  diaper rash, 78–79
  learning, 72
  muscle control, 71–72
  outings, 79
  playtime, 79–80
  routines, 72–73
  sleeping, 73–74
  smiling, 75–76
  toys, 80
  vision, 72
Security blankets, **117–118**, 136
Seizures, 69
Self-feeding, **134–135**, 183
Separation anxiety, 125
Septicemia, 69
Seventh month
  books, 115–116
  left- or right-handedness, 117
  music, 116
  security blankets, 117–118
  toys, 119
  travel, 118–119
Sexist toys, 156
Sexual relations, 216, 222, **237–238**, **259–260**
Shampoo, 63, 135
Sharing, 153–154
Shoes, 140, 145, **152**
Siblings, 18, **265–269**
Sickle cell anemia, 193
Side-lying position, **165**, 215
Single mothers, 264
Sit carry, 64, 65
Sitting up, 105, **107–108**

Sitz baths, 214, 215, 221
Sixth month
  checkup, 105–106
  drooling, 109
  language development, 106
  muscle control, 107–108
  playtime, 112–113
  safety tips, 112
  sleeping, 110–112
  teeth, 108–110
  toys, 113
Skin breakouts, 220
Skin color of newborns, 44
Sleeping
  in first month, 55–57
  in second month, 73–74
  in third month, 86–87
  in fifth month, 100–101
  in sixth month, 110–112
  in eighth month, 126
  in ninth month, 136
  in twelfth month, 157
Sleeping positions, 56, 74
Smell, sense of, 51, **52**
Smiling, 31, **75–76**
Smoke alarms, 88
Smoking, 230
Soft spot (fontanel), 42
Solid foods, introduction of, 92, **102**, **179**, 181–182
Soy formula, 181
Spermicidal foam, 243, **244**
Spina bifida manifesta, 191–192
Spitting up, 55, **177**, 194
Spoiling, 58–59
Sponge baths, 61
Spoons, 183
Stair guards, 112
Standing, **123**, **132**, 139, **145**, 152
Stepping reflex, 29–30
Sterilization
  as birth control, 247–248
  of bottles, 175
Stork bites (nevus simplex), 45
Stranger anxiety, **124–125**, 131, 147
Strawberry hemangioma, 45
Stress, 142, 220
Stretch marks, 223
Stroller accessories, 10

Strollers, **10**, 65, 79
Sucking, **76**, 94
Sucking blisters, 165
Suctioning, **22–23**, 188
Sudden infant death syndrome (SIDS), 56, **74–75**
Suffocation, 8, 9, 75
Sugary foods, 134, **135**
Surfactant, 187, 188
Swaddling, 55, **57**, 65, 78
Sweating, 223
Swings, 13

Tachycardic episodes, 74
Talc, 33
Taste, sense of, 52
Tay-Sachs disease, 193
Tears during delivery, 201, 202, 208, **213–214**
Teeth
    cleaning, 109–110
    first visit to dentist, 153
    grinding, 142–143
    prenatal development, 102
    in sixth month, 108–110
Teething, 94, **101–102**, 103, 105, 168
Temperature control, 28–29
Tenth month
    body language, 141
    cruising, 139
    fears, 143
    feet, 140
    hair pulling/teeth grinding/ear tugging, 142–143
    head banging, 141–142
    messy baby, 140–141
    muscle control, 139
    toys, 143
Testicles, 46, 194
Thalassemia, 193–194
Third month
    gurgling and chuckling, 85
    learning, 85–86
    muscle control, 85
    pediatric care by phone, 83–84
    playtime, 86, **88**, 89
    safety tips, 88
    sleeping, 86–87
    toys, 88–89

vision, 85
"This Little Piggy," 140
Thrush, **60–61**, 168
Thumb sucking, 94
Time alone, 65–66
Tonic neck (fencer's) reflex, 29, **30**
Toxic shock syndrome, 240, 243
Toys
    for first month, 66
    for second month, 80
    for third month, 88–89
    for fourth month, 95, **96**
    for fifth month, 104
    for sixth month, 113
    for seventh month, 119
    for eighth month, 129
    for ninth month, 137
    for tenth month, 143
    for eleventh month, 149
    for twelfth month, 159–160
    for newborns, 13
    sexist, 156
    storage of, 140
Train travel, 118
Travel, **118–119**, 274
Tubal ligation, 247, 248
Tuberculin (TB) test, 131, **151**
Tucks, 209
TV shows, 156–157
Twelfth month
    biting, 154–155
    checkup, 151
    gender differences, 155–156
    playtime, 153–154
    safety tips, 158–159
    sharing, 153–154
    shoes, 152
    sleeping, 157
    toys, 159–160
    TV shows and videos, 156–157
    visit to dentist, 153
    walking, 152
Twins, 271
Tylenol, 68, 92
Type A babies, 50

Umbilical cord, 33
    care of, 60, 61

Umbilical cord (*continued*)
  cutting, 22
Undescended testicles, 46, **194**
Urinary catheter, **203–204**, 209,
  210
Urinary incontinence, 218–219
Urination
  in newborns, 32
  postpartum, **209**, 219
Uterine involution, **213**, 223

Vagina, 47
Vasectomy, 247–248
Vernix, 44
Videos, 156
Vision
  in second month, 72
  in third month, 85
  in fourth month, 93
  newborns, **31–32**, 43

Vitamin K injection, 30
Vitamins, 132, **167–168**, **228**
Vomiting, 177, 194

Walkers, 112, **123**, **124**
Walking
  as postpartum exercise, 232, 234
  in twelfth month, 152
Water, 182, 229
Weak ankles, 151
Weaning, 177–178
Weight, 182
  birth, **25**, 186–187
  second month, 70–71
  fourth month, 92
  fifth month, 99
Weight loss, postpartum, 225–226
Withdrawal method of birth control, 245
Working mothers, 259, 262, **283–286**
Worrying, 250–251